KUNTI KUNTALA SHAKUNTALA

KUNTI KUNTALA SHAKUNTALA

Binapani Mohanty
A.K. Mohanty

Publications

KALPAZ PUBLICATIONS
DELHI-110 052

Kunti Kuntala Shakuntala

Rs. 790

ISBN : 81-7835-418-7

Published in 2005 in India by
Kalpaz Publications,
C-30, Satyawati Nagar,
Delhi-110 052
Email : kalpaz@hotmail.com

Lasertype Setting by: Tact Computer Graphics, Delhi
Printed at: Salasar Imaging System, Delhi

CONTENTS

Dedication

Bou,

You had a great deal of hope that I will write a novel some day and you will get to read it. Unfortunately, I had not been able to publish a novel in book form during your lifetime even though there were many short story collections published as books. You had always encouraged me to write about the problems faced by women in their lives. Could I ever forget that ?

You are no longer present in this mortal world. But I have seen your reflection on the faces of numerous mothers. No one has ever been able to keep count of the myriads of dreams these mothers have seen and the countless sacrifices they have made in order to rear this world amid continuous struggles.

Hence, many 'Kuntis' dare to dream with open, hopeful eyes in the silent revolution going on in this world. Countless 'Kuntalas' get ready for the battles of life. And numerous 'Shakuntalas' immolate themselves. The existence of women is ever alive among all of them. You among them and they among you are forever immersed in meditation.

Bou ! This is my first offering to that ever bright consciousness of yours.

Mahalaya
1989

Bina

My Own Tale

I have no desire to write a foreword to my own novel. Just as I picked up pen and paper to write short stories, in the same manner, I have written two complete novels. The first novel had been published under the title "Sita Ra Shonita" as a serial in the magazine "Aasantakali." It has not as yet been published as a book. Some others are still in an incomplete form.

This novel 'Kunti Kuntala Shakuntala' had been published in 1986 in the magazine 'Jhankara' under the title 'Bahni-Lagnaa'. Keeping the theme of 'Bahni-Lagnaa' intact, I have only increased its size in deference to requests made by many of my friends as also Sri Sahadev Pradhan, the publisher. The name of the novel has also changed in that context.

Many programmes have been undertaken from the villages to the cities in order to give recognition to the freedom of women as also to free women from exploitation. And yet, a daughter or a daughter-in-law or a wife or a mother or a woman is being tortured and oppressed everyday somewhere or other. I have only made an effort to point a finger in that direction in this novel. No one can positively indicate what path is open for whom in order to be free from one's own typical prison. But I am of the firm opinion that the woman of today would be in a position to confront her problems and the inhuman oppression that she has to contend with everyday. I am positive that she can dedicate herself in order to hold aloft the light of freedom for the next generation.

I am grateful to the publisher, Sri Sahadev Pradhan and the printer, Sri Rajkishore Singh for their sincere efforts and cooperation even though the novel took a long time in seeing the light of the day. The efforts of Sri Saroj Ranjan Mohanty, the editor of 'Jhankar' would always be remembered by me in the compilation of the manuscript and its publication as a novel.

I express my deep gratitude to everyone at this auspicious moment of the publication of the novel. I am also waiting to receive the feedback from my dear readers.

Binapani Mohanty

Translator's Note

I had no idea what I was letting myself in for when I accepted the assignment to translate 'Kunti Kuntala Shakuntala' into English. Until now, I had confined myself to translate Oriya short stories into English. Translating a novel of this kind proved to be as tough as crossing the Matto Grosso on bare feet.

For almost four months, Kunti has held me under her spell. I have had to take an unofficial sabbatical in order to complete the translation work. I have tried to be as faithful to the text as it has been humanly possible. The going has been tough. If there are certain patches which turn out to be baffling to the reader, it is only because of my own inadequacy. It ought not to reflect on the author.

I am grateful to the author who gave me an absolutely free hand in the translation. I am most grateful to my dear friend, Prof. Himansu S. Mohapatra, Professor of English, Utkal University, Bhubaneswar who went through the manuscript and smoothened the rough edges. I am also grateful to him for having taken the trouble of writing a wonderful foreword to the novel. Thanks, dear friend.

My wife, Dr. Anjali Das, deserves a special mention. For the time that I was busy in the translation work, her constant refrain was that Kunti meant a great deal more to me than her. I would like to place on record here that nothing could be farther from truth and that I would never have been able to complete a work of this magnitude without her constant support and encouragement.

Ashok K. Mohanty

FOREWORD

It is not often that in telling the simple story of an Oriya village girl's journey from innocence to experience a novel manages to unlock the deep-lying sources of the malaise of the contemporary Oriya society. This is what Kunti Kuntala Shakuntala, the first published novel by the acclaimed Oriya writer Binapani Mohanty, does with a certain aplomb. The novel gives an insight into the commodification that is a woman's historical condition. It augments that critical vision by showing the complicity of the mythical icons of Indian womanhood such as Kunti, Draupadi and Shakuntala in that condition. One can in fact underline another aspect of the novel's appeal, which is its echoing of the theme of Thomas Hardy's Tess in the story of Kunti, pulled as she is between an Alec-like sensualist and an Angel-like romanticist.

The novel can justly lay claim to classic status in contemporary women's writing in Orissa. It makes a bold new exploration into an Oriya, nay Indian, woman's life, psyche and circumstances. The three female names in the title suggest, on the face of it, different facets of iconic Indian womanhood. Yet the names, being only plays on the root name of Kunti, speak of sameness, the chilling and disabling sameness of female identity in the Third World, bred by poverty, patriarchy, tradition and a misguided modernity.

The novel tells the story of Kunti, a poor village girl, in three roughly equal parts. The three parts not only correspond to three phases of her life; they are also set in three social spaces. While Kunti's adolescence is set in a superstition-ridden village, her youth is set amid the false urban glitter. The last part, corresponding to her early womanhood, is set in a limbo-like space that bears only a nominal relation with a hermitage. Brought into focus through this three-part structure is a solitary woman's journey from innocence to experience. It is a journey, however, which singularly fails to break through the barriers created by money, power and gender. It is through this compelling and paradoxical picture of Kunti going through new incarnations, but actually going nowhere that the novelist indicts a society that specialises in the commoditisation of women.

Caught between a blind tradition and a false modernity, and knowing full well that she can never ever be free from the Alecs of this world to find her Angel, Kunti can only perform in the end a Tess-like gesture of self-purification through murder. This is what she does as she kills Laltu alias Satyabrata who, like Alec, wants to violate her soul, having already violated her body. In the end and in an ending that is un-Tess-like, the flickering possibility of a connection with Tapan, who, Angel-like, has reappeared in her life, fades into the distant horizon.

The authentic portrayal of a woman's story in this novel has the potential for triggering off for woman, and, I suppose, for us all, a search for 'a literature of their own.' The English translation of the novel by Ashok K. Mohanty, faithful and reader-friendly as it is, will surely do its bit in causing it to be appreciated among a wider readership.

Himansu S. Mohapatra
Professor of English
Utkal University
Bhubaneswar-751004

1
Kunti's Story

It was as if new wings were growing on her. With those tender wings she wanted to fly away to some distant horizon or high above some green field or on to some river flowing away aimlessly at an infinite distance. At times she was lost watching a portion of the sky standing in some mango grove. At other times, she was beside herself with joy on seeing her reflection as she stood alone on the edge of some pond. She was elated hearing the caw, caw calls of the crow, the song of the cuckoo and the calls of the cricket. She could not concentrate on anything.

She was slowly getting possessed by some kind of quiet restlessness.

But then there were strict rules at home. She was not to step out of the house. She was not supposed to laugh or giggle. Everyone reminded her at all times that she had outgrown the time when she could relax by gossiping with her friends. Every opportunity was good enough to remind her that a girl was supposed to end up in the kitchen. The village school was enough to teach her how to write a couple of lines to her mother-in-law's place. There was no need for any further education for girls. The more they read, the more trouble they would beget. That meant passing the fifth grade in the village school was enough. There was no need for any girl to trudge across three villages to go to the minor school. What was the need of any further education? When it was tough to feed a boy and send him to school, who gave a damn about girls?

Kunti burst into tears and rolled on the floor. She went without food for two days. Forget the father; even her mother did not bother to look at her sideways. On the other hand, she was rebuked because she did not do the household work. The village women made digs at her mother. The boys of the village made fun looking at her sobbing face.

Everyone stared hard and upbraided her without holding anything back.

She was forbidden to go to the river to bathe. She was warned not to look at anyone with uplifted eyes. She was told that she could not walk freely.

It was as if someone was whispering into Kunti's ears the strange tale of her transformation from a girl into a woman.

Without being aware of it, Kunti had accepted everything in silence. Her flapping wings had become tired. How much could she cry? How much of tear was left in her anyway? Was there anyone around who could wipe away her tear? Was there anyone who could hold her by her hand and take her across the fields and the river to the minor school?

She would have felt a bit confident to have Nima Bhai around her. Nima Bhai was always there to comfort everyone in case of any mishap. He used to have a lot of affection for Kunti's mother. But her mother was extremely intolerant of him. She had no love lost for him since he was a stepson. Kunti's father had five daughters and a son from his first wife. He had somehow managed to marry the girls off by selling some of his land. He had borrowed money too for the purpose. Mother always cursed father. She always quarrelled with father saying that they were going to be drowned in debt in taking care of her own children. If father paid Nima Bhai's school fees, mother got angry and went to sleep without eating dinner. Kunti did not like her mother's ways. Kunti had snatched it out of her hand when her mother beat Nima Bhai last year with a piece of burning wood. Mother had turned on her and had beaten her with a broom. Nima Bhai was bleeding from the face. Father returned home and saw everything, but did not say a word. That day no food had been cooked at home.

Kunti was lighting a lamp near the *chaura** in the evening. From behind the mango tree, Nima Bhai called, "Kunti!"

Kunti looked up with startled eyes while making obeisance near the *chaura*.

Nima Bhai was signalling her to be quiet by pressing his finger to his lips. Kunti carefully looked around her and went near him.

Nima said softly, "Would you give me something if I asked for it?"

"What is it?"

"Give me two rupees. I will go to Cuttack."

Cuttack was far away. He had to board a bus, then a train, and a rickshaw after that, and then...."

"Kunti! I will go away to Cuttack along with Gaura Bhai. He would find me a job there. I will study in the high school. You will not tell it to anyone. And I will return your money through Gaura Bhai."

Kunti thought something and then said, "You will go away on the sly. When mother comes to know of it, she will send people to kill you there."

"You're nuts! How could she know? I will slip away in the night with Gaura Bhai. But we don't have any money for the transport."

Kunti understood that Nima Bhai was asking her to steal two rupees from the small amount of money that mother had kept. But if she came to know of it, she was going to tear her to pieces. What was she to do? How could she do it? Still, she collected herself and said, "You go away now. Mother will come here to make obeisance. Come near the window of the kitchen in the night when everyone is asleep. I will roll the money in a paper and put it on the window sill. But Nima Bhai! You will go away. You will be studying at Cuttack. But mother does not

---

* a stone structure placed in the courtyard where a lamp is lit in the evening.

want to send me to school any more. You take me along with you."

"I will take you some day, but this is not the proper time. Once I get a job there, I will come back for you. You too would have to slip away in the night. You keep on studying now. Never give up studies whatever mother might say. I will definitely come back to take you to Cuttack."

At this time mother's voice could be heard, "Kunti! How long are you going to pray there? Come inside and light the hearth. Do you want your father to go to sleep in the night without food? The kids are sleepy. I am not feeling well. Don't call me again.You take care of things along with your father. Why don't you come here ...?"

Nima Bhai sprinted away on hearing mother's voice. Her insides were in a churn on looking at the sad, emaciated face of Nima Bhai. Kunti wished him well and again made obeisance near the *chaura*, "Oh Mother Goddess! Take care of Nima Bhai. Let not anyone know about him!"

Just as she finished cooking rice and dal, her younger brothers and sisters surrounded her with plates in hand. Some vegetables had been chopped for a curry. But Kunti did not feel like cooking anything else. Nima Bhai was going away. Apart from that, no one bothered whether he ate anything or not. Even no one bothered why he hadn't returned home until then. Father came home and woke up mother. Both of them had dinner. No one asked about Nima Bhai. Kunti also did not say anything. Father and mother had a *paan* each and went out to sit on the outside verandah. Father needed a massage there and mother was going to talk about everything under the sun sitting near him. This was the right time. Kunti went inside the bedroom of her father. The idol of Krishna had been placed on a small wooden platform. Mother hid all her money behind the idol. No one knew about it other then Kunti. Maybe Nima Bhai also knew about it. Kunti was going to hand over all the money to Nima Bhai that night. He was leaving home with such a heavy heart. He hadn't eaten anything throughout the night. She was going to tell him to eat something first using that money.

Kunti came outside and looked around. Mother's bedroom was open. The kids were sleeping on mats on the floor. It was dark all around. The lantern had gone out.

Kunti entered inside with soft steps. She went near the idol. She made obeisance there and said, "Oh Lord! Please forgive me. I am stealing the money as Nima Bhai needs it for his studies. Punish me any way you like. But let Nima Bhai make something of himself after studying well."

Kunti picked up the money and tied it to a corner of her saree. She had started sweating. Everything was in a blur. It was as if someone was whispering in her ears that stealing was the greatest sin on earth. Yamaraj was going to nail her to a tree for that or perhaps fry her in a pot of hot oil. She seemed to be feeling severe physical pain all over.

She walked outside somehow with her eyes closed. It was dark all around as before. A lamp was burning in the kitchen. It seemed that ghosts were dancing all around in that light. The straws were hanging from the thatched roof. Kunti seemed to be seeing horrifying shapes around her. She closed her eyes. Why was Nima Bhai as late as this? Perhaps father and mother were still awake.

Kunti hadn't eaten anything either. Why didn't mother have any affection for Nima Bhai? Why did she stop him from studying any further? Nima Bhai did all the work at home from morning till evening. He did everything that was asked of him. But mother did not even give him enough rice to eat. She gave him an extremely small quantity of curry. If anyone sent home sweets, Nima Bhai never saw anything of it. Mother gave everything away to her own children. But Kunti could not bear it. She always kept aside something for Nima Bhai from her share. Nima Bhai never said anything to mother. He only kept looking at the *chaura* with his eyes filled with tears. Ah! how sad he looked! Father never argued with mother out of fear. Instigated by mother, at times he tied up Nima Bhai and hammered him. Otherwise, father never ever beat anyone else. Father was married once earlier. Nima Bhai was the son of that woman. But so what? Nima Bhai was such a nice soul. He sat on guard for nights on end if either father or mother fell sick. He went without food and shed tears. Who else was going to caress Kunti on the face and talk sweetly if Nima Bhai went away! Who was going to hunt for berries and pears for her!

Suddenly, there was a knock on the windows. Oh God! If it is some kind of a ghost! Who knew! It could be Nima Bhai's mother who might have come in the shape of a witch! Mother was saying that Nima Bhai's mother had turned into a witch and lived on that mango tree. On all festive occasions, she liked to have her share of sweetmeats and hence she broke the branches of the mango tree. She stopped children going that way and sucked their blood through straws. When people slept in their houses in the dead of the night, she entered their kitchens and threw the utensils on to the floor. Nima Bhai's mother was extremely wicked. That was the reason why mother had tied charms around everyone's arm. She herself had one charm on each arm.

Once Kunti had said, " Mother! We are all wearing charms. Why don't you make one for Nima Bhai? He is going to school on that lonely road everyday!"

Mother had said with heavy sarcasm, "Save your love for your brother! Why would that witch touch Nima? She can if she likes wring the neck of her own child and have him for dinner. But she will go up in flames if she comes anywhere near my children." That day Kunti had understood very well that mother could never take a liking to Nima Bhai. If anyone loved Nima Bhai, she had to face the wrath of mother. That was why....

Again she could hear someone knocking. In the faint light, Kunti could see Nima Bhai standing on the other side of the window. He was signalling her to keep quiet, afraid that she might blurt out something. Kunti walked scared to the window and passed on a packet towards Nima. Gaura Bhai was standing behind Nima. Nima wanted to say something. But Gaura Bhai restrained him by putting his palm over his mouth. Kunti's palm had been sweating inside the palm of Nima. Kunti wanted to cry. Was Nima Bhai going away for ever?

Gaura said softly, "Now, now! Don't cry, Kunti. Nima will come back and take you to Cuttack. You too are going to study at Cuttack."

Kunti could not say anything. She was crying with her face pressed against the window. Patting her softly on her head, Nima Bhai disappeared into the darkness along with Gaura Bhai.

Kunti came back and fell on the mat, her body racked by sobs. She felt very hungry. But she had no mind to touch the food.

She kept on hallucinating throughout the night. There seemed to be a tree laden with deep red flowers. Large nails had been embedded in the trunk of the tree. Two mustachioed men were carrying Kunti and hitting her against the nails. Kunti came awake. She said to herself, "Oh Lord! Please forgive my sins this time. I will never steal again! I will never tell lies again!"

Kunti saw that it was getting to be dawn. The morning star was dazzling big and bright on the eastern sky. A cold breeze was blowing. She saw herself standing atop a mountain. There was a gaping hole in the middle of the mountain. Two demons were running towards her, baring their huge teeth. She started running to save her skin. The fire singed her all over. With a shriek, she came awake. She saw mother come towards her while brushing her teeth. Her eyes seemed to be burning with anger. Kunti drifted back to sleep again.

Mother kicked her with her left foot and said, "You scoundrel! What has come over you? The kitchen door is open. The rice pot has not been filled with water. And you are sleeping till the late afternoon. Have you been dreaming throughout the night? Save your tears for someone else!"

Kunti got up while rubbing her eyes. Mother had still not stopped kicking her. When father tried to restrain her, she shouted, "Don't you try to come to her rescue. In a few days, she is going to complete fourteen and step on fifteen. At that age I was doing all the household work besides taking care of six kids. There was a child every year. Who was there to help me out? This girl only believes in eating and enjoying herself. Why don't you die, you wretch! I have the tough luck to have five step daughters. And more daughters from my own womb. Oh! Why didn't my mother step on my neck when I was born?"

Mother went on and on. Kunti could not hear anything. She would come out with ten stinging sentences if ever father opened his mouth even once. She would curse her step children first. After that she would not spare her own children. Once she got tired of cursing, she would start wailing.

Kunti carried the utensils near the pond to clean them. She was never more scared than she was today. She had decided that she would make any sacrifice needed to ensure that Nima Bhai could continue with his studies. Mother could never stand him as he was not her own son. One day she would also run away from home like Nima Bhai. And then she would also take away her younger brother and sister. They will study at the city and will remain happily in Nima Bhai's house. No more would they come back to this village ...no...never.

Kani Bhauja*, her next door neighbour, said near the pond, "Why are you weeping like this? Is any negotiation going on for your marriage? Your mother was talking of so many things sitting in our house. She seems to be really worried for you. She has to be. You are so beautiful!"

Kani Bhauja smiled slightly. Kunti herself was not aware when she was weeping. What could she say now?

The other women of the neighbourhood were enjoying the fun and laughing. She had no idea why they were after her

*sister-in-law

right in the morning. Kani Bhauja was throwing water on her and she was getting wet. Now she was staring at her from head to foot and laughing.

At this time, her younger sister Shanti came running and said, "Apa*! Apa! Come quickly. Someone has stolen mother's money. Mother is howling!" She ran away in a flash just the way she had come. Kunti carried the utensils and ran home. A sledgehammer seemed to be hitting her inside her chest. O Lord! Let Nima Bhai be out of the village. If mother would lay her hand on him, she was going to skin him alive.

There was pandemonium inside the house. The younger brothers and sisters had joined mother in the wailing. Father was sitting thunderstruck with his hand placed on his head. Kunti came and stood there.

The grandmother from the next door neighbour's family asked Kunti, "Hey Kunti! Has Nima told you anything before leaving? Kulia's son Gaura and Nima were going somewhere across the fields at dawn. Naria had gone to see the *jatra**. He saw them and asked them where they were going. Both of them ran away like thieves. Has that rascal vanished with your mother's money? Oh no! The woman had starved and saved the money for her children. But a stepson is a stepson after all! Blood, as they say, is thicker then water!"

Mother let out a big wail, "I know, Aunty. That brat has taken the money. No thief has entered my house! He has opened the kitchen in the night and cleaned out all the food. He has stolen the money from behind Krishna's idol. There were some snacks in a tin. He has also carried it away. Who knows what else he has taken away or sold off? It is all because of his father and his lofty wishes. He wanted his son to study in the high school. He wanted him to be a deputy collector. Ultimately, he has ended up as a thief. His mother was a thief. How could he be otherwise...?"

Kunti put the utensils aside and sat down with a sigh. She had not eaten anything throughout yesterday. Her limbs were

*sister

** a play enacted during night time

tired. She had nothing to say to her mother. Mother would beat her to death if she so much as suspected her. She was trembling all over out of fright. It was as if she was in the grip of an icy chill. She leaned against the earthen wall. Her eyelids began to droop. The old lady started shouting, "What has happened to that girl? Why has she gone limp like that…!" That was all that Kunti had heard. She seemed to have passed out after that. She could only hear voices at intervals. Kunti had absolutely no inclination to talk. The old lady felt Kunti's head and said, "She has a high fever. How come none of you knows about it?"

Two persons picked her up and carried her to the bedroom of her mother. They made her sleep on the mat and closed the door. Kunti could not keep awake. Both her eyes were heavy with sleep. She did not have enough strength in her to raise her eyelids and look at the idol of Krishna resting on the platform a few feet away.

Someone lifted her up and made her drink half a bowl of some bitter medicine. Why should it taste so bitter if it were not some kind of medicine? So mother had not shied away from spending money on her! Mother might be an ill-tempered person. But she definitely had some affection for her. Kunti went back to sleep. She was feeling light-headed; as if she was floating somewhere high in the sky.

A lamp was burning near the door. So the day had turned into the night. She had been sleeping in that room since the morning.

At intervals, someone was coming inside to feed her either that bitter medicine or some barley. She had broken into a hot sweat which was providing her with some relief. But try as she might, she could not lift her head. The kids were playing in the courtyard. She had no idea where her parents were. Kunti looked at the idol of Krishna and lifted her hands with difficulty to make obeisance. Again she slipped back into a deep slumber.

A cricket was singing somewhere near the ears. She had no idea what time of the night it was. The kids were sleeping with their feet pointing at the door. Her parents were perhaps talking to each other on the outside verandah as always. Kunti sat up on the mat. Her head had stopped reeling. She was feeling a little better. But the breeze carried a sobbing sound from somewhere. Was mother still weeping thinking about the money?

Kunti came outside with soft steps and looked furtively around. No one was to be seen. She started walking towards the outside verandah holding on to the wall. That was it. Father was smoking *ganja* leaning against the wall. And mother was weeping leaning against the pillar. Mother could do nothing else except weep when father smoked *ganja*. Mother had to take care of the deficit household as best as she could manage. It was difficult to feed everyone twice a day, and hence, mother only cursed her fate and wept when father spent money on *ganja*. Father was always quiet whenever mother went on a chatter. He never said anything. But father got mad if mother tried to restrain him from smoking *ganja*. He even beat her up at times without any mercy. Mother was always very scared of getting a hiding from him.

Kunti was coming back. She had been seeing the same scene being repeated every evening. But, at this time, father said, "That brat left home and went away. Everyone will point a finger at you. People will say that the stepmother could not stand the stepson…."

Mother shot back, "Why would they say that? Why should I get a bad name? No one bothers that my son, in the prime of his youth, has stolen my savings and vanished. I was the one who made him grow up to be a man from a child. Now that he grew wings, he flew away with my lifetime savings. I am going to curse him…."

Father said, "Lower your voice. Where is the time for your curse to take effect? He has left home for ever. My grown-up son has not only left home. He has torn away both my arms."

Mother roared, "Your arms have been torn away? Why

don't you go running after him? I will do hard labour to take care of the children. Don't you try to scare me. You have disposed of all the landed property to get the daughters of the first wife married off. What have you got for me or my children? I am not so easily scared! Ha!" Father's voice seemed to have turned gruff. Coughing intermittently, he said, "Why are you shouting, Nima *Bou**? Nima's maternal grandfather had bequeathed that land to his daughter. Even this homestead belongs to Nima. You never know about the villagers. They might instigate Nima. It is better for us to keep quiet."

"Don't you dare call me Nima *Bou*. I have no relationship with that brat. On the other hand, he has cut my throat with a dagger. He will not live in peace.... You are going to see for yourself. I am going to pray to Lord Shiva...."

Kunti thought this time father was positively going to kill mother. Just like the other night when she was bleeding all over after getting beaten up. But father did not even make a sound. How could mother be so harsh? Even after knowing that Nima Bhai had gone away from home, she was still frothing at the mouth. And why couldn't father get tough with mother? Finally, mother had ruled that she was not to be addressed as Nima's mother. So she had decided to obliterate the name of Nima Bhai from the household for ever! But she had no idea why and under what circumstances Nima Bhai had left home. How could she even know that everyone was going to follow in the footsteps of Nima Bhai! Their parents wanted that the children should give up studies and obey them only to scrape out a living somehow.

Kunti could not stand any longer. She went back to the mat and lay down. She felt as if her wings in flight had been chopped off by someone with a battle axe.

What was sorrow and what was happiness in a poor family? What was the distinction between life and death? She was not like her rich friend Jharana that everyone would remain awake, standing guard over her throughout the night if she fell ill! It was not as if friends and relations would come running! *Pujas**

* mother

would be offered so she would recover fast! Father would bring fruits and cajole her to eat them! No, no. All those were dreams. In a poor family, death was as colourless as life. If someone fell sick, there were only pains and sufferings. Expecting any kind of comfort at such times was unthinkable. One could not die always even if one wanted to. On the other hand, there was no end to the sufferings. Kunti poured a glass of water for herself and drank it. Who knew how long the night was going to be before the dawn broke!

Word spread like wildfire in the morning itself. Ganesh had seen Nima along with Gaura moving in a rickshaw in Cuttack. Hagura had a grocery shop in the village. He had gone to Cuttack to buy provisions for his store. Nima came face to face with him but did not talk to him. Again, fresh news arrived in the evening. The zemindar was returning from Kolkata by train. He saw Nima and Gaura on the platform with tickets in hand, bound for Jamshedpur. They paid their respects to the zemindar and requested him to inform at home that they were going to Jamshedpur in search of jobs. They would live there if they found jobs. Otherwise, they would die there. They were not going to return home. The train left as the zemindar was about to tell them something. This spread through the entire street in a flash. Everyone respected the zemindar. He could not be disbelieved. Radhu Mahajan was also with the zemindar. He had gone to the banks of the Ganges to offer the *pinda*** of his father. Why should he be telling a lie coming back from the *tirth*?

That Radhu Mahajan was closeted with father for an hour and talked in a conspiring voice. But mother dismissed him deprecatingly. She was lying near the idol of Krishna.

The grandmother of the next door neighbour walked inside the house and said, "Nima *Bou*, the boy left home in a huff. But he might have informed you people about it. He has taken away the money in the middle of the night. Why are you worried? You have your own children. Who would look after them?"

---

* worshipping

** annual rites for the dead

Something seemed to have got hold of mother. She started howling loudly. Tears were running down her eyes. She caught hold of the feet of the old woman and said, "Aunty! I am going crazy. Just tell me what I can do. Just get me some poison. How can I stay in this house? My grown-up son, who would have looked after the family, has gone away from home. Why didn't I die before this came to pass...."

Kunti fell from the skies. Was she hearing this from her mother? Or was it someone else's voice? Or had the ghost of Nima Bhai's mother entered her?

The old woman said, "Have patience, Nima *Bou*. People these days have nothing to do except talk nonsense. Don't take the women of this street at their face value. They can persuade you to believe anything. Don't bother about that. Who doesn't know about your affection for Nima? The child grew into a young man under your care. But he did not bother about you. God will punish him...."

"No, Aunty, don't say that. He is my eldest son. I cannot see him suffer. Let God look after him wherever he might be."

The old lady was wiping away the sham tears from her eyes. There was no trace of any tear in the eyes of mother. But one felt that they would compel the leaves to fall down from the trees through their wailings. In the middle of the night she forbade everyone to address her as Nima *Bou*. She had not shirked from burying him in curses. How could she change like this all of a sudden? But Kunti could not understand anything. She had not been able to understand either of his parents or anyone else from the village until then. Everything seemed to be changing in a moment including her beliefs. Perhaps she might have been able to understand these if she would have studied at the minor school. She had passed class five and had been sitting at home for the last two years. She had not remembered anything that she had studied at school. She had no time to read it even if she borrowed a story book some time from someone. Mother had that one refrain that a daughter was meant for the mother-in-law's household. If she learnt to write a letter to her mother, that was enough. Where was the need for any further study?

Nobody had the guts in the house to take on mother in an argument.

Holding on to his waist, father went outside. As if he had no strength left in him. He was looking weak. Kunti had been staring. Radhu Mahajan took out a packet and put it in the palm of father. Father looked here and there and put it inside his waist. Radhu Mahajan knew how to talk. He had usurped the properties of many people by conning them.

Kunti went towards the back of the house. In a corner of the sky, there was just a trace of the moon. It could be barely seen through the leaves of the mango trees. There was some kind of an eerie silence everywhere. It was very scary. Mother said that Nima Bhai's mother lived on that mango tree. She loved sweets. Hence, she asked for them on every festive occasion by shaking the branches and leaves. Sometimes she got angry. Then she plucked off leaves from the branches or threw stones on to the thatched roof. That was why no one went near that mango tree after dark. But Kunti was not afraid today. His mother must have known how much Nima Bhai loved Kunti. Suddenly, a few leaves fell down from the trees making an eerie sound. Her chest began thumping. Oh yes, someone was coming this way. Who was it? Ha! Shame on her! It was her friend Jharana walking towards her very softly.

Kunti was sitting near the *chaura*. She stood up on seeing Jharana.

"Hello, friend. You were not well. How come you are sitting alone in this darkness?" Kunti did not answer the question. She said, "I was suffering from fever ever since the departure of Nima Bhai. I have just managed to get up on my own this evening. When did you come?"

"Just now. Yesterday your mother was at our place. She cried a great deal for Nima Bhai. I heard about your illness only from her. I returned from my uncle's place only yesterday."

Kunti could recall it now. Jharana had gone to her uncle's place for a holiday. Her mother was saying that a groom had been fixed for her there. The groom was supposed to be highly educated. Only he was not very fair to look at. Kunti spoke in Jharana's ear, "Is it fixed? Have you seen your groom with your own eyes?"

"Aw, come on! Mother always talks like that. I have said no."

"Why did you do that? The groom is highly educated. He has a good job. There is no one else at home except his parents. His sisters have already been married off. They have huge properties...."

Jharana put her palm across Kunti's mouth to stop her. In an emotion-filled voice, she said, "Do you know, friend? Mother has made up her mind to get me married to him. But I will drink poison in that case."

"Why?"

Speaking into Kunti's ears, Jharana said, "Do you know, friend? I heard that he has another woman at his workplace. My aunty said no to the proposal. But uncle is adamant. So is mother. Only if my father were alive...."

Jharana broke into a wail. Kunti had no idea how to comfort her. Jharana collected herself at length and said, "I had pinned a great deal of hope on Nima Bhai. Maybe he could have done something at this juncture. At least, I would have run away with him."

"What ...? What did you say? Pray, come again!"

"It's true, friend. Where is another man like Nima Bhai in our village? He has comforted me so many times in the past. We have spent a great deal of time together. He will study ... earn money ... I will also study...."

"Friend, why haven't you ever told me about it?"

"How would I know that Nima Bhai would run away from home like this?"

Kunti's eyes were filled with tears. Both of them held each other's hands and looked anew at each other. At this time mother's voice could be heard, "Hey, Kunti! Jhari! What are you talking about in the backyard in the nighttime? Come inside. Kunti, get a *paan* for aunty."

Both of them had a start. In the darkness, they walked back inside the house quietly. Neither of them had anything to say. It was as if two strangers had met in some unknown island for the first time.

Jharana and her mother returned to their home after a while. Aunty and mother had been talking to each other for a long time in a conspiring voice. Jharana and Kunti were not able to overhear anything. Jharana clasped Kunti's palm in her own while leaving and said, "Hadn't Nima Bhai told you anything while leaving home? He always loved you a great deal."

Kunti could not even gulp. No, she was not going to tell anything to her friend. Who knew when Nima Bhai was going to return? Was Jharana going to wait for him until then? Besides, would she be spared by aunty, mother and other villagefolk?

Kunti had been standing absentmindedly. Mother said in a voice that clearly reached them, "Oh yes. A girl is born to be given away elsewhere. Why not send them somewhere where they would at least be assured of two square meals? They cannot understand anything now as they are kids. They would understand it in due course."

Jharana walked behind her mother with her head lowered.

Mother said, "Why are you looking like that? Your hair looks dry. Why don't you apply a bit of oil to your hair? Different kinds of people are coming to the house. We cannot leave home just because Nima ran away!"

Kunti entered inside the house with an effort to keep her mouth shut. She was not able to understand what mother was saying to whom since yesterday. No one would be spared when sparks stated flying inside her head.

Kunti passed out at the place where she was sitting. Mother asked her to eat before going to sleep. But Kunti went to sleep just like that. The kids also slept all around. There was rice left from the morning. Who was going to cook again in the night? Father did not eat anything in the night half the days. Mother often managed with a bit of snacks. At the most she took a bit of watered rice.

Even in her sleep Kunti could know that father had returned home. Mother got up and went outside. Father would either go on talking incessantly under the influence of *ganja* or mother would start weeping while massaging father's feet. When mother wept at midnight, the breeze carried it in waves. Kunti felt the insides of her chest in a churn. A cold shiver ran down her spine. Her throat got parched. Breathless, she only stared vacantly leaning against the wall. She wondered what she could do under the circumstances. Didn't she have the power to wipe away the tears of mother? Couldn't she provide some comfort to mother just because she was the daughter? She could. But then why didn't she do it? She had no answer to that question. Didn't she know that it was a crime for her to speak out her mind? That she was not supposed to break the rules? She was only a daughter. Not a son. Not just a daughter. She was only a burden on everyone, and like the proverbial last straw on the camel, she was beautiful too. Too much beauty was not a crown in a poor family. It was a burning pyre of curses and sufferings. Only the person possessing it understood what it entailed. Just as she lived with her body, she died every moment with it.

Mother had put too many restrictions on her these past few days. She didn't allow her to go to the river bank. She had restricted her from moving about with friends. On festive occasions, she wanted to deck herself up and move around the village. But that too became a strict no.

These days she felt ill at ease stepping out on the streets even if it was only to visit her friend Jharana or the neighbourhood sister-in-law. She felt that the entire village tried to go beyond her unkempt hair and dried up skin and discover something else inside her. What was it? What was there in her body? Shivering and shrinking unto herself, she returned home. The kids of the village were the worst. They coughed knowingly when she passed their way. Sometime they broke into a vulgar song or passed comments. Some of them were older than Kunti, some were her age and some were many years younger than her. But they were male. Kunti's chest always thumped when she saw them. Many a time she returned home immediately on spotting them. She opened the school books of her childhood to read. Or she picked up the *Mahabharata* or the *Ramayana* to scan them. That was a lot better. She could not face the devouring stares of so many people. Already she had been sitting at home for three years after giving up studies. Only if she had passed minor examination! Luckily, Nima Bhai had taught her the English alphabets. If he would not have left in a hurry, she might have been able to read English in a few more days. She would not be so scared of the village brats if Nima Bhai would have been around. Who knew when he was going to return?

It was true indeed! Mother was weeping. Kunti sat up. When mother wept, it always seemed as if trees, plants and the breeze too wept. Kunti might be very angry with mother. But she could not bear her weeping. She wished to tear the sky, the earth and the atmosphere into pieces at such times. But she could not succeed in doing that. No, today she would go and ask mother why she was crying. Let her think anything, let father beat her up ....

Kunti walked without making a sound. The lantern was flickering in the breeze near the front door. A streak of light from the lantern had fallen on the outside verandah. Mother was massaging oil on the feet of father and was sobbing. Kunti didn't know what to say. There were no clothes on the body of father. How could she go there? At this time father asked affectionately, "Nima *Bou*, are you sleeping? You are working throughout the day. You must be tired." Mother said while continuing to sob, "No, why should I be asleep? You must be feeling sleepy. That's why you are pointing at me. I have not been able to drop my eyelids every since having a grown up girl at home."

Father said something. Kunti couldn't hear it. The sobbing sound from mother was no longer clearly audible in the breeze of the spring. Mother could not sleep because Kunti had grown up. That was why she restrained her in everything. But girls like her were still going to bathe in the river or see the *jatra* in the other streets or visit the temples on festive occasions with their parents. But Kunti's parents were not going to take her anywhere… they would let her rot inside the house calling her a grown up girl.

Father's voice could be heard again, "Nima *Bou*, are you sleeping? I have been thinking of telling it to you a number of times. But I keep forgetting every time. The entire village is talking about it. She is looking so beautiful while eating watered rice and spinach. She would be dazzling like a queen if she would be eating *palau* and mutton. Don't think that I am exaggerating because she is my daughter….but everything is fate."

Mother had perhaps dozed off for a moment. Sleepily she said, "Yes…everything is fate. We might have given birth to her. But we have no control over her fate. You listen to me. Somehow you get her married off this year. I am not able to have any control over myself seeing these village brats moving around like hounds. You never know what might happen when. I am not able to sit for a while to pray to the gods because of her. On top of that, the girl has been missing Nima so much that her health has started to fail."

Father got angry, "Why are you shouting so loudly? She might hear you."

"What more shame do I have? The grown up girl is waiting to be married off. On the other hand I am going to give birth to a child soon. How can I show my face to the son-in-law? Jhari's mother was saying that if we went to Cuttack, the doctors could do the operation …."

Father started at the top of his voice, "What? Do you know what you are saying? People are not getting a child. After all, it is the child of your own husband. Why should you go for the operation? The mother of Jhari is intolerant of you. She cannot see anyone prosper since her husband has died. Take heed, don't allow her to enter this house again."

Mother whispered, "Why are you getting angry? I know all about that intolerant woman ... I was just testing you.... My mother has given birth to three sons after my marriage with you. Why should I bother about it at this age?"

In the faint light through the door, Kunti saw her father embracing her mother. He said, "Shall we kill a life just because we are half dead working just to keep our children alive? The children will go their own separate ways tomorrow. We still have to remain as a family."

Mother said, "You do anything you like. But get the girl married off this year. Everything would be ruined if she ran away with someone."

"Why are you so scared? Just because the girl is beautiful? She is going to be a queen because of her beauty. I have got her horoscope examined by the village astrologer. Sadhu Parida has been after me since morning after seeing that horoscope. He made many entreaties. But I didn't make any commitment."

"What are you saying? I am not able to understand anything. I know all the tricks of that rascal Radhua. He must be casting his net so he can grab that mango tree. Don't get caught in his net. That is the only thing we have." Mother got up and sat leaning against a pillar.

"I know it. All you women are alike. Sadhu Parida was right in telling me not to discuss anything with you. That you are going to spoil everything."

"Hunh! Sadhu is also the seed of the same fruit."

Father moved near mother. He looked around and said, "No, Nima *Bou*, it is not like that. Sadhu Parida came on his own and gave the proposal on behalf of Radhu Mahajan.

Straightaway, I said no. Finally Radhu himself came and said that there was no need for us to return the money we have borrowed from him. He assured me that he was going to destroy all the papers. He is prepared to marry Kunti just like that. He is not asking for anything ...."

Mother said, " Save those sugary words. I had thought he was moved by our sorrows and that was why he was willing to forego the money. The bloody son of a bitch! Two of his wives have already hung themselves to death. There is not a child at home, and he must have crossed forty already! So he could not find anyone else! He has his sights fixed on my kid daughter! Why doesn't the bastard die!"

Father was not prepared to let go. He came out with an even stronger voice, "You are saying that there is no child at his home. The two wives died because of their own follies. One left for her mother's home eight days after the marriage never to return again. And the second one died of cholera. Who could have helped that? But the astrologer says that Radhu's planets are in the ascendance right now. *Shani* has already completed its course of twelve years. Good time has come for him now! Get that into your head!"

Mother said, "Whatever you might say I am not going to give my daughter away to Radhua. I will rather poison her. Or I will wring her neck. Haggard old man ... how can he even say this?"

Father said in an even stronger voice, "All women are stupid. I am not a fool that I will take lessons from you. Nima *Bou*, I have brought about my own downfall because I have been guided by you all these days. You have got three of my daughters married off to sprightly young men. Tell me if they are happy. There is not even a handful of rice available during the whole day. Are they going to eat the youth of their husbands and live on that? Try to get this into that silly head of yours. A woman's life is worth nothing if there is no food for the stomach and cloth for the body. I have told Sadhu Parida already. Let Radhu return the title deeds of my land and pay me seven thousand rupees towards marriage expenses. After that, I will discuss with the girl's mother and give the final word. I am not the one who could be tricked so easily."

Mother had been sitting as if she was terribly exhausted. Father started filling *ganja* into his *chillam* again. The weak legs of Kunti had been trembling. If mother would come to know of it.... Why was she so scared of such small things? Nima Bhai used to say that you could not live like human beings in this village if you were afraid of words and deeds. He ran away because he could not live in this timid village. Apparently, he was going to turn all the cowards of the village into heroes when he returned after completing his studies. If only Kunti would be alive until then!

Kunti could not hear what her mother was saying. Father was coughing intermittently. The naughty cloud was playing hide and seek with the moon. Kunti's body was getting colder by the minute in fear and apprehension. The chill wind was not helping matters.

Mother's laughter could be heard at length. She was saying, "So! That's it! But how could I know all these things? You are indeed clever. Why didn't you tell it to me earlier? When he has stashed away so much of wealth at home, he will come to our rescue in future. Besides, we have other girls at home to be married off. The sons can take care of themselves. But, at least, we would have a roof over our head. Poor Nima left home worrying about that. The Lord only knows when he will return."

Mother started sobbing again. Mother was thinking of Nima Bhai and weeping. Did that mean she liked him after all?

Father said, "Why are you crying? If someone went away, it is over and done with. And besides, it is not as if you do not have children of your own ...."

Father continued in the same vein for some time. Kunti could not hear what he was saying. Mother said half-angry and half-affectionately, "Let him live long by the grace of God."

"So what do I tell Mahajan? Sadhu Parida will arrive in the morning. It will be to our disadvantage if we defer the decision any longer. He has wealth. He can always find a bride for himself. He is after me only because he is a pious man."

Mother said, "Why are you asking me again? When he is doing good to us, we should return the favour. Otherwise, the gods would despise us. But that Mahajan is forty or is he even older that that?"

"Nima *Bou*! Don't make me angry. What would you get from age? You were fourteen when you had married me. I had already crossed forty by the time. But have I neglected you even for a moment? The more aged you are, the more clever you become. Riches will be sweeping your feet. You women are only concerned with appearance and age. Go, it is already late in the night. Let me close the front door."

Kunti sprinted away to her sleeping space in one breath. Father and mother perhaps had gone to sleep. That silence seemed to be biting Kunti like a bunch of bedbugs. On top of that she felt something tying her feet like a snake. She understood quickly that she had no deliverance from that. She had come to understand that it was no longer possible to escape the wealth of Radhu Mahajan. Her hands and feet had been tied. She could no longer swim in the river or run on the side of the paddy fields or lose herself in the greenery of the distant horizon while calling some strange bird. She knew she could not request her parents not to give her in marriage to Radhu Mahajan because she did not want to marry him. She could have told everything frankly to only one person. And perhaps he had the courage to dissuade her parents from going through with the proposal. But that Nima Bhai was not with her now. When would he return after completing his studies ...! Racking sobs were trying to escape her. She had been sleeping on the mat as if she had fainted out of tiredness.

Sleeping lightly, Kunti dreamt that some demon had come, cut her wings in flight and thrown them into the sea. And she had been sleeping on some unknown land bleeding all over. Try as she might to call for help, no sound escaped from her mouth. Heavy stones seemed to have been loaded on her chest. The two sides of the pillow were wet with her tears. As she came awake, she moved her hands over the mat as if she was searching for something. The psyche of a fifteen-year-old bird in flight – neither could it smell the wetness of the earth nor could it touch the whiteness of the horizon. She felt like a bird which had lost its nest and had been shot by an arrow in midair. She was swirling in that state in the dark skies.

Like the other womenfolk of the village, Kunti abided by all the religious chores round the year. But no one came forward to relieve her of the cruel sufferings that she was undergoing. Kunti had a feeling that she had been lying in some unknown, deserted place bleeding all over since God knows when. It was no recent phenomenon. Her whole body was burning ... it had continued to burn .... In phases and effortlessly. However much she tried to make the world a more beautiful place by getting crucified on the cross of the society and bleeding all over in the process, she became that much more exhausted. It seemed ages had passed. She had died a hundred times and been born a hundred times while the seasons kept changing in their natural way. And yet she experienced no peace. Her emaciated body had no rest either. Nor had the filth of the earth lessened in any way. There were only storms. Her soul kept moving in the kingdoms of heaven, earth and hell being a prey to the anger of the storms extending till the horizon. Where could she find peace? Who could say where the heavenly beauty of exquisitely graceful women had been scattered? Kunti could not understand why the Lord had been so prejudiced.

Kunti got up from the bed. She did not feel scared any more. Everyone was asleep. Only the moon was playing hide and seek with the clouds intoxicated by the breeze of the spring. The owl seemed to be weeping intermittently in the deodar tree. Nima Bhai was absolutely right when he said that no one could continue to live while being scared all the time. There was no glory in accepting anything that came your way. There was glory when one succeeded in somehow tackling the problems that came your way.

Could Kunti do that?

All hell broke loose in the morning. Kanhu Pradhan's daughter Jharana had become unconscious after drinking poison. No one knew whether she was going to live or not. One of the boys from the village had gone on a bicycle to get a doctor. All the people of the village had congregated before the door of Kanhu Pradhan's house to watch the scene. She had already been made to drink tamarind water, cat stool and what not. But her stomach was still not cleaned out.

Kunti reached there along with her mother. She could not believe that her friend was going to drink poison in the middle of the night just like that. Her mother had been lying unconscious. At times, she was shouting 'Jhari' when she came round for a while. The people of the street were whispering to each other. As if Jharana was some kind of a female cobra. She would have bitten many people. It was better that she was gone. Otherwise, the whole village would have come to grief because of her. The village brats were following her all the time. They were writing bawdy songs about her on walls. The girl thought that there was no one as beautiful as her on earth. Who knew why she decided to kick the bucket in this manner? Her mother was responsible for all this. She went around a thousand places in search of a groom for her. The girl was young. She could not take it any more. Hence, she decided to take the easy way out. Kunti was not aware how long she had continued to stare at her friend. Was it a fact that she drank poison because Nima Bhai went away without telling her anything? But she had never told her that she was contemplating any such thing! Did she drink poison because she was not happy with the marriage proposal put forth by her mother? What might have transpired during the course of one night ...?

"Hey Nima *Bou*? What are you staring at? Are you getting the message or not?"

Both Kunti and her mother had a start. The old woman Geli from down the street was standing. She was distantly related to Kunti as a grandmother. She had been staring at them leaning on her walking stick. Kunti's mother bowed and touched her feet. She directed Kunti to do likewise.

Old women Geli said, "Take heed of my words, Nima *Bou*. I have turned old seeing scenes of these kinds. This will be the situation if you keep young girls at home. All of you turned blind in spite of having eyes being swayed by the radio, that block office and the women's *morcha*. We have certain rules which guide us through life. But you can see for yourself what happens when you don't abide by them. I had advised Jhari's mother long back to get her married off. But she did not bother about me. She urged the girl to pursue higher studies. Now take it! Tie the misdeeds of the girl to a corner of your saree!"

The old woman sat down as if she was exhausted. Her ferret-like eyes were scanning Kunti from head to toe. Kunti had the uncomfortable feeling that someone was poking her all over with a burning stick. Mother was sitting on the floor and whispering something in the ears of the old woman.

There was a hush at this time. Had the doctor arrived?

No, Sadhu Parida, Radhu Mahajan and two fat young men arrived at the scene together. Those two fat people did not belong to the village. Sadhu Parida said, "Manu dear! Please check the pulse. The heart seems to have stopped since the morning. What more can the doctor do? You have been treating everyone in your village, no?"

One of the two young men was pitch dark in complexion. He sat down near Jharana and checked her pulse. Then he grimaced. Radhu Mahajan said, "Hey Manua! Check carefully. If any medicines could help, talk to us freely!"

Manu did not say anything. Radhu Mahajan had been staring at Jharana tying his red towel around his head. He was half bald. Kunti had seen him many times during festivities. He was not very tall. He had a slight paunch even though he could not be called fat. He had a mixture of black and white hair on his chest and back. Oil seemed to be dripping from his extremely fair face. Kunti recalled the conversation between her father and mother last night. Her head started reeling. Everything looked dark around her. She thought she was going to faint. Her friend had not died. She had found deliverance. But why was she alive? To set up home with Radhu Mahajan as a husband?

Kunti could feel vomit rise from deep inside her stomach. Fever, the work at home, sleepless nights and her friend drinking poison - all these seemed to have sucked out all her energy. Like a tree falling in storm, she fell on the floor with a thud. People surrounded her on all sides. Everyone seemed to be bothered about her. As her mother picked her up and put her against her chest, Father's roar could be heard, "You have enough troubles of your own. What are you doing here along with your daughter? Have you come here to give counsel? Are you leaving this place immediately or not? Ha.... If the woman had only a little bit of sense...." Kunti had been staring. Radhu Mahajan was wiping away the sweat from the brow of her father. He said, "Okay, okay. Don't lose your temper. You will fall sick. She is only a child ...." Kunti saw that Radhu Mahajan was staring at her. He looked away when their eyes locked. As if he was feeling shy. Mother said, "Hey! What for are you staring like that? Pull the corner of your saree over your head. Move. Let us go home. Don't keep on wailing 'friend'! Can't you see that your father is furious? Come, let us go."

Kunti returned home with her head lowered. Two people were running on the road with bamboos in their hands to carry away the body of her friend. Mother said, "If someone is gone, she is gone. How are we bothered about it? Everything is okay if we are okay. Let us go home. You haven't eaten anything since last night. You eat something and sleep for a while. You will feel much better after that."

Kunti lay down straight on the mat. Mother said, "Go and have a bath. You have touched a dead body."

Kunti did not answer. Mother said, "Can't you hear me? I am telling you to go and have a bath." At this time father's voice could be heard, "Hey Nima *Bou*! What advice are you giving her? Get a pot of water and pour it over her here. She will not go near any well or pond to have her bath. How many days are left anyway? Get some water and give her a bath in that corner room. I am not going to be guided by you any more. Times are really bad."

"What makes you get angry with me? Just because I said that she had touched a dead body?"

"Shut up, you stupid woman. If you talk back at me, I will break your goddamned teeth. From today onwards, bathe the girl with turmeric and oil at home. And guard her every moment. Radhu Mahajan has promised to send food from the temple. In three days time, everything would be over."

Kunti's eyelids which were shutting down became open again. She had never seen her father smoking *ganja* with the *chillam* during the day time. But mother did not say anything. She simply carried a bundle of currency notes from his hand and went inside. Perhaps she hadn't remembered that she too had touched the dead body. Kunti lost herself in the darkness when she closed her eyes again. She did not have the energy to think of anything. The man floating on a boat in deep sea could neither count the waves not dream about the shore. The tiny mind and body of Kunti floated away into deep darkness.

She had no idea how she had spent the next three days amid all kinds of uncertainties. Her friend's body was burnt. The police tried to harass the family. But Radhu Mahajan paid them enough bribe to hush the matter up. Everyone in the village was praising Radhu Mahajan. The dry face of her friend came floating before her repeatedly. What could she ask anyone? Father and mother kept whispering between themselves all the time. She could not fathom from her mother's face whether there was happiness or sorrow in her. Kunti was in one world. They were in another.

On the evening of the third day, two other men came and talked to her father along with Sadhu Parida and Geli's mother. Kunti had no idea what was going on. But she was convinced that something was going to happen soon. Suddenly, mother came inside the house crying all the way. She sat near Kunti and caressed her head. Tears went on flowing incessantly. Kunti was worried. She asked, "What has happened? Why are you crying?"

Mother started crying even louder. Geli's mother came inside the house and said, "Why, do you think that you alone have given birth to a girl? It is not as if she is going away somewhere far. She would respond if you call her from this place. You get away from this place. The barber woman has arrived. Let her massage Kunti with turmeric powder. That Mahajan must be scared witless by this time. There is more love because the girl does not take a dowry with her."

The old woman went away. Mother too went away wiping her nose. The barber woman applied turmeric powder to Kunti and made her wear a new saree. Kunti could neither cry nor say anything. It was as if she was just a doll. Anyone could make her dance the way they liked. For some reason, her mother fainted when she sat on the palanquin. Tear and saliva were flowing freely. The younger brother and sister started howling. Even a couple of drops of tear ran down from the dry eyes of her father. But not a drop fell from the sea-like eyes of Kunti. She had been staring ahead without blinking her eyes. She could not recall for a moment that she was in this house for fifteen years along with her father, mother, brothers and sisters. She had turned into an idiot looking at the faces of all those strangers. The palanquin pushed its way through the mango and coconut trees. Her childhood and all the memories associated with it had been left behind. Dreams, mango flowers, friends, river, pond, kewra plants, the burial ground – the palanquin passed through all these. In the process, it seemed Kunti's name was wiped out from that village for all time to come. There was not a drop of tear in her eyes. No one was Kunti's own that she would miss him or her if she left her home or village. There was no such person for whom she would shed tears wherever in the world she might be. So much so that she did not even miss Nima Bhai any more after the death of her friend. Let everyone go in search of his own happiness. Kunti was not going to worry about anyone.

She had no idea what time of the night it was. Kunti saw five to six men standing under a tree with a gas light in hand. Someone blew a conch even before the palanquin had reached there. Kunti was startled by that sound and fainted inside the palanquin.

After that what? She felt that some people lifted her away from inside the palanquin. They sprinkled water on her face. There was the distant sound of a clarionet. There was a fire burning in front. A priest was chanting *mantras*. Kunti was opening her eyes to close them again. It was as if she had been surrounded by demons. She was half awake and half asleep. Knots were tied with Radhu Mahajan in that state. Kunti fell down in a heap from the platform at the time the knot was tied. She had lost consciousness yet again.

The night passed and the morning came. Kunti opened her eyes slowly. What place was this? She was not on her usual mat surrounded by earthen walls. She was sleeping on a bed wearing a red silk saree. There were gold bangles on her wrist and *alta** on her feet. Surely she was not dreaming?

Some unknown women entered inside the room. Kunti closed her eyes the moment she saw them. One of them said in jest, "Look at her! She has been showing off ever since she has arrived here. Her excuse is that she is exhausted after fasting for a day."

Another woman came out harshly, "Aw, I have seen many women like her. Would the stomach be filled only if you are buried in ornaments? And why does this dame lose consciousness time and again? Gunduri, wake her up! Isn't she going to bathe? What is the time now? The gods are still waiting to receive offerings from her hand."

Gunduri said, "Why don't you people leave? I will wake her and bathe her. Radhu Bhai has said that she will bathe near the well. She will not go to the river or any pond."

"What for? Is someone going to carry her away? There is a saying that when the hungry man gets hold of a hilsa fish, he

* a red liquid applied on feet on festive occasions

chews up the bones as well." Kunti had no idea who said that.

This time Kunti sat up. She pulled down the veil over her head. It was as if she had been staying in that house since ancient times and was going to stay there till eternity. She walked out to the verandah at a fast pace. Someone caught hold of her by her arm and said, "Hold it, you show-off. Your feet are not steady even now. You will again lose consciousness. I will help you walk. I might not be your own sister-in-law. But Radhu Bhai is more dear to me than my own brother. Call me Apa. I am Gunduri."

Kunti looked at the face of Gunduri. She did not have any bangles on her wrists. Half of her head had turned grey. She was wearing a white saree with a thin border. A dirty blouse to go with that. But there was love and affection in her eyes. There was a hint of tear in the corner of her eyes.

Kunti took her bath near the well and changed in to a new silk saree. Ornaments had been lined up on the bed. Cosmetics too had been arranged neatly. New sarees and blouses had been stacked in the cupboard.

Gunduri said, "Bhauja, the women of the street will say many things. Just ignore them. They are highly intolerant. Go ahead and wear your ornaments. There is no one at this place. You have got to take care of yourself. I am not going to touch anything."

Tears welled up in the eyes of Gunduri Apa. Kunti wanted to say something. But she thought better of it. In fact, she was not able to comprehend the events that were unfolding around her like a bad dream.

A little while later Gunduri Apa arrived with a bowl of watered rice, fish fry and pickles. She said, "Eat this. You must be famished. You haven't eaten anything since yesterday."

Kunti was terribly hungry. She sat down near the rice bowl. Then she thought something and pulled Gunduri near her holding her by the hand. She had to act out the role of the daughter-in-law at this place. That had escaped her altogether.

Gunduri Apa wiped the tears from the corner of her eyes and said, "I am not so lucky. How can I eat fish? You go ahead." Kunti had finished eating. But she was sitting there without washing her hand. Gunduri Apa was nowhere to be seen. Not even a kitten was to be seen anywhere. There was not another person in such a huge house. How was she going to live there? She stepped outside slowly. No, there was no one around. Someone could be heard talking from the other side of the house.

She washed her hand quickly and came back to lie down on the bed. It seemed that she had not slept for ages. Sleep simply overtook her.

As she came awake, she found that many people had come inside the house. Conversation was going on. But she could not see any women other than Gunduri Apa. The sun was about to set on the other side of the window. How long had she slept? Why had no one called her? Kunti was feeling so tired that she did not even want to get up. Gunduri Apa sauntered into the room after a long time and said, "Bhauja, have you got up? The priest has come. There are no auspicious moments tomorrow. The priest is preparing the *chaturthi* puja. The astrologer also agrees with the priest. You come quickly and have a bath. Your father has arrived with some gifts. I did not call you as you were sleeping."

Kunti was startled. She asked, "Father? Whose father?"

"Father of who else? Radhu Bhai's father has expired before ten years. Your father has arrived with gifts for the *chaturthi*." Gunduri Apa had a *paan* in her mouth. She was smiling.

At this time father came inside the room and embraced Kunti. He said, "My darling! After your departure there is only darkness in my house. Your mother has taken to bed. Why are you looking so dark?" Kunti had been staring at her father. Her eyes held no tears in them. There was no grief in her heart either. What could she tell her father? The tears in her father's eyes were as good as lines drawn on water.

Gunduri Apa said, "Do you see, uncle? Your daughter has forgotten you in a day's time. She won't have any problems in our house. You tell aunty not to worry about anything. I will tell Radhu Bhai to send her to your house for a few days when things quieten down a bit."

Father said, "Daughter! You are like the mother of this girl. Try to manage everything. She is so young. Don't take offense at anything."

The barber woman was in a hurry. So Kunti left with Gunduri Apa to have her bath. She did not think that she had ever met someone who now tried to masquerade as her father.

The rituals of the *chaturthi* puja were over. All the people of the village sat in the courtyard and had dinner. Radhu Mahajan had spent lavishly to win everyone over. He was also moving around making everyone comfortable. Kunti had been looking from inside her room through the opening in the door. Gunduri Apa was preparing *paan* leaning against the door. She smiled at Kunti and said, "You are a lucky girl. My brother has pulled out all stops and he is spending freely. It was not so in the earlier two marriages."

Kunti asked, "Where are the other two?"

"They are dead and gone. Don't talk about them any more. My insides get all churned up when I think about them."

"Why? Were they suffering from any disease?"

Gunduri said, "Let it be. I will tell you some other day. Here, your father has come to take leave."

Kunti saw that man masquerading as her father was coming with Radhu Mahajan. There was a wide grin on his face. Kunti lowered her head. For some reason her chest thumped when she looked at Radhu Mahajan. After a while, father said, "I am leaving. I have invited my son-in-law. Both of you come at the time of the full moon. I hope my son-in-law does not forget his poor father-in-law."

Radhu Mahajan bowed low and paid his respects. Then he said, "Gunduri! Give that dhoti to uncle so he can wear it . And make a packet of sweets. There are small children in the house."

Father said, "Let it be. I will not take anything from the daughter's house. If you could give me some money, I could get that bullock released. Other things can wait. There is no hurry."

Radhu Mahajan extended a cloth packet and said, "No, father, I am a religious man. I always keep my word. Everything is inside this packet. Sadhu Parida has already taken the paper relating to your land. The rest is inside the packet. Besides, this is not the end of everything. I promise to help out in the future when there is a need. Don't worry about anything."

Father moved his left palm over Kunti's head affectionately and said, "I am leaving, my dear. Everyone at home would be waiting for my return. Hey Gunduri, hand over the packet of sweets to the barber. I can't say no to the son-in-law. I am leaving, my dear. God bless."

Holding the new dhoti under the armpit and carrying the packet of currency notes in his hand, father left while wiping his eyes. Kunti had been staring dumbly. An owl hooting somewhere in the distance seemed to be making faces at her. To her luck, the women of the village had not come in the evening. Gunduri Apa was saying that women never went outside to eat in the evenings. That was good. Now they would have said all kind of things to make her miserable.

Gunduri Apa would not be persuaded however much she insisted that she did not feel like eating anything. She made her eat some sweets. She laughed and said, "Bhauja, you must eat well and be strong when you have come to this house. What other happiness is there in the life of a woman? You don't lack for anything. You can do anything you want. My brother is a pet. He will do anything you ask him to do. But there would be no happiness if it is not ordained. Everything depends on your fate."

She pulled Kunti and took her to another room. A lantern had been lit in that room. Radhu Mahajan had been sitting on a huge bed. There was a cotton towel around his neck. Gunduri pushed Kunti inside and closed the door after her.

She had no idea that she was going to stand on the gallows so soon. She trembled all over with fear. She held on to the door and sat down on the floor.

"Hey! Why are you sitting there? Come here and sleep."

Kunti did not answer. Radhu Mahajan yawned loudly. Then he rubbed himself all over with the towel. He made obeisance before the deity Radhamadhav and went forth to lock the door. He looked at Kunti for a while and said, "Are you scared? Come, come with me."

He held Kunti by her hand and made her sit on the bed. He asked, "Aren't you feeling well? I heard that you have given up food since the day your friend died. The dead is gone. How does it matter any longer? Now come and sleep."

Kunti could not sleep even then. Radhu Mahajan picked up her soft body and made her sleep against the wall. He asked, "Are you feeling unwell? Shall I give you a massage on the waist?"

Kunti did not answer. Radhu Mahajan embraced her and caressed her all over. He made her sleep on his chest and caressed her head. He mumbled a lot of sweet nothings which did not mean a thing to Kunti. After a long while, he said, "You must be tired. Sleep. Don't be scared. Call me if you want to go outside."

He started snoring as he finished saying that. Kunti pushed herself against the wall with fright watching his bare body, open mouth and the dirt under his nails. Radhu Mahajan had been sleeping like a demon. As if he was not bothered about anything. Kunti was amazed looking around the room. A soft breeze coming through the half open window was playing hide and seek in the faint light of the lantern. Someone's ghost seemed to be dancing in the shade. A faint moon could also be seen in a corner of the sky. Her entire being seemed to long for a bit of light and breeze. She wanted to get off the bed and sleep on the floor. Or else she wanted to go and sleep with Gunduri Apa. Or maybe just go away somewhere. Her friend could die. Nima Bhai could leave home and go away. Couldn't she take one small step in any direction? Suddenly, Radhu Mahajan turned sides and started talking incoherently in his sleep. In a moment, he started snoring again. There was no way Kunti could sleep.

She got down from the bed slowly and stood on the floor. The gold ornaments in her hands, feet and neck gave her the uncomfortable feeling that she was covered all over with snakes. She was sweating heavily under the heavy silk saree. Kunti opened the window and stood near it.

What had happened to her past? She could not recall the face of her father, mother, Nima Bhai, Jharana, Geli's mother or anyone else connected with her past. She was not very sure that they all existed at one time. A large number of ghosts seemed to have surrounded her and devouring her silently.

And this Radhu Mahajan! How grotesque was his appearance, laughter and conversation! He lifted her from her house just like that and married her. And today was supposed to be the nuptial. Her husband was asleep peacefully after ensuring that she was laden with silk saree and gold ornaments. How stupid this man was! And yet how cunning! Only he knew what he was talking about while caressing her all over. So this was her dream of the nuptial night!

Kunti turned around to look at her husband. He was fast asleep. So this was her nuptial night? Was this the first night of meeting the husband? There was no limit to the romantic stories she had heard about this night from the women of the village. And yet ...!

She had started sweating heavily in the sweltering heat. The ornaments were heavy on her frail body. She took off the ornaments one by one and kept them on the floor. The sweat beads dropping from her forehead into her eyes seemed to make her blind.

Kunti had fallen down and injured herself in her childhood while running to catch butterflies. The butterfly was flapping its wings on the branch of a plant just beyond her reach even as she was having difficulty in getting up. Kunti had tried to get up and fallen again ... the butterfly had flown away. Even as she was watching it, it flew away and disappeared. She could never forget the sadness which had enveloped her that day because of that sheer defeat. That sadness and that defeat had kneaded her to a pulp going beyond the setting moon and the bright stars of the sky and the fragrance of the Henaa flower blossoming all around. She could not get away from it. Kunti was not able to understand that however much she tried to cling to her youth, it had already turned into a handful of dust.

She did not have enough strength to stand there any longer. She slept prostrate on the floor. The breeze was no longer playing hide and seek with the mixture of light coming from the lantern and the moon. It was staring fixedly at Kunti. At the despondent Kunti. At her virginity which had blossomed as a flower. At the drop of glistening sweat under the lips of time. At the trace of a smile that was fast disappearing.

There was no change in Kunti's routine the next day or on the days that followed. Gunduri Apa cooked and fed her. She also made the bed. Guria, the servant boy, swept the rooms and cleaned utensils. He also massaged Radhu Mahajan. He grinded *bhaang* and made sorbet for his master. He also carried flowers for Kunti. Kunti did not have to do any chore. Being idle all the time, she neither felt hungry nor could she sleep easily. Kunti sat down near Gunduri Apa one day while she was cooking and said, "Apa, let me chop the vegetables today."

Gunduri Apa was aghast. She said, "Why, am I already dead? I will be nowhere if Radhu Bhai comes to know of it."

"Why? Are you a servant in this house? You ... why, you are ...."

"Oh, yes. In the manner of speaking I am a sister. Otherwise, I am even less than any paid servant. It's all my fate .... Why should I blame anyone?"

Kunti had been staring amazed. As she was cutting brinjals, Gunduri said, "But how are you concerned with any of these things?"

With the eagerness of hearing a good story, Kunti held on to Gunduri's palm and said, "No, Apa. Please tell me. Why are you staying here and not at your mother-in-law's place? What about your children?" Kunti fell silent not knowing what else to ask. Gunduri did not say anything.

"Apa!"

"Yes."

"Why are you here? What about your family?"

"Do you feel uncomfortable about it?"

Kunti broke into a wail and held Gunduri by her feet. She said, "Don't talk like that. Or else I will take my life with my own hands."

Gunduri became pensive. She looked at the thatch of the kitchen. She went outside and took a peek. No, there was no one around. The office of Radhu Mahajan was open in the first floor. Interest on loans must be getting computed there. The clerk must be explaining the various transactions. Radhu Mahajan must be getting tired of counting the money. He must be dozing leaning against the pillow. Apart from that, why should anyone come to this house unless there was a dire need?

Gunduri wiped her running nose. She cut a patato into two pieces with a flourish. The fire was burning brightly in the hearth.

"You do not know anything about the world, Bhauja. You were born only yesterday. My daughter would have been two years older than you had she survived. But the gods even snatched her away from me."

"Who all are there in your husband's place?" there was curiosity in Kunti's voice.

"Not a damned soul who matters. In two years, I have seen my husband's face twice only. He was always smoking *ganja* and was never in his senses. Everyone said that a truck ran over him when he was working in some factory."

"But there would be your father-in-law, mother-in-law, landed properties ...?"

"Are you nuts? My husband's younger brother left me on the streets the day he expired. He had his own wife at home. But it was as if he had waited since a long time for his brother to conk out somehow. I bore all the indignities staying in the barn for a couple of days. The parents-in-law did not intervene even for a moment. Even my sister-in-law remained mum in spite of seeing me suffer. Anyway, she had no guts to take on her husband head on. She was always sick. Always on the bed with back pain."

"What are you saying, Apa? Even if no one at home said anything, didn't anyone in the village intervene?"

Gunduri lost her cool and said, "People of the village? What could they do? Those bastards were waiting in the wings to see the fun. This happens in every village. Who came to her rescue when your friend died? The police might have created all kinds of problems. Okay, Radhu Bhai is supposed to be a miser. But he came to their rescue by dishing out the required amount."

Kunti lowered her head. Even with her limited intelligence, she had come to realise that one could achieve the impossible if there was enough money around.

As she was giving the finishing touches to the curry, Gunduri said, "Everyone closed his eyes. Even that sonofabitch Yamaraj pulled away my child from my lap. All my problems would have been over if he would have taken me in stead. But I am ordained to suffer. Who can I blame?"

Kunti tried to bring about a twist in the tale. She said, "Was that why you came to your brother?"

"Nah! How could I come on my own? Father and mother had already expired by then. Even the homestead land had been mortgaged to Radhu Bhai. I had once sent a message to him. But Radhu Bhai did not bother to answer. He said he could not take care of every destitute on earth.

"So you came on your own?"

"It's all very complicated. A kid like you cannot understand. But when Radhu Bhai's second wife became very sick, it was a big problem to run this household. She had drunk some kind of poison. The child in her womb died as a result. When Radhu Bhai found the woman take to her bed for six months, he finally yielded. He quarrelled with my husband's younger brother and brought me back. Everyone is scared of him, you know."

"Scared? Why?" It seemed as if the two words dropped out of her mouth suddenly.

"And why should not they be scared? People in about ten nearby villages have borrowed money from him. Who would come to their rescue in hard times? My husband's younger brother was a goonda, demon and a dacoit. But he went and hid himself in the granary when he saw Radhu Bhai. Financial muscle is always stronger than physical muscle."

Kunti did not answer. She was drawing lines on the floor and seemed to be lost in thought. She wanted to say something. But it was difficult for her to pop the question. Should she ask why that woman drank poison even if she was carrying a child in her womb? And why Radhu Mahajan's first wife too had died young? If Gunduri Apa got angry and scolded her, that would be too bad.

Gunduri Apa put the pot of curry on the floor and said, "Come Bhauja, eat now. Radhu Bhai won't eat until late. He will get angry if I don't serve you early."

"Aren't you going to eat?"

"Forget about me. I can eat only after I have served food for my master. All said and done, I am still only a maid servant... no one bothers about me."

There were tears in Gunduri Apa's eyes. Her lovely face seemed to have been singed in smoke and sweat. Her weak frame in a dirty, white saree seemed to be shaking like the leaves of the bamboo plant. She had never talked for such a long time with Kunti ever since she had stepped into this house after marriage. This was an odd village. No grown up woman had ever stepped inside the house. Gunduri Apa also never went anywhere. She did not even chat with Kunti for any length of time. She was extremely careful in conducting herself. Only now could Kunti understand why Gunduri Apa went on working round the clock with a sad face. Kunti said slowly, "Apa! Shall I tell you something? Couldn't we go for a bath in the river in the evening? I don't like the water of the well."

"No way. How can you talk so stupidly? Will Radhu Bhai spare me if he comes to know that the newly married woman had gone to bathe in the river? The women of the street will make fun of us. They wouid threaten to leave the river bank and go away...."

"Why? What sin have I committed?"

"No, you haven't done anything. It is all your *karma*."

"Apa!" Kunti broke into a wail.

"Quiet! What is sorrow and what is happiness for a poor girl? People will make fun of you. No one ever steps into this accursed house for this reason. No one looks at his face with the belief that no food would be available if one looked at Radhu Mahajan's face in the morning. People think that their children would fall sick if they crossed his path in the morning. And, on top of that, Radhu Mahajan cannot bear anyone else dropping in to the house to converse with his wife."

"Father had asked me to come to our village after a few days. You tell your brother...."

"You are really stupid. You would have gone if your father would have sent a formal invitation along with the usual gifts. On the other hand, he is taking money, rice and oil from his son-in-law everyday through someone or other. The rituals of temples may stop. But your father's begging would never stop. And you think he will take you home? He believes that a man's responsibilities are over once he gives a daughter away in marriage. Forget about your father's house. Your father is heartless."

There was a churning inside Kunti's stomach. Everything looked dark around her. She had a feeling that she was falling into some kind of a bottomless pit. A terrible demon was standing at the bottom with his hand extended and mouth open. No, no.

No one would save her. She tried to get up. But she collapsed back clutching on to her stomach. Gunduri had gone out at that time with a pot in hand to get drinking water. Or else, she might have started wondering about her state. Radhu Mahajan would have got angry for no reason at all.

Guria arrived at this time and said, "Maa, why are you sitting here on the floor? The master will not be pleased. Where is Apa?"

Kunti had not properly seen Guria until then. What was the need after all? Why should she talk to him? She motioned towards the well in the backyard with her finger.

"No, I am not going that way. The master said that the barber has come from uncle's house. Tell Apa to serve him food in the upper storey."

At this time Gunduri Apa arrived and screamed, "You bloody rascal! Why have you got up on the verandah? Have you washed your feet or not?"

Guria jumped down the verandah and said, "No, Apa. Nothing is the matter. Why don't you see for yourself? I have just now taken a bath in the pond. The master asked me to tell you …."

"Yeah, I have heard. The barber has come. I will send food for him. Brother was saying that Manua and his friends will eat here…."

"No, they are not going to eat this stuff. They are holding some kind of a feast under the tree. They have slaughtered a he-goat."

"Are you going to eat there, you rascal? You are moving around the place for that reason. Is that right?"

"No, I was not going there. The master ordered me to help in serving the food there."

"Okay, okay. Leave this place. Don't get any of those non-vegetarian stuff here."

Guria went away wringing his palms. Gunduri Apa put the pot of water on the floor and said, "Radhu Bhai always behaves like a child when Manua comes along. He comes with a bunch of his friends. They enjoy themselves here. Who is going to work so hard for them?"

Kunti asked, "Who is this Manua, Apa?"

"Your own nephew. He is the son of Khira Apa who was Radhu Bhai's own sister. Khira Apa was seven years older than Radhu Bhai. She is dead since long. Manua is working somewhere in Kolkata. He comes to his uncle on holidays and makes demands on him. As if Radhu Bhai was his friend. He had come during the marriage."

Who was this Manua? How old was he? He was working at Kolkata. And yet he made demands on his uncle when he came here on holidays. But Kunti had never seen him.

"Why are you staring like that? Haven't you seen Manua?"

Kunti remained silent. How could she make anyone understand that she had not as yet seen her husband properly? Manua was a rank outsider.

"It is that mustachioed fellow. Pitch black in complexion. Looks like a demon. The two red eyes keep burning all the time. When you fainted at the time of the nuptial puja, he was the one who had taken you on to his lap."

Kunti still did not answer. Gunduri Apa was talking to herself as she was arranging the utensils. She was cursing someone too. Kunti was not bothered about that. She had a feeling that her feet were getting dragged down some bottomless pit. The dark pit seemed to be unusually cold. That demon was there still with his hands raised and mouth open. No other soul was present.

Silently, Kunti got up and moved towards her bedroom without telling anything to Gunduri Apa. She passed out on the bed. Gunduri Apa's voice could be heard intermittently. She had no idea how long she had slept. All of a sudden, she came awake hearing the voice of Gunduri Apa near her. Apa was wiping her face with a wet towel. Who was this in front of her? Radhu

Mahajan? Her husband? There was a concerned look on his face. He seemed to be making an appeal to her. On his left, someone looking like a demon was staring at her leaning against the bed. His moustache was almost a foot long. The eyes were bloodshot. As if he could devour someone whole. There were a couple of others on the other side. Kunti could not bring herself to look at them.

Radhu Mahajan shouted, "Gunduri, how many times have I told you that food has to be served at the right time? She seems totally famished. What would people say?"

Someone broke into a guffaw. It was perhaps that Manua. He said, "Just hold it. Let me check her pulse. Everything is all right, uncle. You are worrying unnecessarily. Aunty was perhaps feeling a bit sleepy...."

"No, Manu. I see her withering away everyday ever since she has left her father's place. But I do not have the time to look into everything."

"Oh, hell! In Kolkata, girls work round the clock and eat only once a day. How slim they are! And beautiful too! In our place everyone only eats and sleeps."

As he removed his hand from her wrist, Manua pinched Kunti on her back. Kunti shrieked and sat up. Oh God! What a nasty sight he was! Was he going to devour her right away? Kunti closed her eyes out of fright.

Gunduri Apa said, "Is it proper to make fun of your Aunty? Manu, you push off. No more of that stuff. Let me feed her."

"Why don't you allow me to feed her?"

Manua pinched Kunti below her armpit in a flash. Kunti shouted in pain, "Oh my God, I am going to die!"

"Hey Manua, your aunt is extremely delicate. Don't touch her again. You are extremely naughty. Come, let us go from here."

Radhu Mhajan pulled Manua by his hand. As he was leaving, Manua said mischievously, "Aunty! Don't forget me! I'll be back." A streak of lightning seemed to pass in his eyes.

Gunduri Apa wiped her tears and said, “That fellow is a vagabond. On top of that, he knows that Radhu Bhai dotes on him.”

Kunti had been staring outside towards the afternoon sun amid the tears and saliva running down her face. The food served in front of her had been staring at her. Where was the hunger? Or the thirst? There was only darkness all around....

She broke into a loud wail looking at Gunduri Apa, “I will die, Apa. I am surely going to die.”

Not a word escaped the throat of Gunduri Apa.

The night passed after the day. Again the day came followed by the night. No tears would come out of Kunti’s eyes. She only kept staring outside in silence. If she talked a great deal, Gunduri Apa chided and silenced her. At times she talked about her own sorrows just so Kunti would understand that one had to live even with extreme sufferings. Everyday would not be smooth sailing. In its own time, things would change for the better.

Kunti could never tell anything to Radhu Mahajan. The reason was that he lowered his bashful eyes whenever Kunti looked at him. He could not look straight at his own wife. As if Radhu Mahajan’s eyes would get burnt and turn to ashes dazzled by her beauty. When he entered the room at night, he put out the lantern and embraced Kunti. He caressed her. He asked her fondly if she would like to eat or wear something in particular. Whether she fancied any particular ornament. As if Kunti was a small girl. She was sulking. She was not talking. And the rich businessman was patting her on the back and trying to placate her. Kunti could not understand what was the meaning of husband, family and the deeper meaning of married life. She shivered when at times Radhu Mahajan caressed her passionately. She felt that the spring would rush out this time tearing the chest of the mountain. At such times, she saw tides of dreams within herself. Amid that tide, she shivered within herself at the possibility of getting hold of the sun after breaking the cover of the fog. But the shivers remained as shivers only. The waves of dreams moved only for a moment on the barren land. The dreams of her unmarried years frightened her like the ghosts of married life. They made faces at her at times. The gold ornaments on the wrists, the expensive sarees on her body, the properties of the landlord, his unlimited wealth – nothing could give her peace. If only she could get away once from the four walls of this house!

Gunduri Apa had left for the marriage of a nephew for the past two days. She was not at all willing to go. Radhu Mahajan chided her. He said, "You cannot bear a grudge for all time to come." He also gave her some money by way of gift for the nephew. He sent Gunduri Apa to her mother-in-law's place in a palanquin. When Kunti cried, Radhu Mahajan said, "She will come back in two days. She is not going to stay there for ever. Why are you crying? How would this household run without her? Don't be scared. I am always available on the first floor. Guria will provide everything. You cook whatever you can. I will get some sweets. There won't be any problem."

Kunti was astounded. What was this? How could a husband talk like this to his wife? She had left home for three months. Kunti had never cooked for a day. She hadn't cut vegetables. She hadn't swept the house nor cleaned utensils. Her palms had become softer. The nails were clean like a whistle. The feet were dazzling being massaged with oil and turmeric paste. At times Kunti was startled on looking at herself. The psyche buried in sarees, ornaments and pleasures were twitching in the process of getting burnt in the fire. No amount of water or air could put out the fire that had enveloped her body and mind.

As she was leaving, Gunduri Apa had whispered to her, "I am leaving because I cannot disobey Radhu Bhai. I will be back in two days. Don't be afraid. Make sure that Guria is always available nearby. Nothing is beyond that rascal Manua. Lock the door properly before you sleep in the afternoon. Radhu Bhai will always stay in the first floor. I will be back in two days...."

Kunti nodded her head in agreement. Let Gunduri Apa go. After all, she had a family. She had to go there at times.

Kunti cooked for the first time that evening. Guria was smoking a bidi and dozing in the courtyard. The moon was shining bright in the sky. Some wild flower was swaying in the breeze on top of the wall of the courtyard. Kunti felt quite a bit lighthearted. She was in her husband's house and cooking for him. And yet she had no idea what her husband liked to eat. She had not even sat once near him when he took his food - the way mother always sat near father or Kani Bhauja sat near Sura Bhai, talking to each other. Why was it so?

There was a knock on the door. Who had come? Manua? No.... From inside the kitchen, she could see her husband going into the bed room with a mug of water. Guria asked, "Sir, shall I ask Maa to serve?"

"No, I will serve myself. Tell Maa to eat and go to sleep. I have to work for two more hours. I will eat later."

It was so everyday. Kunti never had any idea what time of the day and night Radhu Mahajan had his lunch and dinner. God only knew what kind of accounts he had to keep everyday.

Kunti got up after a while. She told Guria, "You and your master finish dinner at your own time. I am feeling sleepy. I am going in."

Guria was sitting on the verandah, dozing all the time. What else could he do?

Was Kunti going to die if she did not eat one day? She had starved for days on end at her father's place. Nothing had happened to her. As such, she did not feel hungry these days. How much could she eat? Had she come as a daughter-in-law to this house only to eat? Damn it! She couldn't even discuss this with anyone.

Guria's voice came floating over after some time, "Maa! If you have already eaten, it is well and good. Or else you finish your dinner. The master might eat something or he might skip dinner. Nothing is certain with him. How long into the night are you going to wait?"

Kunti did not answer. Should she ask why the two earlier wives of Mahajan died young? Both of them passed away within a year or two from marriage. There was so much of wealth and plentifulness in this house. So why did they commit suicide? The other night her father and mother were whispering to each other about it. But she had not been able to hear it. But it could not be denied that she had a lot of eagerness to know in detail about what had happened. Whenever she had asked Gunduri Apa, she had received that one stock answer. She did not know anything. Should she ask Guria?

Kunti came near the door and said, "Guria! Would you tell me the truth if I asked you a question?"

Guria was out of his wits. Maa was talking to him standing only at an arm's length. Was it some kind of a dream?

"Maa...!"

No words would come to Kunti's lips. Was she really going to ask? What would happen if someone else came to know of it? She took a detour and asked, "Why doesn't any woman from the village come here? Is there any kind of misunderstanding?"

"No, Maa! Ever since the master's first wife died, no one comes here. Please don't tell anyone. She had set fire to herself in that kitchen. That is why the master has asked me to stand guard. In case you get scared."

A cold wave ran all over Kunti. She stammered, "Why did she set fire to herself? Was there any kind of a fight? Were father-in-law and mother-in-law alive then?"

"No, father and mother had expired before the marriage of the master. The first wife used to only sit and weep all the time. I had no idea why. She would not say anything if someone asked her about it. The women of the village used to drop in at times and engaged in merriments. But *Bada* Saantani*** never seemed to be happy. She went to her father's place. But she could not stay there long. The master brought her back. She used to long for a child. She had slyly fetched many medicines through me. She made pujas in the temples. Made offering to the gods. But

* elder

** mistress

the gods did not heed the prayers of that golden image. Whether she set herself on fire because of that or whether Agnidev pulled her to His laps would remain a mystery for ever. Only He who makes days and nights knows about it."

Guria fell quiet with his hand placed on his head. Kunti did not stop there. She asked, "And what about *Majhi* Saantani*?"

I cannot say anything about her. She was extremely hot-tempered. The entire street would reverberate when she lashed out at the master. The master had borne everything quietly. He never said anything to her. He took her to different places to placate her. *Bada Saantani* had only gone once to her father's place. But *Majhi Saantani* went around the whole country. The master also went around with her. But that was not enough .... She used to have epileptic fits in the middle of the night. *Saantani* used to howl. The master was depressed...."

"Why? Because *Saantani* was having fits?"

"No. The master was worried about having a kid. *Bada Saantani* did not have any issues. But the master took *Saantani* and prayed hard at uncle's village. God incarnate is present there... all wishes came true when someone prayed hard. The master went there with *Saantani*. They stayed there for ten days and then returned." Guria exhaled a deep breath.

Kunti asked eagerly, "What happened after that? Was epilepsy cured after that?"

"No, *Saantani*. Even such a great lord also did not listen to them. But *Saantani* was sitting glumly since the day she returned. She kept talking to herself. At times, she used to laugh so much that she used to roll on the floor. At other times, she used to howl loudly. Finally, the Lord answered her prayer. There was a child in the womb, but...." Guria became silent. He put out the candle that was burning. It was difficult to see his face clearly in the darkness.

"What happened after that? Go on, Guria. Why are you quiet?"

* middle

"What is the use of talking about it? My heart seems to burst. *Saantani* went mad from the moment the child came into the womb. She howled at midnight, 'Take out this child from my womb. This is the child of Satan'. Sometimes she shouted, 'Get me some poison.' And she went on talking in this manner. She moved around like a mad woman. The master called many doctors. But she never became normal again. The master was spending money lavishly in the hope of getting a child. He never even shouted at her.

"But the best laid plans of men go awry. One day *Saantani* fainted near the bank of the pond. No one knew when she had consumed poison. She was lifted home. The doctor said that the child was already dead in the womb. The master lost consciousness the moment he heard it."

"And what about *Saantani*?"

"She was oblivious of everything. She kept on laughing and crying alternately. The women of the street were keeping vigil. But how long could they do that? She was made to vomit and the poison got expelled from her stomach. But the four month old foetus had died inside the womb. She was lying unconscious. No one from the street came to this house. Finally, Gunduri Apa came from her mother-in-law's place.... A few days after that *Majhi Saantani* passed away. Ah! Her golden frame had turned into charcoal in the last few days."

Kunti was astounded as she listened to everything. What was this? So both his earlier wives had committed suicide. But why? Why did *Majhi Saantani* poison herself even when there was a child in her womb? What was the story of the Satan's child that she was talking about in her madness? How could there be a Satan's child if someone was not married to Satan?

Guria implored, "*Saantani*! Don't tell anyone about all this. The master will chop off my head if he comes to know of it."

Kunti asked, 'Guria, did no one come from the house of *Majhi Saantani*?"

"Maybe things would have been different if they would have been informed. But there was no one in her family except the old mother."

"Guria! What do you mean by Satan's child? Did Satan get married?"

Guria bit his tongue and moved away. He boxed his ears with his own hands and said, "*Saantani*! The matter is a bit thick. You won't be able to understand that now. Are you sure you won't be scared? The master has called tantrics and shut out everything before your arrival. Who knows what might happen at what time? Co-wives seem to have a bond with each other, you know."

"Guria! Are they going to scare me?"

"No way! They just cannot enter this place. Everything has been nailed. Outside on the verandah, in the backyard and on the bank of the pond. Who could cross that? But *Saantani*, this is the reason why the women of the village do not come to this house. As such, no child has ever been born in this house. On top of that, ghosts abound...."

"Guria! I can hear voices at times in the backyard. I am scared. It's as if someone is running."

"That is nothing, *Saantani*. Manu *Saante** and his friends play cards there and make picnic. They make merry throughout the night."

"Does Manu *Saante* live here?"

"No *Saantani*. He is your own nephew. Khira Dei's son. He comes here from Kolkata on holidays. There is no one at home. Besides, he loves his uncle dearly. He is a kid. But he is extremely moody. Everyday he enquires about you...."

Kunti said suddenly, "Guria! I cannot stand any more. I am feeling sleepy. I am leaving."

As she said this, there was a dryness in her throat and lips. Her limbs started shaking out of sheer fright. So Manua

* master

was staying here and besides, he seems to have taken a fancy to aunty. Enquiring about her everyday. Instead of her co-wife witches, this live ghost Manua seemed to be sucking her blood all the time. If Kunti saw him again, she was either going to set fire to herself or drink poison or jump into the pond. If nothing else was possible, she would hang herself from the roof. She could not take any more of this.

"Who is it?" Kunti was startled out of sleep when someone touched her.

"It's only me, Kunti. Did you get scared?"

Kunti did not reply. She had not been able to know when Radhu Mahajan had entered the room.

"Have you eaten?"

Kunti nodded in the affirmative.

"You lock the door and go to sleep. The children have cooked something in the backyard. Manua is insistent. I have to go and sit with them for a while. Guria is sleeping on the verandah. So don't be afraid. Do you get it?"

Kunti moved away. Mahajan was swaying from one side to the other. Perhaps he had consumed more *bhaang* than usual. Kunti became quiet.

As Mahajan left, Kunti locked the door and the windows. She raised the flame of the lantern and slept with her face down. She felt as if she herself had consumed quite a bit of *bhaang*. Or maybe she had been possessed by ghosts and hobgoblins. Covering her head with the corner of her saree, Kunti had been lying in the darkness with her eyes closed. She had no idea when she had slept. Every human being had a limit of tolerance. Once that limit was crossed, human beings did not remain human beings any more. After that, events, untoward happenings and accidents meant the same thing to them.

The next morning she felt that Mahajan was moving from the first floor to the ground floor and from the bedroom to the granary. He seemed to be quite active. He seemed to be happy too. Kunti was watching him from inside the kitchen window while she was cooking. But she did not seem to have any interest in what he was doing. What was the point of poking one's nose in affairs where it was not wanted. She was going to spend her entire life in this manner. Why was life such a lengthy affair? How harsh and insipid life was! And then how much of anxiety and indecisiveness was there! Kunti could not answer any of these questions making rounds inside her mind. Only a deep breath of despair escaped her, tearing her chest in the process.

After a while Guria arrived and asked, "*Saantani*! Have you finished cooking?"

Kunti lifted her face as she was dressing drumsticks.

"The master said that he would eat here in the ground floor."

Kunti had never seen Radhu Mahajan eat in the ground floor in the last three months. She did not know what to do.

"Don't worry, *Saantani*. The master is not very finicky about food. Whatever you serve, he would eat it with a great deal of satisfaction. He does not distinguish between mutton and spinach. Are you afraid?"

Kunti said, "I have no idea. Whatever you have brought and asked me to cook, I have done that."

Guria nodded and went away. He too seemed to be in a happy mood.

Radhu Mahajan came to eat and sat happily on the verandah of the kitchen. The usual red towel was on his shoulder. He was clean shaven. There was a mixture of black and white hair all over the body. As he put a bit of rice into the mouth, she said, "I had no idea that you were such a good cook. But you must be exhausted. Gunduri is also not likely to come soon. Her brother-in-law has sent a message that she is going to stay there for another fifteen days."

What could Kunti answer? It was difficult on her part to say anything with a smile on her face to an aged man like Radhu

Mahajan. She was extremely sad to know that Gunduri Apa was going to return after a fortnight. As she served the curry, Mahajan told Kunti, "You look exhausted. You go and eat. I will have food served to Guria."

Kunti had been standing holding on to the kitchen door. She said nothing. Mahajan finished everything licking his fingers and then drank a glass of water. He looked at Kunti and said, "I have been thinking of telling you something for the past two days. But somehow I am getting distracted."

He drank another glass of water and rested for a moment. He moved his hand around his stomach and said, "This is what I wanted to say. Grandmother has sent word from uncle's house. She could not come to the marriage because she cannot see very well these days. Besides, she has to do puja twice a day and take care of all the rituals. The *Jhulan Jatra** is in the offing. There will be *jatra* and *pala*** for three days. That is what the old woman says. I do not have the time to die. Where could I go? What I think.... You must be tired of sitting at home. You make a round of that place. The old woman would be happy. She prays God everyday for us. This will solve all the problems."

Kunti hid her face behind the door. She had never gone to the *Jhulan Jatra*. Her parents went there. One had to walk a long way. She had always wept in private because she could never go to see the *Jatra*. But when there was *jatra* in her village at the time of the Raja festival, she and her friends always grabbed space in the front row. The night passed in the process of watching *jatra*. By morning, half the people were always asleep on the ground. Even the confectioner, the balloon seller and the bangle seller fell asleep. But the *jatra* continued. How enjoyable those days were! For the past two years, her mother had not allowed her to go outside. Forget the *jatra*. Mother was getting very angry if she borrowed a story book from Kani Bhauja and read it.

---

* a *jatra* held at the time of Holi

** a folk song sung by a chief singer and his sidekick

Mahajan's voice could be heard, "Why don't you say something? I am telling this for your sake. Besides, how much longer would the old woman live?"

Mahajan had come near her and was staring at her. Oh no! What would Guria think? Kunti stepped back with her face lowered. He caught hold of her hand in a flash and said, "Why do you feel shy? After all, it is uncle's house. Grandmother is still alive. You stay there for a couple of days and enjoy yourself. I know you are feeling lonely here by yourself. But business is making me dance all the twenty four hours of the day. I would feel much better if you make a round of that place. The deity Radhamadhav of that village is the moving image of Lord Vishnu. Whatever you will ask, He will grant...."

For some reason Kunti started sweating. Mahajan was talking sweetly resting his hand on her shoulder. Guria was looking at them from a corner of his eyes and smiling. It was midday. If someone came around! Mahajan looked at Kunti's face and said playfully, "What makes you so shy of me?"

When Kunti glanced at Guria. Mahajan laughed and said, "Guria! Finish your food quickly and go to the market. Buy some sweets and bananas from there. One cannot go just like that. The barber was saying that the old woman loves laddus."

Turning towards Kunti, Mahajan said, "Select a few silk sarees to carry with you. There will be many people around there. Deck yourself up with the ornaments. Carry some money with you so you can make offerings at the temple. Oh yes, don't forget the real thing. There has to be a bit of business mixed with pleasure. You talk as much as you want with the old woman. I don't mind that. But don't forget to ask the deity to give us a son. There has to be someone to offer *pinda* after we are gone. Otherwise, this soul will not be get deliverance. Are you getting me? What use is all this wealth? For whom do I keep sweating everyday?"

Kunti was startled for a moment and looked at the face of Mahajan. Her head started reeling. What was this? Was God going to drop a son in her lap from the heavens? Mahajan could not understand this simple thing. And he was trying to placate the gods. In spite of her young age, Kunti could understand that there was no value attached to the pompous words of the important man. For some reason she felt like laughing, looking at the sweating and imploring face of Mahajan. She looked down to the floor pressing a corner of her saree to her mouth. Mahajan went on chattering a lot of sweet nothings happily, seeing Kunti smile. Not a single word registered on Kunti. She wished she could laugh wildly and roll on the floor. She would laugh so loudly that the people of that whole street would gather there to look at her. Her laughter would not cease even if gods descended from the heaven....

"*Saantani*! Why are you crying like this? Has the master told you anything?"

"Why, no...I am laughing. Can't you see that?" Startled, Kunti saw that Guria was staring at her, his eyes having turned round. And, in fact, hot tears were streaming down her cheeks.

"No, no. An insect fell in the eye". Kunti got up suddenly and went inside the bedroom. Who knew what Guria might have thought. Luckily, Mahajan had already gone to the first floor. He slept there on a mat for an hour in the afternoon.

That day and night passed too like all other days and nights. In the morning, arrangements were made for her departure. Whatever it may be, she might feel a little bit better if she went away for a few days. Any place would do. She felt totally suffocated in this dungeon. Mahajan was opening the suitcase time and again to check the clothes, ornaments and money. He also checked the ornaments which Kunti was wearing.

As the evening was approaching, a palanquin arrived near the house. The young bride, laden with ornaments and draped in a twelve feet long Berhampuri silk saree proceeded towards the palanquin slowly and sat inside it. The door of the palanquin was still half open. Suddenly, a huge man resembling a bull arrived on the scene and blocked the path. Mahajan came and pulled him on to the verandah. Kunti had a hunch that she had seen him somewhere earlier. Why was she shivering like that? Why did all the enthusiasm to step outside the house disappear in a moment at the glimpse of that man?

They returned near the palanquin after a while. Tomorrow it would be the full moon day. Hence, there was a bright moon in the sky. The light was shining on top of the trees, roofs of houses and the village street. Moon was reigning everywhere. The features of that pitch dark man amid that were creating the illusion of ghosts.

Radhu Mahajan extended a packet of money to that man. He said in a voice loud enough for Kunti to hear, "Son, keep this money with you. Spend some money out of this to buy some snacks and sweets if you feel hungry on the way. Be careful on the way. Your aunt is extremely shy. So watch it when you talk to her. Explain everything to your grandmother. Come back the day after the *Jhulan Jatra*. My house is dark now. Don't keep it in darkness much longer."

Mahajan wiped a tear from the corner of her eyes after saying this. Then he shook Kunti by her arm and said, "Be happy! You are going to the place of the deity. Obey the grandmother. The deity is there for our good, to make sure that nothing goes wrong with our dynasty. Don't be afraid. My queen! My pet! Come back soon. It would be difficult for me to continue to live if I don't see you soon."

"Hey Manua! Get Aunty back the day after the *Jhulan Jatra*. Pray to the deity for me. Do all the rituals. I am kept busy in all kinds of work. I do not have the good fortune of making a *darshan* of the deity. But I have never neglected in paying Him his due. I have spent my entire life serving Him. Why should I go through life if He does not come to my rescue? To hell with my life! To hell with my tears! To hell with my dynasty! This time I am going to hang myself or jump into the pond. God is great! But I am a poor man. But I am not afraid of death!"

"Uncle! Uncle! Why are you getting so worked up? You have nothing to worry as long as I am alive. Don't you have any faith on me? Just watch how your blood is boiling inside my system."

"No, son. I am not blaming you. It is all my fate. But my faith has been reinforced after coming in contact with Kunti. The two of you can either save me from the deluge or burn me to ashes. I don't need anything else in life, Manu. All I need is a son. My ancestors are cursing me. My life would go in vain if I don't get *pinda* after my death. Pray to Radhamadhav so your aunt can have a son. The dynasty must continue somehow. I do not need anything else in life. Just pray to Radhamadhav for a son for me. I am not a greedy man. The deity knows my psyche. I am simply telling this to you to console myself...."

Kunti had been staring. Radhu Mahajan had been wiping his tears with his red towel. It was as if he could not live even a couple of days in the absence of Kunti.

Radhu Mahajan was standing on the verandah and praying with folded hands as the palanquin started moving. It was as if he had made one of the biggest sacrifices of his life which had no equal in history or scriptures. He was not bothered whether Kunti was aware of it. But he was concerned about Manua. He was from Kolkata and he knew how to talk. Mahajan knew that Manua could make a fool out of his uncle by asking numerous questions and quoting the scriptures at him. That is why, he always behaved deferentially with him. But how could Kunti come to know of it?

The pitch black face of Manua seemed to have swallowed all the dreams of Kunti in a flash and taken a dip in the sea. The palanquin had continued on its way across fields. There was no way out for Kunti. She could not keep herself at a distance and see a bit of dream for herself. Manua had been walking in step with the palanquin like a ghost. In the light of the moon, his huge moustache seemed to forge ahead in pace with the palanquin.

The palanquin kept on moving in the darkness. And as it proceeded on its way, everything was over. It did not matter whether Kunti understood it or not. Was there any other sorrow on earth than the sorrow of knowing something? And what happiness was there in ignorance too? There was no other path except one's own fate. Kunti pulled back her eyes from the moon and shut them. Everything was dark. And then how many people had seen the light in their lives?

The palanquin had crossed the village limits. It was going by the side of the river. Where was that uncle's house? Who was that grandmother? Where was that moving image Radhamadhav? Kunti could not think of anything. There was darkness if she closed her eyes. Even when she opened her eyes, there were patches of darkness inside the moon. The huge moustache of Manua seemed to dazzle sometime ahead of the palanquin and sometime behind it.

Kunti had no idea about the time of the night. Suddenly, the palanquin came to a stop. Kunti came wide awake inside the palanquin. She lifted her head a bit only to be confronted with the cat-like eyes of Manua burning in the darkness.

At this time a silver-haired old woman came walking from inside the house. She was bent from the waist. She lifted the lantern and looked at the face of Kunti and said, "O my image of gold! Goddess Laxmi! Look at her! She is totally worn out. Come inside, my dear."

Holding on to Kunti's waist, the old woman walked inside. From the way she had held her, Kunti could know that the old woman was still strong even if all her hair had turned grey.

The old woman fawned on Kunti. She fed her and made her sleep. Kunti thought that she was hearing some affectionate words for the first time in her life. No one had talked like that to her before. She slept very comfortably. The grandmother gave her a massage intermittently in spite of Kunti's protests. After a long time, the old woman said, "I have a lot of work in the morning. Sweetmeats are being prepared as *bhog* for the deity. I have to supervise that. I am going to make some laddus and jalebis. If I don't stand guard, the workers will spoil everything."

Kunti got up. The old woman could understand that she was scared. She said, "The sweets are being prepared in the backyard. Why are you afraid? You lock the door from inside. Oh God! I have forgotten! I had made offerings to Lord Mahadev this evening. You take a bit of *bhog*."

The old woman brought a large brass glass full of sorbet and held it near the lips of Kunti. Kunti drank it at one go and said, "Why is it smelling like this?"

"Many things have been added to the sorbet to make it tasty. Shouldn't it smell? Has your mother never given you sorbet?" Kunti did not answer. She had smelled that odour earlier. It was the odour of *bhaang*. Mother used to grind it for father. Once or twice Kunti had done the grinding. Her chest started thumping. Her insides were burning. She drank some water from the mug kept nearby. Someone called the old woman at that time. She went outside leaving the door ajar. Kunti knew that the door was open. The light of the lamp might go out any time in the breeze coming through the window. But she was overcome by the heavy food and *bhaang*. In spite of her, she was not able to get up. Was she going to get intoxicated and shout at people? Radhu Mahajan was going to get a bad name in the process. She closed her eyes and slept quietly. Musical instruments were playing somewhere outside. But today was not the *Jhulan Jatra*. So...so... Kunti went to sleep thinking of different things.

She came awake in the middle of the night. She felt that many people had surrounded her and staring at her. Who were they? Where had Radhu Mahajan gone? Where had her parents gone? Who were these people? Where was she? She could not understand anything. Her head was in a swim. In spite of her best efforts, she could not sit up. Who was this? Standing near her with his moustache spread regally on both sides of the face. But this was Manua. And who were the others? Everything looked hazy in the light of the lamp. Oh yes, she had come to the house of the grandmother. Manua had accompanied her. He had left immediately after reaching this place to see the *jatra*. Kunti tried to scream 'Grandmother'. But her lips did not part.

Someone seemed to be holding her down with a mountain on top of her. In spite of making every effort, she could not even touch the mountain... in due course of time, she turned deaf. She was losing and regaining consciousness time and again. Again she was losing consciousness falling prey to the grotesque laughter of those people. Kunti could not understand whether they finally turned to stone or she herself had turned to stone. Time remained suspended at a particular point.

The day had come on its own. And so did the night. Kunti could hear the sound of musical instruments at times. And at some other times, she could hear songs from the *jatra*. Sometimes she opened her eyes and stared a bit. Some other times, she closed her eyes. She did not have the strength to turn on her side even though she had been lying on the bed for the past three days. Kunti could not see the old woman come even once to that room. Where had she gone? So was this the land of the ghosts? It was beyond Kunti's imagination that Manua and his friends could stoop to such a low level. So Radhu Mahajan had sent her knowing everything....

Manua opened the door and stood there, "You only came here to sleep. You did not go to the temple or to the *jatra*. What shall I tell uncle?"

Kunti turned away her face in disgust.

Manua said, "We will go home today. The palanquin will come. You arrange all your clothes. We will start at around three in the morning." He went away.

Kunti sat up. She was trembling all over. Until now she had neither opened her small suitcase nor checked the ornaments and the money. How did it matter to her? Let it go. Let everything go. The person burning live in her own life's pyre could never look back. This was something known only to the person who was burning.

Kunti could not stand straight even after holding on to her waist and knee for support. Where had that grandmother gone? She opened the door and looked out. No one was there. It was already evening by that time. A man resembling a demon was sitting leaning against a pillar a few feet away. He had a big bamboo pole in his hand. When Kunti saw her, she screamed 'O my mother' and fell down. That was it.

After that? She came awake in the house of Radhu Mahajan. Mahajan was sitting with his hand over his head. An aged man was checking her pulse. Manua was sitting on a stool and dozing. Kunti closed her eyes. The aged man said, "Feed her this medicine once at two hour interval. Her body has become hot. You could call it fever. But it will be okay in two days."

Radhu Mahajan whispered something to him and went outside with him. After a while, he said, "Manu dear! You too seem to be exhausted. You go and sleep. I will sit here. You get Gunduri back tomorrow morning. I cannot do this kind of woman's work. You are going back to Kolkata tomorrow. What shall I do?"

Manua yawned and said, "You are always scared of everything. I have already sent the palanquin to fetch Gunduri Aunty the moment I reached this place. I have sent word to her to come immediately. She will reach by the evening. Why are you afraid? There is nothing the matter with Aunty. She is only exhausted because of the journey."

"Oh yes, son. Everything seems to be okay to you. But I have been once bitten. So I am twice shy. I am ill-fated. All I want that the lineage should continue. Someone has to put a drop of water in the lips of the ancestors! Anyway, I accept what the gods would decree. Even though it is not me, it is my blood after all."

Manua spoke something incoherently. Kunti could not understand what he was saying. She had no inclination to look at the face of Radhu Mahajan. She felt like vomitting out of venomous hatred towards him. O God! Why didn't she die drinking poison like her friend Jharana? Why didn't she run away from home like Nima Bhai? In this state, was she alive or dead? She had heard her mother making a reference to Fate at times. But what sin had she committed that she had to bear such punishment? Was she suffering the consequences of the curses heaped on her in an earlier life? What was she in her earlier life? What bad deeds had she done then? Two drops of tears ran down her cheeks. A cow was mooing somewhere. Radhu Mahajan's snores could be heard by Kunti over all these. Mahajan was sleeping peacefully with his mouth hanging open. Kunti closed her eyes when she saw him. Gradually, there was an overpowering silence everywhere.

Kunti had been lying in an unconscious state for a long time. Gunduri Apa arrived as it was just going to be evening. Kunti got up and stared at him. Gunduri Apa bowed low at Mahajan's feet and broke into a wail, "What has happened to my Bhauja? Why on earth did I go away? The image of gold has turned to ashes. Brother, why didn't I die before seeing this? Why am I alive still?"

Radhu Mahajan wiped his eyes with his towel and said, "Gunduri, everything is my fate. She went to uncle's house for a day. But she stayed there for three days. She hit her head on the floor as she was trying to stand up. Her whole body is bruised. The fever has come down a bit from yesterday. I am relieved that you have arrived. All my business has gone to dogs." Radhu Mahajan went away hurriedly.

Gunduri Apa was caressing Kunti. She asked about the grandmother. She asked about the *Jhulan Jatra*. She asked about her journey. She asked a thousand questions. But Kunti just lay there without answering any question.

Guria's voice could be heard after a long time, "*Apa Saantani*, the master has asked you to sleep in that room. He is going to see off Manu *Saante* at the railway station. He would return late."

Gunduri Apa did not reply. All words were insufficient for Kunti at that time. She kept quiet.

Days passed. There were no more smiles on Kunti's face. Even the ever-chattering Gunduri Apa had also turned quiet.

Radhu Mahajan was never free from his business affairs. The silence of the ground floor never disturbed his routine.

How long could the matter remain under cover? Gunduri Apa said once after four months, "Bhauja, why are you moving all the time with a long face? You are going to be a mother. You should remain jolly."

Kunti felt as if someone had set her on fire. She did not say anything. Radhu Mahajan was euphoric. Her blood started boiling with disgust and anger when she set her eyes on him. She had the feeling that she was being hit by numerous spears at the same time. Who? Who was responsible for this? Was it Kunti herself or her parents? Or was it the wealth of Radhu Mahajan? The passion to save the dynasty at all costs? Who could say why the soft flesh of Kunti was sacrificed at the altar? For saving whose dynasty? This passion to save the dynasty was beyond virtue and sin. Man destroyed his present even though he knew everything about the future. Kunti's thought process continued. There was no end to it. Not a drop of tear came to her eyes even if she wanted to cry. At times, she thought she would drink poison like her friend or jump into some well or pond. She could not continue to live with that shameless body. But days passed while she kept on thinking about the whole affair. Her limbs were becoming tired too soon. She was no longer able to do any work. She did not have the courage to throw that child inside her womb to the garbage.

One day her younger brother Tima arrived. He had carried different kinds of sweets. Mahajan said, "Gunduri, father-in-law has sent word. To go to his house for a couple of days. Mother-in-law has sent gifts with her love. But how could she go there now in this state? You never know what might happen."

Gunduri Apa said, "If the childbirth would be taking place there, then she would have gone. But there are many problems in their house. Tima says that his mother is suffering from fever for the past one month. She just wants to see Kunti for a while. After that she would send her back. Okay, let her go. She will come back in the same palanquin."

Kunti looked at Tima. The boy had grown big in the meantime. His eyes were fixed on the gold ornaments of Kunti. Mother was unwell. The kids might not be getting a proper meal. Father might be losing his temper. The wants of the poor household could not be completed in one word. But Kunti neither had any strength in her body nor did her mind have any inclination. Would she help anyone or would she be a burden if she went only for an hour?

As Tima was leaving, he asked, "Apa, won't you come?"

Kunti said no shaking her head. Radhu Mahajan said haltingly, "You would have had a change had you gone for a while. Your mother would also have felt better. Okay… we will see after a few days. Everything will be unburdened in a few days. Hey Tima...explain everything to father."

Tima went away. She was not moved in the least even though she was meeting her brother after such a long time. No one understood that she no longer wanted to meet her parents or put a foot in her village. Let no one understand. Kunti did not want to take the trouble of explaining anything to anyone. Mother would think that her daughter was enjoying herself in the rich man's house. That was why she did not come. Father would say that you could rely neither on a married daughter nor on flowing water. Tima would think that Apa had turned too proud to talk to her. Forget about anyone from the village; she didn't even ask how they were getting on. The younger brothers and sisters would be waiting expectantly. What would Tima return with?

Let them go...let everyone go...Kunti did not want to see anyone's face. She was not going to explain anything to anyone. It was not in her hands to be born into this world. And yet, they had conspired among themselves to snatch death from her control. Hence, she was not going to tell anything to these people. There was no need for that too. Her insides were only churning with hatred and vomit.

But a person could not do everything that she wanted to do. Whatever she got was beyond her imagination and not necessarily according to her own wishes. Whether one was rich or poor, one had to concede this aberration.

Dashing all the hopes and efforts of Radhu Mahajan, Kunti gave birth to a girl child. It was the dead of the night. A midwife was moving inside the room purposelessly. Kunti had been staring at the roof quietly in spite of the unbearable pain. Gunduri Apa was caressing her head and weeping. Kunti was shattered with extreme sadness looking at the baby girl. She wanted to say in a loud voice - why did you come to this world, o daughter; to be born as a girl in this world is a curse. Can you lead the kind of life that your mother has led? Suffering at every stage in life? She was only trembling holding her lips together. Radhu Mahajan had not as yet come to the room to look at the daughter. His voice could be heard outside. Kunti closed her eyes.

After a long time Radhu Mahajan's voice could be heard. He was saying, "Hey Manua, I spent so much money. I went into all those troubles. I dipped myself in knee-deep water. And yet I did not get a son. No one would remain in this dynasty any more. The throats of the ancesters will remain dry. It's a girl. How does that help matters? Shall I spend money only to come to grief."

Kunti's eyelids opened on its own when she heard Manua's name. How had he arrived here? Who informed him? He had left for Kolkata after that *Jhulan Jatra*....

Manua smiled slyly at Kunti's face and said, "Uncle, you get hassled for nothing. Gaji Nahak had made that prediction... that it will be a daughter the first time and then a son will come. Don't you know that Bhima always loses the first round? What can I do if you throw tantrums? I am leaving for Kolkata...."

Radhu Mahajan wiped his tears with the corner of his towel. He said, "Why are you getting so angry? Who do I tell about my sorrows if not to you?"

"Did I disagree? You havn't propitiated the gods properly. You haven't given the Brahmins their due. You try to cut corners everywhere...."

"Okay, son, okay. Whatever money is needed to be spent, you go ahead and do it from now on. Don't wait for me. Make whatever offerings you wish to before Goddess Kali of Kolkata. What shall I do with money?"

Putting his hand on the shoulder of Radhu Mahajan, Manua said, "Okay, uncle. You just have some patience. The next time around I will take Aunty to Kolkata. Gunduri Aunty will also come with us. I will make all the arrangements there. You will see Aunty returning home with a son in her lap. You just keep praying to the gods...."

Radhu Mahajan seemed to be reassured with these words of Manua. He released a deep breath. Raising his hands heavenwards, he said, "Everything depends on Him, Manua. I am an insignificant human being. I can only worry about things. Okay, Son...don't take any offense at my words."

"Ha! Ha! Uncle, sometimes you are just a bit too much."

Radhu Mahajan and Manua left one following the other. Kunti had woken up from sleep as if she had seen a dream. Could all these be true in real life? Could such stories not be dreams?

Gunduri Apa said, "Bhauja! I have made a little barley for you. You have a high fever. You drink a bit of it and go to sleep. You would be depressed when you hear things you don't want to hear. You will deteriorate physically too. Who is going to look after your newborn baby?"

Kunti didn't say anything. She turned her back towards the child and slept. How could she explain the pains of her motherhood to Gunduri Apa? How could she tell the story of her sufferings to anyone which she had tolerated silently so long? Who was going to believe her anyway? Two drops of tears rolled down and made her pillow wet.

The baby started crying. Gunduri Apa took it to her lap.

Kunti realised that she was going to suffer like this if she stayed there. No one was going to share her grief. Nor could she tell it to anyone. Who was going to believe her if she opened up?

Radhu Mahajan had unlimited wealth. He had social status. But people of this village came to the first storey of this house only to take loans, hock their properties or take counsel of Mahajan as to how they could harm other people. No one ever came to the ground floor. Why should anyone know and believe the news of the ground floor? The women of the street never stepped inside the house. Gunduri Apa never stepped out of the house, whatever be the occasion. Kunti thought that her chest would burst open. So was she going to remain a prisoner in this house for all time to come? She would marry someone but spend her life carrying another's man child in her womb! Again it would no longer be possible to see any dream in relation to that life! Had she known this earlier, she would either have poisoned herself or hung from the roof. But she could not do it. Only today she was able to understand how much more clever her friend was than her.

Did anyone on this earth have a husband like this? Perhaps it was so with Draupadi in the Dwapara era. What sufferings she might not have undergone? She might have acquired virtue by being subservient to five husbands. But what peace did she have? It was different with Queen Kunti. She did not have to spend long times with her husbands. Sita had foregone all the pleasures of life in order to acquire the epithet of 'Sati'. Everyone could not do it. There were only examples of sacrificing the self for love or womanhood in the *puranic* characters of Laxmi, Saraswati and Parvati. Whom would Kunti emulate?

She started feeling like a mad woman as the night progressed. She was terribly scared when she recalled the events of the night before the *Jhulan Jatra*. Manua had again arrived that day. He had reassured his uncle that he would send Kunti back next year with a son in her lap. Kunti started shouting, "Here, here...Oh my mother! The demon is rushing at me...it will devour me...catch it, catch it...."

Gunduri Apa shook her awake. Kunti got up and screamed - "Here, she is rushing in. The witch - she is sucking my blood! What is this! Oh God! Please save me! Save me!"

Gunduri shook her again. She wiped her face with a wet cloth. Guria said, "Apa! What is this again? *Majhi Saantani* was hallucinating like this ever since she started carrying a child in her womb. Everyone said that the ghost of *Bada Saantani* wrung the child's neck. She only shouted – 'This is Satan's child, not my child, take it away.' But she had not given birth to the child…you came after that. You know everything."

"Shut up! Shut up, Guria. You would be out of a job if the master came to know about this. Go and tell Brother to ask Apartia to come. He will break the spell. Someone has done something evil. I am not able to go leaving the child alone here. Go!"

Guria perhaps went. Kunti started sweating profusely. Either because of the words of Guria or because there was too much noise. Gunduri Apa was fanning her. She was talking incoherently to herself. The child again started crying. Kunti sat up. She extended her hands to pick the child up but stopped midway. Gunduri Apa said, "Give a bit of milk to the baby, Bhauja. Her throat must be parched."

"No, no! Poison has got mixed up with my system, Apa! Don't ask me to do that. Get me a bit of poison."

"Shame on you! No one talks like this being the mother of a child. Who does not become sick? Your fever too will go away. You take two more doses of medicine and the fever will vanish."

Kunti fell down on the bed. Only half conscious, she could know that someone was chanting *mantras* and caressing her. The smell of camphor and incense sticks was in the air. After some time, Gunduri Apa forced some sweet liquid down her throat. She recalled the drink she had the day before the *Jhulan Jatra*. Were these people going to kill her? She had a lot of faith on Gunduri Apa. But what could she do?

It was the middle of the night. Kunti sat up again in the calmness of the night. Her entire body was experiencing tremor after tremor. She did not have the courage to go outside. She raised the lamp and looked at the face of her daughter. The girl was sleeping peacefully in the lap of Gunduri Apa. She touched her soft body with the tip of her finger. How was that girl going to live in this world? Kunti could not rear her. Who else was there to whom she could offer the baby? Radhu Mahajan might even kill the baby. Out of sheer greed. And Manua? She broke into a cold sweat when his fiendish stare, huge moustache and mountain-like body floated before her. She moved her hand away from the girl and went to sleep.

Her treatment continued for twenty one days. Manua was nowhere to be seen. Radhu Mahajan had never once looked at the face of the baby girl. And yet, the child had continued to grow without any hassles lying on the bed like that. As Mahajan sat down to lunch on the twenty first day, Guria came and asked, "*Saante*! Aren't you going to hold a puja today? The girl has to be given a name today."

Radhu Mahajan became stiff for a moment. He looked here and there and said, "No, we won't do it today. Manua has written asking me to hold the puja at the end of a month. I had asked him to take leave and come. He could not get leave for today. I don't like holding the puja in his absence. We will leave it until the end of the month."

Kunti had been staring at Radhu Mahajan. What a cruel, heartless man he was indeed! For the sake of Manua, for the sake of saving his dynasty, he was sitting on the branch of the tree and hacking at it from the root. Kunti had crossed all limits of endurance. All the festivities would take place only when Manua arrived. And after that, Kunti was supposed to go to Kolkata with him. Why? She felt that she had been set on fire. Angrily, she pressed her lips and remained quiet.

Gunduri Apa came inside the room and said, "Now, look at this, Bhauja. There was never a child in this house. This is one of the best things that has happened here in a long time. But Brother did not get some bananas even for *bhog*. Forget any gift, your father and brother did not even bother to come. What use is the life of a girl in this world! You have given birth to such an image of gold. But she is ill-fated. Why don't I die...okay,

okay, don't grieve. I will send Guria on the sly to make an offering. He will make the offering to Lord Mahadev and get the *bhog* in the night. The little goddess has come after such a long wait...."

Gunduri Apa had continued caressing the girl even as tears were running down her cheeks. It was almost as if she herself had given birth to the girl with her own flesh and blood. She could not bear it for a moment if the girl was neglected.

Kunti had been staring at Gunduri Apa. Tears were streaming down from her loving eyes. Her face was filled with joy like a mother. Suddenly Kunti said, "Apa! I will tell you something. Would you do it for me?"

Gunduri turned her eyes from the girl and looked at Kunti.

"Go ahead."

"I am not going to live much longer. I am getting weaker by the day. I might die any moment. And this girl...."

"Oh, you are more worried about your own death than the child. One always feels weak after giving birth to a child. You are taking medicines. You would get back to good shape in a few days."

"No, Apa...You have to take care of this child. It is all right if I live. It is even better if I die. She is your daughter. Take her. As God is my witness, I am offering her to you. You are her mother from today onwards."

Kunti bowed her head near Gunduri Apa's feet after putting down the girl near her. Tears were streaming down from her eyes. The last link of her life had got blended with some deep darkness. Gunduri Apa picked up the girl and clasped her on to her chest. She too said emotionally, "How lucky I am, Bhauja. I had never thought that any one would address me as mother in this life."

Kunti replied smilingly, "I feel relieved at long last today. I was terribly worried ever since the girl was born. You can very well see that I am no longer in the pink of health...."

Radhu Mahajan entered inside the room at this time and said, "Why are you getting worried because you have a girl. This year it is a girl. Next year there will be a son. Manua had said that he would get you examined by a doctor at Kolkata. Everything is possible these days. You go and stay in Kolkata for a month when you get better. Gunduri is here. She can look after the girl." Kunti felt that someone had set her on fire. She started shaking with anger and hatred. O God! Radhu Mahajan was not content after taking revenge on her once. He wanted to take revenge on her yet again! Radhu Mahajan may be past his prime. But Kunti and Manua were young. And Mahajan had wealth to boot. But was the earth going to put up with such sin? The earth will break in halves. The skies will be pierced. What would Kunti do if that did not come to pass?

"Oh, no, Bhauja. Why are you shaking like this? Why are you getting so angry when the discussion turns to children? You are young. You still have long years of fertility."

Mahajan said, "This life goes waste if you do not give birth to eight to ten children. Why else are you born a woman? Only to eat, wear silk sarees and ornaments, and sleep? I have spent money like water to bring you home. Is it just to sit and eat?"

"Ah, Brother! You will never change! After all, she is only a kid!"

"Kid, my foot! You were married at eleven and a mother at twelve! You were doing all the household chores. You are in this state today because you were ill-fated. I get heart-stricken when I look at you...."

Gunduri Apa said, "Let it go, Brother. I am perfectly happy here. What is the difference between your child and my child?" Kunti broke into a nerve-wracking laughter shaking from head to toe. She had not laughed liked that since ages. A streak of lightning seemed to have spread all around with that laughter. Guria came and stood there hearing that laughter. Kunti told him, "Guria! This is the Satan's child! This is the ghost child of *Majhi Saantani*! Move her, move her! Take her away from my sight!"

"What are you saying, *Saantani*! Why are you behaving l'‿e this? Are you scared of something?" Guria was stammering. Kunti did not stop there. She kept on her chatter incessantly.

Gunduri said finally, "Either the first or the second one is playing all these tricks. The intensity will increase as the night progresses. And on top of that, today is the new moon day." Kunti gnashed her teeth and said, "Look! Don't try to give me that kind of bull. I know everything. I will tell everything. Guria, take away this ghost child. Or else I will wring its neck."

"Oh, my God! Brother! Ask Apartia to come. I am taking the girl away to the other side." Gunduri Apa took the girl away to a room on the other side. As if Kunti was going to eat her alive. Kunti tried to follow her. But she fell in a heap as she tried to get up. Mahajan poured a mug of water on her head and shouted, "Hey, Guria! What are you staring at? Go quickly and call Apartia. Tell him to hold a puja and finish the work in one night. Just tinkering with things would not serve the purpose."

Mahajan went away after him. He did not even wait for a moment to check whether Kunti had regained consciousness. Good. It is a lot better if Gunduri Apa slept in the other room today with the girl. Something churned inside her chest when she looked at the girl. Her blood was getting all dried up. She couldn't do any work for the last eight days when she looked at the girl. Kunti had been lying like that, feigning sleep. Let one hour or two pass...or let the night pass....

Apartia came and perhaps lighted some resin inside the room. There was smoke everywhere. It was not possible to either open the eyes or breathe. Kunti blinked and felt ill at ease. She thought that she was going to roar. Everyone will think that her co-wives' ghosts had taken hold of her. That was her biggest weapon. But someone sounded a bell somewhere. Kunti's voice was drowned in that. Apartia was talking something incoherently while moving around the room. After some time Apartia said, "*Saante*, this is *Bada Saantani*. She always wanted a child. She must have told me many times...."

"Shut up! Tell her to wring the neck of the child and take her away if she always wanted a child. I have nothing to do with that girl. But I will nail her against the tamarind tree if she as much as touches Kunti. Aparti, you start offering the *bhog**. She has to leave this place tonight anyhow. Otherwise, I will send for the experienced witch-doctor from uncle's place."

"Ah! Do you think this is beyond Aparti? Where is the need for the witch-doctor from your uncle's house when I am still around? Everyday I have been throwing a couple like this into the drain after squeezing them like shrimps in this hand. Are there any ghosts in the five surrounding villages? *Saante*, only because I am scared of you, I don't touch any of the trees around here. I am not the man who is easily scared if only I get the nod from you."

Radhu Mahajan whispered something in Aparti's ears. Kunti could not hear anything. Aparti was happily engaged in counting the currency notes. Kunti was already getting breathless in the smoke. She had witnessed many such witchcraft during her childhood. But....

Aparti said, "*Saante*, I am keeping a pot full of water at the door leading to the backyard. *Saantani* has to hold the pot in her teeth and run outside in the dead of the night. I will follow her. I am sitting on this verandah...I will do the rest as *Saantani* reaches near the burial ground. Send a little bit of *bhog* for the Mashanichandi**. Guria and me will sit here."

Gunduri said, "Do you mean to say that the young woman would be left alone in her room?"

"Why, you are in the nearby room. Keep a vigil. You will see how *Bada Saantani* will leave this place with a great deal of fanfare.

"Aren't you going to eat?"

"*Ram, Ram*! I have given blood from my hand! What kind of puja shall I do if I eat? You go and sleep near the child. I

*offering made to the gods

** goddess of the burial ground

haven't done a puja since a long time. I want to feel totally pure at heart."

"Aparti, are you sure that she will not come to any harm? Where could the young woman go with the pot of water in the dead of the night?"

"Where else? She will become unconscious once she crosses the mango tree. I will call you after that. Guria, me and you will bathe her in medicated water and bring her back. I will hit nails at the place where she falls. To make sure that no evil spirit ever comes this way again. *Apa Saantani*, there is an unsatiated feeling when one dies without any children." Who knows what reply did Gunduri Apa give. Kunti turned on her side and looked. The room was in pitch darkness. A bit of smoke was coming out near one corner of the verandah. The smell of resin was still there in the air.

Gradually everything became quiet. Even Kunti could no longer hear her daughter crying. Who knew where Aparti and Guria had gone. Smoke had gathered in the courtyard giving the impression of an overlying fog.

Kunti rolled near the door and craned her neck to see what was happening outside. Aparti and Guria had been sitting leaning against the wall. Each one was holding a *chillam*. She had seen *ganja chillams* in her father's hands ever since her birth. She could not be mistaken about that. So this was the sorcery of Aparti.

Kunti had been staring. Aparti and Guria had been lighting *chillam* after *chillam*. Guria said after a long while, "Aparti, there is no more ghee in the lamp. Let me pour a bit of ghee and sleep for a while. You call me when it's time."

"Oh, yes...make sure the lamp lights properly. You sleep a bit. I will call you. She won't come out now. It has to be in the dead of the night."

Aparti smoked on his *chillam* again and looked here and there. He laughed a bit and talked to himself. Again he smoked on the *chillam*. His eyes were burning like the eyes of a cat in the faint light. They were closing and opening intermittently. Kunti had rested her head near the door. She had been staring at Aparti.

It was over! Aparti went and lay down near Guria. Father always went to sleep like that! He did not reply if anyone called.

Kunti stood up. Her legs were shaking. There was no strength in her body. But if she missed this opportunity, another was unlikely to come. Luckily, her daughter was sleeping in the other room. Nothing was there which could pull her feet back. There were indeed the burial ground, river, pond and paddy fields ahead of her...buses were available beyond that...a little farther away there was the railway station...! Where would Kunti go? To her father's house? She shrank unto herself with anger and hatred.

Suddenly, Guria was heard coughing. Sleepily, he asked, "Aparti! Are you sleeping? What is the time now? Call me when *Saantani* goes out with the pot."

"Shut up! Don't shout! It is still not the proper time. Nothing can be done for two more hours. There is a particular time for that. I will call you."

Aparti sounded intoxicated. He covered himself with the bed sheet and slept again.

Kunti rested for a while. She drank a bit of water and came to stand near the door. Some time passed. She stepped into the courtyard and looked here and there. She went near the place where Aparti and Guria were sleeping.The place was reverberating with their snoring. Both of them were sleeping peacefully. Kunti was trying to know the time of the night by looking at the sky. Some unknown bird was chirping somewhere. Kunti was startled for a while with the bird's call. No...if she delayed things any more, she was going to die at this place suffering every day of her life. Enough was enough....

She opened the door to the backyard slowly. She heard some kind of a sound. Perhaps the street dog was sleeping on the verandah. Or did someone wake up at home? Kunti was scared beyond her wits. What was she going to do? She jumped down from the verandah without being able to comprehend anything. And then she started running....

How could she muster so much energy? So much strength? She was running like mad. She felt that she was being chased by Aparti, Guria, Radhu Mahajan, Gunduri Apa and everyone else. They were calling her by name. The words filtering through the cool breeze seemed to be going off like bombs. But Kunti did not stop. Her limbs were shaking out of sheer fatigue. Her feet were scratched and bleeding all over. She was running ahead without thinking of anything. She had no idea where she was headed. Suddenly, she felt that someone had held on to a corner of her saree. Loudly, she shouted 'O mother' and fell on the ground. It must be that Apartia. What was this? Her saree had got stuck to a broken branch sticking out of a tree. There was a tear in the saree. She rested for a while. One side of the sky was getting lighter. The large stars were dazzling and looking down at her. She could see a village at a distance. Paddy fields were ahead of her. A narrow road could be seen faintly between two fields. A light seemed to be burning at a distance. Was it a witch? They came out in the nights - but...! She had a feeling that she had seen a big light like this some time before! What was this? Oh, she recalled. It was the railway station! Once she had gone to her uncle's place in the train with her father. She had never gone there again. But they had started to walk early in the morning that day and caught the train in the evening. But this was morning....

Kunti turned around. Someone seemed to be coming from a distance in the darkness. She started running again. She could not see any other way out at the present time.

The horn of the train was blaring. O God! The skies had become clearer! if anyone recognised her now, she would be back again at Mahajan's place. What would happen after that? The horn of the train seemed to blast her ears. Another twenty yards and she would reach the station. She was getting out of breath. Her throat was parched. Her eyes had been blinded with sweat. If the train went away? Kunti thought she could not make it any more. She was going to fall on the ground never to get up again. Holding on to her stomach, she ran again. Someone shouted, 'Hey, the train is leaving. Don't go near the rails...don't go...." Kunti was in no state to see what was happening. The person who was going to present life to death could not stop on seeing the features of death. She was not going to be afraid!

The huge train was just in front of her! Kunti could not understand what was happening to her. She slowed her pace. She moved away from the rails and went to one side. There were people everywhere. The people of that side would come over to this side and catch hold of her. She might have died if the train would have been on the move. But it was standing like a demon with its mouth hanging open. She had no way out...somehow she pulled herself inside a compartment and fell all on a heap. It seemed that a lot of people were entering inside the compartment making a lot of noise. As someone's cold hand touched her forehead amid all the pandemonium, Kunti lost her consciousness. There was darkness on all sides. She was not able to realise that numerous ghosts were making a great deal of noise and countless demons with huge, frightening eyes were eating her alive. There was nothing more comforting than not being aware of what was happening around you!

2
Kuntala's Story

"Kunti! My dear! Why are you standing there like that?" Kunti looked back. That good-looking, grave woman had been staring at her. Consolation was oozing out of her voice.

"How many times do I have to tell you that I am extremely pained when you sit sadly like that? Happiness does not come everyone's way easily in spite of all the efforts. Happiness and sorrow come in equal measure on this earth."

Sumitra Devi held Kunti by her hand and made her sit on the chair. She arranged her wayward hair and asked, "Are you thinking of your home? Your children?"

Kunti's eyes were filled with tears when she looked at her. The weeping face of that cherubic girl floated before her eyes. How could she say that she had deserted the month-old daughter at home and run away?

Observing her silence, Sumitra Devi said in a sad voice, "I don't want to hurt you. But I feel that you have undergone a lot of sufferings. Perhaps your child has also suffered. Not today. You get well first. I will listen to the whole story some other day. You go and rest now."

Sumitra Devi went away. Two drops of tear welled up in Kunti's eyes. How did she come here? Who brought her? She had no idea in the least. She remembered that she had left home at midnight. There were rivers, ponds and narrow roads ahead of her. There were trees devoid of any leaves. Boulders were lying on the high road. The train was coming from the front.... Many people were running on all sides making a great deal of noise...she could not remember anything after that. Who could she ask when and how she landed up at this place?

There were only a servant and a cook in such a large house like this. There was no other woman at home except Sumitra Devi. She was busy all the time. She was always surrounded by people when she was at home. Tea and sorbet were being prepared and served by the cook and the servant all the time.

Some days she did not even get a chance to eat. Kunti had her food by herself and went to sleep. She did not have the courage to ask anything to either the servant or the cook. They also never volunteered anything.

She could not recall the exact day of her arrival at the place. No one ever entered her room to ask her about anything. She was always a prisoner wherever she went. A deep breath escaped her.

The cook carried her food to her room and said, "Sister, you take your food. Maa would be delayed."

Kunti was startled. The cook was old. One eye was very small. It was almost as if he was blind. Still Kunti had observed that he cooked well. The servant's name was Kantha. But he did not come much inside her room. The cook was talking for the first time looking her straight in the face. Should Kunti ask why Maa would be delayed? But she could not muster up enough courage to look at the face of the cook. The cook sat down on the floor and said, "Maa was saying that you are like her daughter. Where is your village?"

Kunti did not answer. What answer could she give to such a question?

"Maa was really worried for you ever since the day of your arrival. You had a very high fever. You were lying with your eyes closed. The doctor was called. Medicines were given. Injections were administered. Maa sat with you for two days and nights at a stretch. At times she broke into a wail. She had a decent meal only yesterday. Ah! There is no one quite like her!"

She could not recall at all that she was suffering from fever and was unconscious at the time of her arrival.

"Why don't you eat? Maa will be angry if she comes to know of it. She has cautioned me a number of times to take care of you properly. I will cook whatever you want to eat."

Kunti said, "*Nana*, I am not able to recall anything. Even I don't remember how I met Maa. How did I come to this place...?"

"How could you remember anything? You lost your consciousness the moment you got up on the train. Maa was sitting at the place where you fell inside the train. The moment she saw you she could immediately know that you were the daughter of a cousin of hers. Hence, you are like a daughter to her."

Kunti thought that she was listening to some kind of a fairy tale. She did not think that she had ever seen Sumitra Devi before in her life. Mother never said anything anyway.

"Now you conduct yourself here like this is your own home. You have nothing to worry about. Maa will take care of everything for you. She will solve any problem that might have arisen at your home. Don't worry about anything. Let me go. I have work to do. You finish your food."

Somehow Kunti ate something and lay down on the bed. She thought that perhaps she had lost her way and reached that place. She could not find the way and go elsewhere again. It was not in her fate to talk with anyone with her guards down. Who could she call her own? Her father, mother, brother, sister, husband, daughter – no one's memory was in her mind. And she had no idea who Sumitra Devi was and what was her relationship with Kunti. One could not ask her any question. She was always grave. It was not possible on any one's part to know what went through her mind.

"Kunti!"

She came out of the light sleep. Someone had her hand on her forehead. She opened her eyes.

"Are you feeling all right?"

"Yes...." Kunti got up in a huddle.

"You don't have to worry about anything. You stay here happily as if it is your own home. I do not want to know anything about you. I do not have any curiosity either. Besides, I know about your entire past from my informants. Do you know? When you entered the train and fell on the floor in the compartment, I had a feeling that you are related to me very closely. You forget the past. Life never gets destroyed. I will give you a new life."

Kunti had started crying on hearing that. It seemed that nectar was dripping from that voice. Ahalya, the stone, had come awake after a long, long time. She wanted to say many things to her. But she had been overtaken by tears and emotion.

Sumitra Devi said smilingly, "You are still young. You can still make something of yourself. You prepare yourself from today onwards. Try to be someone just like the girls of the city who are building their lives by studying hard. There are Oriya, Bengali and English books in my library. You sit there and read books for a few days."

"I can read Oriya. but I do not know Bengali and English."

"You read Oriya books first. I will teach you Bengali and English in due course. There won't be any lack of time or guru if one wants to read. Besides, you can learn the alphabets from Trivashi. And, it is not a very difficult thing to either speak or read Hindi. You can realise your latent power if you read. Kunti lowered her head. It was beyond her imagination that there were such decent people on earth who derived pleasure out of helping strangers. What did Kunti know about this world? She was happy that perhaps finally her fate was dealing her a good hand.

Different books had been arranged in the glass almirahs in the library of Sumitra Devi. There were many Oriya and English newspapers. Glossy magazines were there too. Did she read all these during the nights? She had never any time during the day. Some men and women from outside often sat and gossiped in that room. Kunti had seen them. But she had no idea who they were. Maa never called her if any outsider was present in the house. As if she was trying to hide Kunti all the time.

Kunti opened many volumes of *Ramayana*, *Mahabharata* and other collections. She moved her fingers through many short story collections. She thought of Kani Bhauja. Suria Bhai was getting many books for Kani Bhauja to read. She was giving these to Kunti. She was being scolded because she was reading them slyly at the time of cooking or under the pretext of cleaning utensils near the pond. At times, Nima Bhai also got books for her. Mother always got very angry. Her eyes were filled with tears when she thought of Nima Bhai after a long time. She wiped her face with the corner of her saree. As her eyes moved around the room, she was startled to see Maa standing near her for quite some time. Maa looked at her and said, "No one can make anything of her if she gets perturbed with small things. It is necessary to rein in the mind. Many men and women come to me for advice. How do I show my face to them?"

Mustering up enough courage, Kunti said, "Give me some work to do, Maa. I will be a burden on you if I just sit here alone."

"Can you do any work?"

"Cooking, cleaning, washing clothes...."

"Cut it out. I have got many people to do those kind of work. What would the cook and servant do? Would they only sit and eat? I will find a job for you if you study well."

Kantha entered the room at this time and said, "Maa! Shanti has come with petticoats and blouses. She says that she wants to measure the size."

"Call her here."

A thirty to thirty five year old widow entered the room. She wished Maa and said, "I want to check the measurements."

Kunti had only one blouse with her. The saree had been torn. The bangles on her wrists had got broken. Her husband had directed Gunduri Apa to remove all the gold ornaments from her body when Kunti was about to give birth to the child. Hence, there was no precious ornament on her. She had continued to wear the blouses and petticoats of Sumitra Devi until then. She had not even remembered to apply any vermilion on her head. Shanti was watching her face with a blouse in hand. Sumitra Devi took the blouse from Shanti and said, "Open that door near the almirah. Change in that prayer room."

Shanti seemed to have been overcome by grief, "She looks like Goddess Laxmi! How could the gods be so harsh on her at this tender age!"

A lamp was burning in that prayer room. Perhaps someone had just then completed puja. There was the smell of incense sticks, flowers and sandalwood. There were images of Radha and Krishna, Jagannatha, Balabhadra, Subhadra, Rama and Sita, and Hanuman. A part of the kitchen could be seen through the small window at the back of the room. Kunti had never been able to set her foot in that room even though she had been there for such a long time. She had no idea that puja was performed in that house.

Maa was saying loud enough for everyone to hear, "Yes, Shanti! She is my cousin's daughter. Her fate turned against her. So I brought her near me."

"Doesn't she have children?"

The question of Shanti hit her on the ears like a large stone.

"God has been kind. A woman has as much peace as disquiet with that. You are a mother. Don't you know with what difficulty you are feeding your children?"

Kunti could not hear Shanti's answer. But she was startled by the emotionless voice of Sumitra Devi. The soft face of that tiny girl floated before her eyes. As if she was calling her with her arms wide open. Even now milk was secreting from her breasts at times. Fate had indeed many strange things in store for her. As Kunti came outside and stood, Maa said, "You know

Shanti, Kunti would look good whatever she wears. Let a few days pass. Things would come back to normal. I am teaching her at home. You find some time to teach her stitching. It is not safe for her to go outside. I don't want her to go out."

"Okay, Maa. Do you think that I would not do something if you ask me? I am alive because of you. Or else Shanti would be begging today on the streets."

Absentmindedly, Sumitra Devi was clearing dust from the books with a brush. She had heard everything. But she ignored it. Shanti put her hand on Kunti's back and said, "I am going now. But I will come and teach you stitching. You get some cloth, needles and thread."

Shanti went away. Sumitra Devi turned and came near Kunti. She said, "Never tell anything about you to Shanti. People are suspicious. They always exaggerate things. A person does not become a widow if she is called a widow. But the cover of a widow is sometimes needed for one's own safety."

There were many photographs hanging from the wall. Sumitra Devi's photograph was nowhere to be seen. It was difficult to identify the people in the photographs. She had never seen any relation visiting this place. Who could she ask? Sumitra Devi was living alone like a *sanyasin* in such a huge palace as this. So she did not have a husband or children!

Sumitra Devi said near the dining table, "You must be finding it difficult to eat here. I do not permit any non-vegetarian food in here."

Kunti had no idea what answer she could give to such a question. How did it matter what she ate? After a while, Sumitra Devi said, "Forget it. There is no point in discussing these silly things. There are many other chores to be done. You have already learnt to write the English alphabets for the past eight days. Can you sign your name?"

"I had learnt to write the alphabets in the village. Nima Bhai had taught them to me without the knowledge of mother."

"Nima Bhai? Who is he?"

"He is my brother. Not from my mother's womb. But he was better than my own brother. Mother stopped him from studying further. After that, he left home and went away."

"Oh...! I am very happy that you have a great desire to learn. Besides, I think you should do something as you are getting bored by only sitting in the house. I will get your name registered tomorrow. We will see if some job comes along."

"No, no. I will do the household work. If someone discovers me outside...?" There was fear and anxiety in her voice.

"Don't be silly. Why should anyone recognise you here? And then you are not aware that a transformation has taken place in your appearance and demeanour in the past few days. Have you looked at your face in the mirror of late?

Kunti had been staring with her hand resting against her cheek.

Sumitra Devi said gravely, "I have held my head high after many fights with this society. I do a lot of work in the company of many dregs of humanity. I lost everyone in the family at your age. I have a son who is absolutely worthless. He has been living in some foreign country. I do not know when he would be back. I pin no hopes on him. My job is to serve people. Period. That is all I know. Now you have arrived. You too follow the same principle. Husband, children, wealth, youth – everything is transitory in life."

Kunti had remained quiet. Sumitra Devi had continued, "You don't have to worry about what I do. I will make all arrangements for you while I am alive. No one can put a fingertip on you. I am assuring you of that. I am toiling day and night to ensure that women get all the facilities. That is why, I always pick up fights with the government."

The lizard on the wall made a concurring sound.

"True, true. I never tell a lie. There is no need for me to tell a lie. If someone dies today because of a dowry death, I have to run there. I have to take care of her children if some woman hangs herself to death because she is beaten everyday by her husband. I am ready with the relief materials when there is a drought or famine. I reach with girls like you to work day and night if houses get burnt somewhere. I spend days in villages – I have to run to ten villages. You too have to do the same thing. There won't be any problems if you make your mind up."

Kunti had been staring at her face. She was able to understand a few things. Many things were unintelligible for her. Sumitra Devi was a storehouse of wonders for her. She seemed to have been blinded by plenty of light after reaching some unknown land. Sumitra Devi had continued speaking with absolute bliss, "Can I do everything alone? It is my habit to fight from my childhood. Now all the parties want me as a member because I have established myself. I will definitely become a minister if I contest the elections. But I do not want to enter into the politics of power. There is need to have a pure heart to serve without expecting anything in return considering the state of affairs in this country. You would know when you step out. Many women try to take advantage for themselves in the garb of serving the people. You would be hurt when you expect something in return."

It was not easy to understand the weighty words. It was difficult to know why Sumitra Devi was saying all these to Kunti. Kunti had been seeing from the day of her arrival that Sumitra Devi did not talk at all. And she never tried to find out whether anyone was listening to her or not once she got started. Out of shame, Kunti could not say that there was no formula within the ambit of her education to understand her discourse. But Kunti had no way of blocking the speed of that fast-flowing river.

"Do you understand, Kunti? I have been toiling hard throughout my life. I am tired. No one could understand me until now. I only want that women should lead a happy life and they should be treated as equal to men in the society. Girls like you can provide a lead to others provided you study and work hard."

Sumitra Devi had a coughing fit as she said this. Her face looked crimson. Kunti caressed her back and said, "You are working throughout the day and night. You don't even cover yourself in winter nights. What is this? I think you have a fever."

"No, no. that is nothing. Hundreds of children in this country do not cover themselves in winter nights. They don't get any medicines even when they have high fever. I cannot sleep in the nights when I think of that. Kunti, tell me who has written this – 'Let me lie in hell till eternity, but let the world be delivered.' You are studying. So tell me."

Kunti had gone on caressing her back as if she had not heard anything. Sumitra Devi took a pause and said, "Where is the time to look after my own health? I haven't had the time to die in the last ten years as I have been too busy in the service of the people. My main dilemma is whether I will go myself to the doctor or take others."

"Yes, Maa! But unless you are in good health...."

"No, no, don't tell me that. The elections are just ahead. Where is the time to die? The opposition is upto its old tricks. They have even composed poems in your name and put them on the walls as posters. Don't get scared by that."

"Maa, what shall I do? If they... they...."

"They cannot do anything. They cannot put their fingertips on you. You don't worry at all. I am there. I will destroy them. Just let the elections be over."

Kunti guided Sumitra Devi and made her lie down on the bed. She pressed her legs gently. Sumitra Devi was talking to herself. Kunti did not bother to listen. She slept after a while. Kunti closed the door and came outside. The dull sunlight of the winter was fading. The cook was dozing leaning against the wall. He got up hurriedly when Kunti called her.

"Oh! The eyelids had dropped a bit. I sleep towards the dawn. There is no rest throughout the day. I do not have the strength any more to work so hard."

"Okay. Maa has gone to sleep. You go and eat. Can I help you in any way? Tell me."

"What are you saying? Five hundred laddus will arrive in a while. I will have to make five hundred packets after adding bananas to that. I have to load them in Maa's car. She will distribute them among children."

"Why? What is so special about today?"

"Don't shout...Maa has a meeting today. She is after a ministerial berth. She does not make any distinction these days. She is sitting down to eat from the same plate with Muslims, Christians and Harijans. How could she keep good health if she does that? She is not able to eat anything at home. But outside of home – the old woman is very greedy. She has stopped all non-vegetarian food since your arrival. She is saying...."

The cook stopped short. Kunti could not contain her curiosity. She asked, "What is Maa saying?"

"She is saying ... please don't tell it to anyone. Otherwise, I might lose my job. My children would starve."

"No, I won't tell anyone."

"She is saying that you would be tempted to eat non-vegetarian food. Then all kinds of evil thoughts would enter your head. She was saying earlier that she would get you married off. Now she is being persuaded by a few people. Don't go by what she says...you will come to grief otherwise."

Kunti felt very awkward by these words. What was this election, distribution of laddus and foregoing non-vegetarian food all about? Kunti did not have the courage to ask any further question after hearing such unpalatable things about someone who had saved her life. She had never come in contact with such things in the world from which she had come. The place where she had spent the first seventeen years of her life. Could she become enlightened in these few days?

Someone was knocking outside the door. Kunti entered her room and bolted it as the cook went to answer the call.

Sumitra Devi had strictly cautioned her not to meet anyone from outside in her absence. But why? How could she keep herself in hiding in a crowd if she was going to stay there for ever? Was she going to suffer for all time to come as a prisoner there? Still...! She feigned sleep the moment she heard Sumitra Devi open the door and go out.

Kunti could not understand what was happening. But she had no doubt about one thing. It was not possible to ask any question of Sumitra Devi. She had no intention of collecting any information from anyone else. She had felt extremely lonely the day she had left home to marry Radhu Mahajan. That loneliness had enveloped her even then. She was overcome with some deep emotion at lonely moments. She had no escape from that. Kunti had absolutely no idea how she could get out of this place. She did not know how she could get a control over herself. But how long could she go on eating here without any work? Could she only go on reading books? At the most, look at the face of some stranger through the window! Listen to the radio if she felt depressed! Her body and soul were restless to be within the confines of these. She was going to leave this limited circumference and get out into the outside world. Kunti went to sleep as she kept thinking about these things. The soft sunlight of the winter was shining on the window.

That day Kunti woke and sat up on the bed a number of times. Again she went to sleep. She stood near the window or sometimes she opened the door and moved on the courtyard. Kunti could never see even a trace of the moon in the evening sky. The cook and Kantha were perhaps sleeping somewhere. There were about eight to ten rooms in the house. Sumitra Devi lived in the upper storey. Kunti too had a room on the same floor. The others were on the ground floor. The rooms in the ground floor were opened and cleaned if anyone from outside stayed at home. The rooms were locked after their departure. Kunti had never had the opportunity of looking at those rooms. She felt scared at times when she looked at those rooms.

Someone called outside at this time.

"Kantha! Kantha!"

Kantha was sleeping like a corpse. The cook too did not respond. Someone was knocking heavily on the door.

What could Kunti do? Should she open the door? No, who knew who it might be! What could she say if she was asked any question?

Was the door going to break?

Kantha got up and yawned disgustedly. He said, "*Dei*, my head is reeling. Can you please open the door? Tapan is calling. He does not have any sense of time."

"No, you open the door. Maa has prohibited me from opening the door. I won't go."

"Maa has asked you not to open the door when she is talking with someone in the drawing room. But Tapan is a friend of her son. Oh, my head is reeling."

Kanta again fell down heavily on the mat.

Having no other way, Kunti went and opened the door. The door would perhaps have broken down otherwise. The neighbours would have gathered near their door.

Kunti leaned against one side after opening the door. A young man ran inside the house breathless and stopped short. He seemed to be a bit startled. Maybe he would have dashed against her in a moment.

The young man lowered his head and stood to a side after examining Kunti from head to toe. He seemed to be a compassionate human being clad plainly in a dhoti and *panjabi* looking amazedly at her. Who was he? Wherefrom had he come? Perhaps that was her question. But this was not the time to ask the question.

"Is Maa there? I mean to say...has she returned...she had asked me to come in the evening."

Kunti was so scared that she did not even have the guts to look at the man. She wanted to escape somehow.

"No, Maa is not here!" Kunti replied softly.

"When would she return?"

Kunti did not answer. She had started sweating even in the winter. She seemed to be shivering.

"Where is Kantha? Where is the cook?"

Kunti went through the shivers every time the man asked her a question. It was strange. She had never felt like that before.

The young man did not know what to say next. He said, "May I know who you are? I mean, I don't recall ever having seen you here before."

Kunti was in no condition to answer. How could the young man know that this was an awkward situation for her?

Suddenly, the young man looked at his watch and seemed to be somewhat disturbed. He said, "Okay, you are perhaps new here. Hence, you are getting perplexed at seeing me.I do not want to create more problems for you."

Kunti raised her face a bit. He was startled when her eyes met those of the young man. She gulped. Again she lowered her head and fell quiet. Not a single word came to her tongue even though she had read a number of books over a long time. The young man extended a bundle of papers towards her and said, "Hand over this packet to Maa when she comes. I will come later. I am leaving."

Kunti shut the door loudly as Tapan extended the packet and crossed the doorstep. The door made such an explosive noise that it seemed as if a heavy stone fell on the earth from the skies. Kunti leaned against the door, startled by that noise.

Tapan's voice could be heard again from outside. Kunti did not respond. Leaning against the door, she was trembling spasmodically.

"*Dei*, you will never reform. Why are you banging on the door like that? I thought that someone had thrown a bomb on the house. Who was calling?"

Kunti extended the packet to the cook and said, "Some Tapan Babu had come with this. Hand it over to Maa."

"I was just falling asleep. I came running when I heard the sound. Were you scared?"

"So you were not asleep? I called so many times. Why didn't you respond?"

The cook struck his back twice with his towel and said, "My body was aching terribly. I took a bit of opium. How much can I take? Maa keeps me engaged all the twenty four hours. There is always a crowd here. How much can I bear in my old age?"

Kunti was amazed to hear that. Until then she had thought that only people in the village took *bhaang*, *ganja* and opium. She had no idea that people were also wayward in the city. Who knew whether Tapan also had come after taking something of that kind!

"I hope you have not been scared, *Dei*. Why are you always so scared and shy? You are living at home like a daughter. Continue doing that. Apart from that, you are educated, You are not an illiterate that you would be scared. How long can Maa keep you under wraps? Let us go tomorrow to see the *jatra*. It has been going on for the past two days at a square not very far from here."

Kunti looked at the cook, scared stiff. It was as if he was joking with her. He was perhaps trying to say that he knew all the stories about watching the *jatra*, selling bananas and breaking coconuts...nothing could be hidden from him.

"Why are you getting angry, *Dei*? I know that you are scared of Maa. But she is not like that...she has transformed and rehabilitated many women. She lectures at huge meetings, But she has taken a fancy to you. Okay, you go and study. Let me go back to cooking."

The cook went away. Walking fast, Kunti went upstairs. No, she was not going to meet anyone or talk to anyone. She would obey the mother who had given her a new life. She was not going to do anything without informing her.

Sumitra Devi returned pretty late in the night. Kunti had her dinner alone and tried to sleep. Tapan's handsome and serene face appeared before her eyes whenever she closed her eyes. What he might have thought about her! Sumitra Devi had perhaps picked up some rustic, unducated girl to keep her as a servant at home. Why else would she be so hesitant in answering such a straight question? Kunti was burning within out of shame. But who was Tapan Babu and why had he come? Where was the necessity of asking her so many questions when he did not even know her? Kunti spent the night amid many bad dreams relating to Tapan. She was half awake and half asleep for the past few days as she was gradually forgetting her past. Her sleep was never disturbed even if she had certain things on her mind. She had again started dreaming while being half asleep. The attraction of a strange fragrance made up of a bit of sweetness and some bitterness had been exciting Kunti.

Kunti woke up in the morning with the caw, caw call of the crow. Her bedroom was adjacent to that of Sumitra Devi. There was only a door in between. Sometimes Sumitra Devi closed it. Sometimes Kunti closed it from her side. Yesterday Kunti had bolted the door from inside.

She opened that door softly and looked inside. Sumitra Devi was lying on the bed reading something attentively. The paper bundle provided by Tapan was lying half open near her. Lifting her head from the papers, Sumitra Devi said, "I am not able to pay any attention to you busy as I have been in my work. Many a time I have thought of asking Tapan to come and teach you a bit of English. He works as an English teacher in a school. He can help you in passing the matriculation examination. Then I will find a job for you."

Matriculation examination! Kunti had passed only class five. How long has it been since she came here? Just because she had read a few assorted books and learnt a bit of English, could she clear the matriculation examination? It wouldn't at all look good if she appeared at the examination and failed. Kunti said unhappily, "No, I cannot appear."

"If you fail, you fail. All I need is a pass or fail certificate for matriculation. No job can be arranged otherwise." Sumitra Devi was smiling.

Tapan opened the front door and entered inside. He was not clad in a dhoti or *panjabi* like the day before. He was looking pretty tall wearing trousers and a shirt. He was going back on seeing Kunti. Sumitra Devi said, "Tapu! Kunti is like my daughter. Why are you shying away from her? I have thought a number of times about introducing you to her. But somehow it has eluded me. I have been quite busy because of this electioneering. My responsibility will be lightened if you could find some time in the morning or evening to teach her a bit of English."

Kunti shook her head gravely. As if she had been exhausted after doing a lot of work.

"Look, Kunti. There is no need to be coy. You concentrate on studies. Apart from that, Tapan is like your brother." Kunti had been standing with her head lowered.

"You know, Tapu. Kunti is disenchanted towards life because she is a widow. She has no interest in doing anything. However much I tried for the emancipation of women, everything came to nought. One cannot secure her position unless one does away with inferiority complex."

Kunti could not look at either Sumitra Devi or Tapan. How could she explain her situation to others?

"She is extremely shy. How can I teach her?" Tapan made the comment. Kunti was yet again shaken by a strange attraction in his words. She did not say anything.

"Oh, yes. You have to do another work. It is necessary to get Kunti's name registered. Come at ten today. You and Kunti will accompany me. You will drop Kunti back at home. I have some work. Besides, who knows how long it will take at the employment exchange. No work is getting done in any of the offices these days. Officers are only interested in their own comforts. They do not do anything. The government is also to blame equally. How would efficiency improve when no strong steps are taken?"

Sumitra Devi went on talking about a lot of things after that. Not a great deal of that registered on Kunti. Tapan had been looking on with the attention of a mesmerised student. The crow went on its routine of caw, caw at intervals.

Sumitra Devi got down from the bed and said in a worried voice, "Ah! It is already so late. Work will not be finished even if one day would have forty eight hours in it. Who knows when death is going to overtake...."

"I am leaving...."

Tapan put a full stop to Maa's tale. Kunti suddenly looked at Tapan. He was signalling to her to keep quiet by pressing his index finger to his lips. There was a naughty smile on his face. Maa had been staring at the wall clock at that time with her back towards them. She turned around and said, "Yes, you get ready. Kunti, you go and make preparations. As a rule, you will work outside for one hour everyday."

"What work? And that too outside?" The words escaped from the unprepared Kunti.

"You will know in due course. Don't be so impatient."

Kunti came inside her room. She was not sure of the awkward situation through which she was passing. Who was this Tapan? He had tied her up all ends with a strange power. All her thoughts were going topsy-turvy. She had been scared of human beings until then, more so the male of the species. Nima Bhai, commanding deep respect and affection, was the only exception.

Whether it was her father or some uncle from the neighborhood, she had been scared of everyone. She had thrown up, thinking about that unseen groom of her friend. Apart from that, she had no love lost for Radhu Mahajan, Manua and his friends. Even now her body recoiled with hatred towards them.

Fear and hatred towards men had almost built a nest in her mind since her childhood. But who was this Tapan? Why did she enjoy thinking about him? Just not once, she wanted to hold him in sight for ever. She was sweating even in the winter...!

At 10 A.M., Kunti sat in the car with Sumitra Devi. Tapan sat in the front. Sumitra Devi had been talking about different things.

There were too many people inside that office. Did one get a job at that place? People had been standing in a queue. Kunti thought that everyone was staring at her. Kunti had been standing after tidying up her white saree. People perhaps stared like that in the cities. She had no further desire to sit on the palanquin. Even she had no desire to see the passing scenery sitting on the train. Any branch she had touched in her life had snapped. She had been standing in the garb of a widow even if she had married and was the mother of a child. She did not have the right to live as the wife of a living man. And yet what hardship she had to go through just in order to be alive!

Sumitra Devi was sitting on a chair and talking to a gentleman. Tapan was reading a paper standing at some distance. Kunti had been immersed in her own thoughts and was standing all by herself without being aware of the noise around her.

She was startled out of her wits when she felt the touch of a palm on her left shoulder. When had Tapan placed his hand on her shoulder?

"Come and sign the papers."

Kunti pushed forward. How had Tapan gathered the courage to touch her in order to call her? Was it because of Sumitra Devi or of herself? Or was it the masculinity of Tapan? What an unpleasant situation it was! Kunti almost lost her temper. But she controlled herself. She had not as yet lost her patience or hope, had she?

Sumitra Devi pointed to a place on the paper and said, "Write your full name here." Full name! What was that? No one had ever called her by any name except Kunti. Many parents in the village fondly called their children "Suna" or "Budhi". But affection or anger had never made a difference in her case - she was the same Kunti all the time. Just the two letters. Nothing else. Kunti became absentminded holding the fountainpen in her hand.

Sumitra Devi seemed to be irritated. She said, "How much time would you take to do the work of others if you take so long to write your name? You know, Hota Babu! No one understands the value of time in our land."

Hota Babu got up from the chair hurriedly and said, "Madam! The girl is perhaps shy. I am going outside. After all, she is a girl...." Hota Babu laughed showing his *paan*-stained teeth after saying that. Kunti was feeling even more uncomfortable by his weird look. Sumitra Devi seemed to be angry. She said, "No, Hota Babu. There is no need for you to go out. What is shyness? This application is being submitted for a job. Why should anyone feel shy about it? One has to forget all these things if she wants to work outside."

Kunti's hand was shaking with the pen held in it. She had heard only one-half of the conversation. The other half had gone beyond her. She would be finished if anyone recognises her as Kunti or as the wife of Radhu Mahajan. Mahajan would send Manua after her and somehow whisk her back to him. Radhu Mahajan slept with all his papers below his head because there was no bigger proof than the proof of papers. Then....?

"Oh, why don't you write your name?" Again there was the soft touch of Tapan's palm on her shoulder.

Without being aware of it, all of a sudden, Kunti blurted out, "My name is Srimati Kuntala....Kuntala...."

"Write Kuntala Devi. The nickname does not mean anything." Sumitra Devi said laughingly.

Over! That was the end of Kunti for all time to come! Kuntala had arrived. Kuntala Devi. The daughter-in-law and mother, who had arrived half-dead and in tattered saree from some dirty village, suddenly stood as an unmarried woman before the world with a little bit of education and a changed name. But she did not think that there had been any basic change in her. The wealth of womanhood was the biggest danger for her. That was all. This was known to Kunti. Kuntala was also aware of it.

Days pass without any hassle when there is hope of better things to come. One got interested in knowing, studying, learning and spending time with other people. At times, dreams visited a person even amid stark reality. Kunti was no exception to the rule. She had tried her best to do the bidding of Sumitra Devi without bothering to find out what she was doing and what dreams she had about the people of the country once she won the elections. She read in the books that opportunity came only once in life. It did not come again. Apart from that, Tapan was a huge attraction for her. His gentle behaviour, sympathy and the desire to help others had provided her the safety of the shore in the mid-sea.

Shanti was coming to teach her stitching. Tapan too used to come everyday for some time to teach her. Some time he taught English, some time Hindi and some other time Bengali. Tapan tried to delve into Kunti's past at times while teaching her. Kunti evaded those questions. The door to her past had been closed. Let that remain closed. A huge snake would come out crawling from that darkness and bite her if the door was opened. Kunti would cease to exist. But others would be destabilised and become poisonous with the pain of that poison. Was there any Nilakhantha who could drink away all the poison of Kunti's life? She did not even have enough courage to think of all these things from the beginning till the end.

One day Tapan asked, "Kunti! Why do you brood all the time? It is not posible to clearely explain why men die and why some people live long without any reason. But a wise person does not spoil his present by brooding over the past. Do you think I am a happy man?"

Kunti was astounded to look at Tapan's face. Tapan had perhaps assumed that she was a widow and that she was sad because she was grieving all the time for her dead husband. That was the biggest tragedy of her life. She had no idea what kind of life and what opportune moment she was waiting for in the shroud of a widow. Her life went on rolling in some unknown direction like a leaf carried away by a stream. Tapan always got worried when Kunti became quiet.

He said again, "Look Kunti, I have again got the inspiration to live after coming in contact with you. I feel encouaged to do something with my life...."

Tapan's words hung in the air. And yet the stupid Kunti did not ask him any question. Controlling all the emotions and grief raising their heads inside her, she said in a disinterested voice, "Let us stop here today. I have to go...."

Tapan returned desolate. He tried to say something. But no words would come.

Kunti's face got covered by a shadow of sorrow. It was not possible to study the language of her eyes correctly.

Tapan asked sometimes, "Kunti! Don't you ever feel like going out? Don't you feel like sitting for an hour on the river bank? Don't you ever want to burst in to a song watching the bird in the skies or the moon?"

Kunti remained silent. She had come across such dialogues spoken by the hero in the books that she had read. She knew how the cunning heroines won over the heros with clever words. But she could not face the situation by placing herself there. She kept her books down and picked up the needle and thread to practice stitching.

Tapan said, "You know, Kunti? I have made a huge plan for you. It is my wish to bring a smile on the face of many women like you But, before that, I want you... I mean, you...."

Kunti lifted her face from the stitching materials and stared. The tangential silence pierced the chest of Tapan like a boomerang. Kunti had no idea what answer she could give to anyone.

One day, neither Sumitra Devi nor Tapan was at home. It was afternoon. The winter was almost getting over. Kunti had been sleeping lightly. The twenty one day old daughter's face floated before her face in a dream. It seemed she was crying nonstop....

Something fell with a thud somewhere. Kunti sat up on the bed. Her insides were churning. Wherefrom so much affection came for that girl when she had not bothered to look sideways at her! She had perhaps covered the memory of her daughter like fire under the ashes in the process of being busy with different chores and reading different books and magazines. But the ash was going to be blown away and the fire would rise sky-high. And everything would be burnt to dust in no time at all. She was only dying within herself for more than six months. Sumitra Devi was assured by providing her shelter. In the guise of teaching her, Tapan was....

"You are crying by yourself in the afternoon? Of whom are you thinking?" Tapan had opened the door and been staring at her.

"Why...no."

She wiped off two drops of tear with her own palm.

"Don't tell a lie, Kunti. You will not suffer within yourself when you share your sorrows with someone. Do I not mean anything to you?"

Kunti was startled. She looked at Tapan. He had bent from the waist standing near the bed. He had empathy, love, affection and tenderness writ large in his eyes.

As Kunti moved back a little, Tapan held her hand and said, "Enough is enough, Kunti. How much more punishment do I have to take in order that you can have peace of mind?"

Kunti's palm was shaking inside the palm of Tapan. Kunti tried to stand up. But the two arms of Tapan suddenly went around her neck and held her in a tight embrace. For the first time in her life Kunti lost total control over herself. Without being aware of it, she leaned against Tapan and burst in to silent tears. Wiping away her tears, Tapan kissed her on the forehead. The hood of the ever awake poison snake in the darkness of the past seemed to lower by that touch. A streak of sunlight seemed to fall in the cave of her dark future. Kunti started wailing with some deep emotion. Kissing her on the head time and again, Tapan tried to quieten her. The screen of the window was fluttering silently in the breeze of the spring.

They had only sat silently on that quiet afternoon. There was no reminder to read books. The sewing machine was standing half open. The pages of the newspapers had been scattered and lying on the floor. Kunti seemed to be in some other world. She had been overwhelmed by the first experience of loving someone in stead of hating the entire mankind as was his wont. Tapan had been lost in some deep thought staring at the sky. There were many things to talk about. But neither of them could say anything. Kunti recalled having read in some book that silence was the only language of love.

A couple of days later the news of Sumitra Devi winning the election spread everywhere. She was constantly meeting people in a happy mood. The rooms had been filled with bouquets and garlands. Along with Kantha and the cook, Kunti had been busy serving tea and snacks. Everyone seemed to be in high spirits. Sumitra Devi was calling Kunti all the time near her introducing her to various people. She took photographs with Kunti. Every newspaper carried stories of her service to society, country and humanity. How much of that could Kunti read? Tapan used to cut the news items and photographs from the newspapers with a pair of scissors and preserve them carefully. He explained to Kunti that all these would prove helpful sometime in the future. Kunti did not understand much of what Tapan said. But Kunti could herself know that there was a glow in her own face and eyes to be part of all that. The intimacy with Tapan and the political victory of Sumitra Devi had spread the colour of the rainbow in Kunti's mind and body. It was beyond her imagination that she could derive so much of happiness out of life. She had even turned a bit talkative of late. As they were listening to the news on the radio one day, Tapan pressed Kunti's palm lightly and said, "I have decided to join politics. I find that public service has no meaning in this country without the ammunition of politics. What do you say?"

Kunti answered, "What can I say? I do not understand politics. But does one need to have ammunition with him in order to do public service."

"You will be able to understand the meaning of these words in a few more days. Not everything that glitters is gold."

Tapan was smiling. But Kunti could not understand the real meaning of what he was saying. She too smiled in order to hide her ignorance.

Tapan was saying, "But my politics is not confined to greed and power. Nobody does anything in today's world if he does not have his own axe to grind. Just see, Kunti. I know the leaders who have come to power in this election. They only intend to beat their own drums, earn money and to reap personal benefits in the guise of making various plans for the upliftment of the poor people. They have no intention to serve anyone."

Kunti said, "I do not know about anyone else. But I have been seeing Maa engaged day and night selflessly in the service of humanity. She is always busy in some work. The country is lucky to have a people's servant like her." Tapan switched the radio off and said, "You are talking beautifully these days. But I have one request. Analyse all the facts. Don't come to a decision hastily."

Kunti had been staring like an idiot. Tapan said, "Like you, I have a great deal of respect for Maa. She has stood by my side in all my misfortunes. I have been able to complete my education and find a job only because of her. Otherwise I might have turned into fertile soil only after being carried away by floods."

Tapan took a deep breath. His sight had been fixed on a dark jungle of a lost past. He again went on as if he was reciting some *mantra*, "I too had parents. I had brothers and sisters. I was studying in class four. Suddenly, the two rivers on both sides of the village rushed inside the village one day. Everything had been razed to the ground by the next morning. Everyone was washed away. I had somehow managed to latch on to the trunk of a large tree...."

"What happened after that? There were no snakes there, I suppose."

"Who bothers about snakes at such a time? Snakes, frogs, cows, calves, human beings, bears and everyone else spend time at one place during the flood. The primary concern at that time is self-preservation.

"So how did you come from that place?"

"Maa, i.e. Sumitra Devi and the people of her party rescued me from that place. I stayed in a hosptial for a long time. Then I came here. After that...."

"What happened? Why did you stop?"

"Many things happened after that. Assume that I stayed in an ashram. I studied. Now I am working. I have plunged into politics and service of people along with Sumitra Devi."

"Maa is great indeed. One night she was telling me that she has saved thousands of orphans and turned them into something in life. She has never eaten or slept peacefully. Only in the process of serving the humanity and the country...."

"Cut it out! That's enough. Have you ever seen the other side of the moon, Kunti?"

"What are you implying?"

"Dark. Very, very dark. Service to the people is only a pastime for her. She hasn't spent a dime for it. On the other hand, she has earned millions in the process. She has built houses and purchased cars. She has kept money in the bank and...."

"Lies! Lies! You are trying to...I mean...."

"Oh yes, Kunti. In spite of immense respect and gratitude, I ... I am not able to express myself properly... I do not love her. On the other hand, I hate her."

Kunti shook Tapan by his arm and said, "What are you saying? I was never aware that you had so much of antagonism towards her…."

"It's not only you. Many people do not know. There is selfishness behind politics always. Service to the nation is only a garb. I have no respect for anyone after seeing the main planks of politics and the way the elections go. Common people like us live only to be mowed down under the elephant's feet. I have no wish to live like that. I had no control over my birth. But my death can be decided by me. And yet…."

"Let it go. I had no idea that you could get so angry. Your face has turned crimson with anger. Can anyone do politics with so much anger? You were telling me only a little earlier that you were going to acquire the ammunition of politics! Is that your promise?"

Tapan was standing holding on to the railings of the windows. He seemed to be lost in some deep thought staring across the road. For the past few days Kunti had noticed that Tapan could not concentrate on anything. He seemed to be absentminded all the time. As if he was thinking about his parents and his village. Or may be he was having some problems at his place of work. Who knew? Even Sumitra Devi might have told him something. Tapan had given of his best in order to bring victory for Sumitra Devi in the elections. He had spent days without eating and sleeping as if he himself had been contesting the elections. And yet, Kunti could not understand the anger of Tapan ever since the news of the victory had reached them. Had Maa said anything to him? She did not have the courage to ask anything, looking at the serious face of Tapan.

Suddenly, three to four vehicles entered inside the gate. Sumitra Devi and her closest allies were sitting inside the first vehicle. Many people had followed them on foot too.

Kunti became active. Sumitra Devi was going to call her now. She had to serve tea, snacks and sorbet. She had to talk with a smile on her face even though she felt depressed. Kunti entered inside the toilet to change her saree. Sumitra Devi always got angry if her clothes were not clean and ironed. She also made her displeasure known when she found anyone with too much cosmetics.

Kunti came out of the toilet and found Tapan missing. Perhaps he had gone inside the drawing room.

He was sitting quietly on a chair in a corner. As if he had been busy in witnessing a scene. As if he had no specific relation with the noise or the congregation. Why had the person, who was so intimately close to everyone, become quiet all on a sudden? Couldn't Sumitra Devi notice that? She did not even call him frequently as she did ordinarily. Or had Tapan created some problems for her?

Kunti found things to be quite a bit odd. Something had been lost somewhere. And yet no one was looking for that precious thing. Kunti could not look for that. It would have had no meaning anyway. How could she judge the helpless condition of someone else when her own situation in life was extremely shaky and when she sat down exhausted a hundred times as she tried to get up? Who was going to appreciate her judgement anyway? Besides, what did she know about Tapan? And how much did she know about this Sumitra Devi, her saviour?

As she was absentmindedly carrying the sorbet tray, she dashed against the tea-poy. The room reverberated with the sound of glasses breaking into pieces on the floor. Sumitra Devi came running towards her and held her and looked questioningly at her. Kunti was a bit embarassed. She said, "No, nothing is the matter. My head reeled...."

Sumitra Devi said solicitously, "How many times have I told you to massage oil properly on your head? I do not have the time to take care of you in every small detail. Apart from that, you are not a child!"

Kunti lowered her head ashamedly. Sumitra Devi did not stop there. She said, "Just see how much hair she has on her head. It is stretching till her knees. You won't get to see such beautiful hair too often."

Sumitra Devi pulled the white saree from her head and untied the knot. Her dry hair cascaded down to her knees. Everyone had been staring at her amazed. In that immobile state, Kunti saw Tapan getting out of his chair and moving outside. Suddenly, Sumitra Devi called him, "Tapu! Tapu! Why are you leaving...?

Tapan stopped near the door and said, "No. Is there any other work? I am tired of sitting here."

"But why are you sitting by yourself? Everyone is enjoying himself. What is wrong with you?"

"Nothing in particular."

"Okay. We will go into that later. Let me tell you the real thing now. Not only to you. I want everyone to hear that. After a long time...."

"I know that, Maa."

"What do you know?" Sumitra Devi furrowed her brows out of vexation.

"Laltu is returning home. He is happy beyond imagination at your victory. Hence, you...."

"Yes. This is for everybody's information. Laltu is my only son. He is returning after a long time. I had told him many times that your own country mattered more than everything else. But he had never understood that. But he is eager to come back after having heard about my victory in the election. It was not my call. But I feel proud as a mother because he has been able to hear your call and the call of the ordinary people. My blood is flowing in his system. He has proved that blood is thicker than water."

Someone came near Sumitra Devi and said, "He has also sent me a letter through a friend. We are all very happy. Your happiness makes us happy too."

An elderly man said in a serious voice, "Sumitra! You refused the proposed civic reception in your honour. Even you did not agree when a few of us tried to host a tea party for you.

You have been making sacrifices and rendering service to the nation selflessly. The nation owes something to you for all these after all!"

Sumitra Devi said coyly, "The country has given birth to me. It has provided me with all the opportunities. I am an ordinary woman. I have done my duty.... Please don't embarrass me by saying anything else."

"We too have a duty. How can you forget that? What would our children learn from us?" Sumitra Devi had been staring at the wall silently. Her presence and demeanour seemed to radiate peace and contentment in some unspoken joy bereft of any desire of indulgence.

"Let it go, Sumitra Devi! There is no point in carrying on in this vein. And who can make you understand all these if you do not want to understand them? Still, we are all like your sons. You have no reason to object if we want to welcome Laltu Babu in a ceremonial manner. He is coming back after a long time. You will not prohibit us from welcoming him. Even if you forbid it, we will still go ahead with our plans. Gentlemen, what do you say?"

Hota Babu smiled at Kunti. She had met him briefly at the time of registering her name for employment. The eyes of the man were piercing the body of Kunti like red-hot iron rods. What an uncivilized man! Couldn't Sumitra Devi know anything?

Everyone clapped and shouted 'Aye, aye.' Someone said loudly that a party would be held to welcome Laltu Babu. Distinguished people would be invited. Laltu Babu loved singing and dancing. He had a great deal of fondness for western music. Hence, different artistes would be invited. The festivities would be conducted in a homely atmosphere rather than on a public pandal. The best place for it was the residence of Sumitra Devi itself. The opposition party cannot raise any hue and cry in that case. Some journalists may also be invited if that was considered necessary.The mouths of the people belonging to the enemy camp would also be shut if a short essay was printed and circulated about the future plans of Laltu Babu.

Sumitra Devi was talking with Hota Babu in a corner. Waves of joy and excitement were playing across her face. Tapan came near Kunti at this time and said, "How long are you going to stand with your hair falling open? This is only the beginning. Wait for the real exhibition. I am leaving."

Kunti was startled. She had in fact been standing for a long time with her hair falling open and no cover on her head. She was the daughter and daughter-in-law of some unknown village where shock waves ran through the streets when she came out on the road. She came from the kind of village where the elderly looked askance and made their displeasure known if she as much as opened her mouth to speak. She could not know how she was standing for such a long time forgetting her surroundings when she had grown to be a woman in a village where she had to remain in hiding all the time. She ran inside the house with lightning speed being startled by the curt remark of Tapan. Oh, no. what a shame! She could not also understand why Sumitra Devi opened her hair in front of others. Kunti had never complained about anything before her. So why was she making this farce?

Kunti spread her hair on the pillow and went to sleep. She wanted to break into a sob. The past was racing towards her like a demon with its hands spread and she had no idea about what lay in store for her in the future. Every moment, the present had kept her in a wretched condition amid uncertainties and doubts. Yet, the love, affection and advice of Tapan had helped her advance in her path. Unfortunately, she was not even able to keep that with herself. Tapan was quite a bit absentminded since yesterday. It seemed that he was thinking deeply about something. Tapan had undertaken infinite hardship to make Sumitra Devi victorious in the election. But why had he become quiet after her victory? And yet he had told Kunti many times that he would have had no existence on earth without the munificence of Sumitra Devi. Tapan was turning into an enigma. Who knew what he wanted from life? Only he was disturbed by the scene of Kunti standing with her hair flowing down before so many people. Why? How did Kunti matter for him?

The chill wind of the late winter was rushing inside through the window. It was cold. Kunti stood up to close the window. Besides, Sumitra Devi never wanted that Kunti should sleep with the window open. The house stood alone by itself. Who knew what might happen! She insisted that women should learn to take care of themselves. She maintained, "Your honour is in your own hands."

A streak of moonlight had been falling on the deodar tree on the other side of the window. There was no vehicle outside. Perhaps everyone had already left. It was quiet everywhere. She had never felt lonely even though she had to often stay alone in such a large house. It seemed a nothingness of having lost something had enveloped her at the moment. There was an emptiness inside her chest.

Footsteps could be heard near the door. The light inside the room was also switched on simultaneously. Sumitra Devi had been standing inside the room. There was a white paper and pen in her hand.

"What are you thinking standing all by yourself? How many times do I have to tell you not to waste your time in thinking about inconsequential things? Sign on this paper. I will feel reassured when I keep your salary in the bank." Sumitra Devi sat on the bed. Kunti was taken aback. She asked, "Salary? But I am holding no job. How could I get a salary?"

"You sign here. I will explain things later. You are holding a job here. That is, you are taking care of me. Even you do the puja in the prayer room when I cannot find enough time. For that, you have to be...."

"Oh no, Maa! Don't speak like that!"

"Come on! I was just joking. Listen, your job is settled. I have talked to Hota Babu and asked him to hold the job for two months. I have a lot of work to do now. I will feel a great deal more comfortable with you around me. You can work from 10 a.m. till 4 p.m. with others after two months. Hota Babu is my own man. A job has been arranged for you in an office through him."

Kunti did not know what to say. Sumitra Devi laughed and said, "You hounded me to find a job for you. You had no peace of mind because you thought that you were a burden on me. Now why do you get scared when a job has been found for you? Okay, you don't have to go out. You can stay at home and help me in my work. In the process, you maintain yourself."

Kunti still could not be happy. She was thinking that she was only witnessing magic shows for the past two days. The more she saw it, the more amazed she was becoming.

Sumitra Devi got up from the bed and came and stood near Kunti. She caressed her hair. She embraced her and kissed her on the cheek. Kunti had only been staring. Sumitra Devi took her right palm in her own and said, "Look, Kunti. There is no reason to be scared. You wrote your name as Kuntala in the office. It was an example of your fear for your past. But you are not aware that God has gifted you with certain divine powers. You have been able to equip yourself in just a few days. You are able to read Oriya, English and Bengali. You know stitching and cooking. You are able to run a household. I am relieved from all these. You have also learnt how to conduct yourself with dignity amid a group of people. Everyone praises you profusely. God has made my dreams come true!"

There was a strange sensation inside Kunti's chest. Kunti was overwhelmed by the magic words. She lowered her head and sat near Sumitra Devi's feet. Sumitra Devi picked her up and said, "Do you understand, Kunti? I will call you as 'Kala' from now on. Krishna, Jagannatha and the poor are dear to me because they are black in colour. Similarly, you are extremely dear to me because you are full of all the good qualities, beauty and the arts. I will explain everything to you another day. Now sign on this paper. I will be at peace once I open an account in your name."

Kunti held the pen without asking any further question. Her eyes had been filled with tears. Kunti always turned sentimental when Sumitra Devi explained things to her with love and affection. Sometimes she turned mute looking at her face. Some other time she lowered her face with eyes filled with tears.

Sumitra Devi wiped the tears from her eyes. She wiped her own face and eyes too. Kunti asked, “Maa, when would Laltu Babu arrive? I have never seen him here ever since my arrival. Where is he?”

“Oh yes. I have forgotten to tell you. Where is time to think about self when so much of work is there to be done? Laltu has been staying in America for the past ten years. He was not coming here as he thought that he could not find any work to do here. He has studied a great deal there. He has done a lot of research work. But he is coming here after a long time and I find that other people are happier than me about his impending arrival. So why should I stand in the way? Apart from that, who is going to manage all these properties and wealth? I do not have any time for that. Who knows when death would overtake?”

Kunti said, “No, no, Maa. Don’t speak like that. What will happen to people like us who are surviving in your shelter?”

“Don’t talk through your head! Nothing has ever stopped in this world for any particular person. What further dreams can I have at the age of seventy? Let everyone live comfortably. Let me die in the process of working for the benefit of the country and the common man. Parents never mean anything to the children.”

Sumitra Devi went away. As if she had no interest in dragging the conversation. At times she went on talking incessantly like a river in full flow. Some other time, she came to a stop midway like all the water had dried up. It was not possible to tell her anything when one looked at her grave face. She belonged to some other world at that time. It was not possible to touch her. Forget about holding her.

Kunti could not sleep throughout that night. She was only exhausted by moving around the room. She came out to the verandah and discovered that the dawn was almost in the offing.

The moon had started to set on the other side of the deodar tree. The morning star was winking from the sky. The scene of the dawn breaking in the village floated before her. The calls of the crow and the cuckoo hit her on the ears. And the scene of her mother sleepily carrying the utensils to the bank of the pond with a stick of the neem tree inside her mouth for brushing. Mother's body was frail. She was all bones. Kunti's insides seemed to churn when the picture of three to four kids huddled together on a mat on the floor, stewing in their own urine and stool, floated before her eyes. Tears welled up in her eyes. Where had Nima Bhai disappeared? Who knew whether he was alive or not? Again, Gunduri Apa with her sad face floated by her. The baby girl had been blinking from inside her lap. A shiver ran down Kunti's spine. Her head reeled. She held on to the pillar and sat down.

The caw, caw call of the crow could be heard a little later. Something flew by her ears with its wings flapping. Kunti stood up. In stead of entering into her bed room, she went inside the library. What was this? The light was burning in the library. Perhaps no one had remembered to switch off the light. She found the prayer room door open too. There was a tremor inside her chest with some kind of weird apprehension. The faint light of the morning was entering inside the room. She turned around and came to a halt near the room of Sumitra Devi. What was this? Her room too was open and she was not on the bed. So? Should she call the cook? No, no. Perhaps Sumitra Devi had gone outside in the night for some work.

A number of photographs were lying on Sumitra Devi's bed in a haphazard manner. A small boy holding a balloon was sitting in her lap in one of the photographs. There was a handsome person near him. There was another photograph of Sumitra Devi and that man sitting adjacent to each other. There was the smile of a newlywed on the face of Sumitra Devi. There were many photographs like that. Suddenly, she found the photograph of a handsome young man holding a badminton racket in his hand. Who was he? Who could it be? Was he Laltu Babu? There was a photograph of a grave, mustachioed young man. It was difficult to look into those eyes....Kunti left the pile of photographs and came away.

She walked softly inside the prayer room and came to a halt there. What was this? Sumitra Devi was lying prostrate there. Two drops of tears had rolled down from her eyes.

Kunti came back. She had never imagined that she was going to find Sumitra Devi ever in such a helpless condition. It was beyond Kunti's imagination that someone could cry like that surrendering herself totally before God in such an agitated state when she had spent every moment of her life in the service of the nation. It seemed improbable for someone who was a symbol of sacrifices and who seemed not to be swayed by victories and adulations. Kunti went inside the bedroom with trembling steps and lay down on her bed fearing that Sumitra Devi might get up and ask her uncomfortable questions.

As she closed her eyes, she found the hazy shape of Tapan standing before her. She had never heard him speaking all these days against Sumitra Devi. On the other hand, he had always maintained that she was indebted to her not only for his present status in life but also his very existence on earth. But what had happened to him yesterday? It was difficult for Kunti to understand why he had become so angry and used such harsh words.

Kunti opened her eyes and looked. No one was to be seen. Her mind was obviously playing tricks with her. She thought that the more she wanted to be closer to Tapan, the farther he was going away. But a detached person could not turn envious. Kunti, who had never experienced hunger, thirst, love and romance in life, sat up on the bed. Why did her chest seem to explode in some unspoken pain? Tapan floated before her eyes even if she did not think about him. A shiver ran through her body till yesterday when she thought of him. But she seemed to be getting singed in silence by some hot and cruel hammering since yesterday. Why did that happen? If Tapan did not come there any more....No, no. He had promised that he would definitely come at the bidding of Kunti wherever in the world he might be or however busy he might be. Tapan had not given her any assurance about anything else. So why should Kunti repose so much faith on him? But she could not give up hope so easily. When she got tired playing merry-go-round amid all uncertainties, she tended to lean against Tapan. Could Tapan save her with his arms spread? Couldn't Tapan understand that she needed him every moment of the day these days? Amid all the uncertainties, only he....

She could hear bhajans on Sumitra Devi's radio. The set was blaring. Kunti closed her eyes. She pretended to be asleep. One corner of the saree was hangng from the bed. Her hair had spread carelessly on the bed. The calendar was getting blown by the breeze and hitting against the wall repeatedly. Kunti was walking slowly in some unknown place all by herself putting her helpless, scared steps forward in sheer darkness. Who knew how much further she had to go!

Kunti went into a deep sleep.

She came awake when she heard the noise made by a lot of people in the house. She sat up. The courtyard was awash in sunlight. Not a drop of dew seemed to be there in the garden which could be seen through the window. Oh! How many flowers had blossomed during the course of a night! For the first time that day she had not gone inside the garden to pluck flowers for the puja. Sumitra Devi must already have finished her puja. Today, her son Laltu Babu was scheduled to arrive!

Kunti came outside with some unknown emotion. The courtyard was being decorated with electric bulbs. Sumitra Devi was looking into some accounts sitting in a corner. The verandah and the courtyard were dotted with new and beautiful chairs and tables. Sumitra Devi looked at Kunti and said smilingly, "Hello, Kala! Were you dousing the fire at sea last night?" Kunti felt ashamed of herself. She could not look at her with a straight face. Sumitra Devi said while checking the accounts, "You have done the right thing. You may not get any further rest today. The party is going to extend late into the night. Laltu is a crazy fellow ... he loves singing and dancing. Hey! I have forgotten to ask something. Can you sing?"

Kunti stood silently. Sumitra Devi said, "What is there to be shy about it? You sing the way you can. You had learnt bhajans ...."

"No, Maa! I have never sung. None of the girls in my village knows how to sing. We are prohibited from opening our mouths to talk. How could I learn how to sing?"

"Haven't you learnt singing in the process of listening to them? There is no one on earth who cannot sing."

Kunti did not answer.

Tapan ran inside the room breathlessly at this time and said, "Maa! Everything would be okay. I have arranged two tape recorders and fifteen to twenty English music cassette. Besides, Sheila and Emily, friends of Laltu Babu, would come. They are experts in dancing."

"That is true. But it would be good if someone sang a couple of bhajans or folk songs."

"There are people for that, Maa. I have invited Samir and Uttara. There would be no problem."

"You don't understand what I was trying to say. If Kunti would have sung a song in this large gathering ...."

Tapan burst into laughter and said, "It would be like a donkey braying. What a rough voice she has! I won't enjoy her singing one bit." He signalled to Kunti to keep quiet as he said this.

"Get lost! Didn't you find any other time or person for your dark humour? I know that Kala can sing. She is just shy and afraid before a crowd. She will have no confidence in her abilities as long as she does not get rid of her shyness. Do you think that all problems will go away if you only pray before the gods?"

The scene of Sumitra Devi lying prostrate in the prayer room in the morning floated before Kunti's eyes. The pathetic picture of the drops of tears flowing down her cheeks also came alive. How could such a self-confident and workaholic woman who seemed to decide her own fate feel so helpless at that time?

But who was Kunti to ask that question? What right did she have to ask that kind of question? Kunti had come to realise that there was a lonely woman shedding tears behind Sumitra Devi's facade of self-confidence, arrogance, status and wealth. She went to the bathroom quietly. She was able to understand the truth that there was no reason to sit for hours together worrying about everything as she had been doing until then. Besides, she accepted the fact that crying was a weakness. In spite of everything, she felt extremely vulnerable at times. But now she had acquired enough strength to combat her weakness.

Kunti did not think that she had been able to understand Tapan properly as yet. Sometimes she felt that she had lived with Tapan for ages. She could not think of the past at that time nor of the future. She felt that the present was the past and the future. Time remained suspended at that time. In another situation and time, Kunti felt as if she was facing an unknown, incomprehensible and intriguing person for the first time in her life. Somehow she ran away picking herself up. What a difference there was between the Tapan of yesterday evening and the Tapan of this morning! How strange indeed was the human being! How changeable!

A large car entered inside the gate sometime in the afternoon. Sumitra Devi's car followed it. Three to four cars and jeeps also followed them. The person sitting in the front seat of the large car had been buried in garlands. Kunti had been staring from the other side of the window. It was difficult for her to recognise Laltu Babu among them. Three persons got down from the car. Everyone had countless garlands around their necks, bouquets in their hands, sandalwood paste and vermilion on the foreheads.

All of a sudden, there were sounds of conches blowing. Who knew who was blowing them. Kunti was startled enough to close her ears with her palms. She had not heard the sound of conches ever since she had left the village. Why was there a tremor inside her chest on hearing that sound?

Why the euphoria building up in her mind was fading? There was a stream of sadness flowing in her heart. Kunti got a hold on herself latching on to the railings of the windows.

Everyone got down from the car and went inside. The house came alive with expressions of joy. Sumitra Devi entered inside her room as Kunti was debating whether to join the rapturous crowd. A young man was behind him. Kunti wished him with folded hands. Sumitra Devi said, "Kala, I have been looking for you since a long time. You are hiding here ... Laltu is like your brother. You don't have to feel shy with him."

Kunti was amazed to look at Laltu. His hair was falling over his shoulders like that of a girl. The hair had turned red. There was a huge moustache on his lips which had stretched quite a bit on both sides. He had a flowing beard. He was busy in caressing the beard with his five fingers which displayed shining rings on each one of them. It was difficult to read the looks on his face. The thick lenses of his spectacles were creating a sense of fear and awe. Laltu Babu removed his spectacles with his right hand and wiped his eyes clean with the left hand. Then he said, "Mummy. You had written about her, no?"

"Yes, Laltu. I love Kala more than anything else in life. I do not believe in building palaces of bricks and concrete with the help of the soil and stone of the country. I have tried to fight and lay down my life to create human beings out of creatures with flesh and blood. This Kala is an example of that. You can see other examples of my creation if you stick around for a few days."

Kunti felt that she was standing before a courthouse. The shining red eyes, the lines on the furrowed brow and the excessively fat body of Laltu Babu had caused a scare in Kunti's mind. She felt that Laltu Babu was examining her from head to toe again and again. There were hundreds of sharp daggers in those eyes. Kunti was bleeding in the mind and body. Whose eyes were they? Kunti had seen them somewhere ... where ... where ...! At times, father looked at mother that way after smoking a lot of *ganja*. Kunti felt extremely tired at these times. She felt very lonely. She feigned sleep covering her head and lying on the torn mat.

She again looked at Laltu Babu. No,no. That stare was intolerable. Who and what was there in those eyes? She knew and recognised it. Its footsteps still troubled her in lonely hours. Who was it? Radhu Mahajan? No, That was not his stare. There was entreaty in his looks. He lowered his eyes when Kunti looked at him straight in the eye. He talked with his sight fixed somewhere else. Sometimes, tears rolled down from his eyes. No, these were not the disinterested looks of Radhu Mahajan. In that case? Oh ... she bit her little finger suddenly. Those eyes ... those stares! The eyes of Manua and his friends had been assimilated in those two round and black eyes. Sumitra Devi shouted at the sound made by Kunti. She said, "You still remain a rustic. Why are you biting your nails like that?"

Kunti saw that Laltu Babu was smiling. It was not a smile. Kunti felt that a lot of burning charcoal was falling on her body. With that smile on his face, he said, "Mummy! You are unnecessarily harassing the girl. She will get over her shyness in due course. I won't allow her to remain shy for long. Don't you worry. Only if someone studies ... you always said one had to learn something else ... what is that, Mummy? I cannot recall the word."

Sumitra Devi burst into laughter and said, "Worldliwise. Only education does not take one far. One needs a bit of intelligence too. And one has to be worldliwise. No one could teach that to anyone. It is essential to have common sense."

"Let her not have it. But I have got it in ample measure. Now that I will take over your entire workload ...."

Sumitra Devi said in feigned anger, "Stop it! You are still a naughty boy! You are just too young to assume any kind of burden."

"Oh, Mummy ...." Laltu Babu embraced her and kissed her on the cheek.

"Leave me alone! You are turning into a kid again! So many people are waiting for me on the other side."

Tapan suddenly entered into the room and said, "Maa! You come this way. Many people have been waiting to meet Laltu Babu."

"I know that. Laltu will not allow me to do any work in a time-bound manner. Come, let us all go. Kala, you too come with us. You won't feel so shy if you meet different types of people." They went out together. Laltu Babu looked back once from beyond the door screen. Tapan was going out with a bowed head. He stopped for a while. But he did not look back.

A lot of events were occurring suddenly in the past two days. Kunti did not know what to make of those events. She was floating only like a straw in the stream of a river in spate. But the straw seemed to have got stuck in a barren land after coming in contact with Laltu Babu. Why? What could he do to her? And yet why couldn't she mingle with the others in their happiness? Why couldn't she just be herself?

It was evening. Kunti knew that the party was scheduled to start. Many people would come. Some of Laltu Babu's friends from overseas were also supposed to come. So she had to dress decently enough. Otherwise, everyone would laugh at her. What would Sumitra Devi think? She had saved her life and provided her with all the facilities to stand on her own feet. She had to ensure that Sumitra Devi was not embarrassed because of her. Kunti could not forgive herself too if she did that.

She could see the front garden through the window. The entire garden had been lit with different coloured bulbs. The moon looked pale before the bright lights. Soft music was playing hide and seek with the breeze. The place was full of young men and women, middle-aged and old people. Two girls with short hair were dancing. Tea, sorbet, *paan* and cigarettes were being distributed. Laltu Babu was going around to supervise everything. What was this? It was difficult to recognise Sumitra Devi. She was wearing a light cream coloured silk saree. A pearl necklace was shining on her, hanging till her waist. There was a string of Rajanigandha flowers around her head. Two huge earrings on her ears. Wow! How beautiful she looked! Kunti had never seen her dressed like that before. She had never once talked about her son either in happiness or in sorrow before his arrival. But the change in her after the arrival of the son flabbergasted Kunti. She had no experience about parties. People sat on the floor and ate from leaves in the village even if they came wearing silk. Mats were put on the floor in case of very rich people. No one was supposed to talk at the time of eating. But Kunti had gathered some knowledge about parties, picnics and dinners by reading books. But the festivities and celebrations before her again created waves of anxiety and helplessness. Kunti thought that she had reached the foothills of a dangerous jungle after moving around a great deal. There were only tigers, bears, elephants and snakes all around her. Fear! It was a lifelong, habitual experience with her to feel scared when others around her were enjoying themselves. But she seemed to be totally suffocated today. Tapan was also nowhere to be seen. It was difficult to know his whereabouts and what he was doing.

As she sat down tired on her bed, she could hear the harsh voice of Sumitra Devi, "Kala! What has come over you? You seem to have gone into a cocoon ever since the arrival of Laltu." Sumitra Devi posed the question with her hand on her waist.

Kunti seemed to be startled. She said, "Not at all, Maa! Why should I be unhappy? I am happy when you are happy. Apart from that, Laltu Babu is like my brother."

"Then why are you sitting depressed?"

Kunti did not answer. She had held on to a corner of the white saree she was wearing. Her head was bowed.

"Oh, now I get it. You are ashamed to go out in a white saree. Isn't that true? I fully agree with that. It had totally escaped me ... you just wait. I will be right back!"

She went inside her room swiftly. She opened an almirah and pulled out a blue silk saree. She said, "Take it, Kala. This blue colour would look gorgeous on you. You wear it. Let me see."

"Maa! What would people say? Everyone knows me to be a widow...!"

"Shut up! People will talk anyway. I have no patience to listen to the cooked up stories of people. I taught you such a great deal. And yet, you haven't been able to rid yourself of the superstitions. Don't widows have a life? Isn't blood flowing inside their veins? It is the menfolk who have loaded us with all kinds of burdens. Shall we go on bearing such burdens for all time to come? We are human beings too."

"Let it be, Maa! You would feel bad if anyone tells you anything on a day like this. Maybe another day ...."

"You are turning wayward! How dare you argue with me? No, you have to wear this saree now and come out. There is nothing the matter with colour. There is no difference between white, red and blue. The main thing is that your mind should remain clean. You have already read a great deal. Try to refute this."

Kunti did not argue any more. She took the blue Benarasi silk from her hand. Kunti's fingers were shaking.

A fire seemed to have enveloped her the moment she touched the saree. The saree seemed to have thrown a spadeful of burning charcoal all over her body. She could not recall the year, month and the day but she had a blood red silk saree on her body. That seemed to have turned blue today. How could she fathom how much poison was there in that blue sea? She had only known this much that there was not a single Nilakantha near her to drink that poison to the brim.

Somehow Kunti managed to wrap the saree around her. But she could not enter inside the garden. She stood leaning against a pillar on the verandah with hesitant steps. As she came out of her room, some people were watching her. Some others just ignored her. She wondered how many people had been invited to the party. People had gathered as if there was some kind of an exhibition.

Suddenly, someone came near her and placed his hand silently on her shoulders. Before Kunti could turn around, he asked, "You are looking very sad ...!"

Tapan had been staring stupidly at her. Kunti felt uncomfortable. She knew that Tapan had not failed to notice the blue silk.

"You, you are looking beautiful today, Kala."

Kunti was amazed. What had happened to Tapan? He did not seem to have any control over her hand. He seemed to be stammering a bit. There was a bit of smell coming out of his mouth. One day he was saying that he did not touch alcohol, *ganja* or cigarettes. How could he change like this all of a sudden? She removed Tapan's hand from her shoulder and said, "You are not in a proper state now. Take some rest somewhere. Then you may come here. How could you stoop so low ...?

"Please, Kunti. Don't shout. I will tell you everything at the proper time. Laltu has mixed something in the sorbet and got me intoxicated. But I am in complete control of myself. I want you to go away from this place. I don't have much time to talk to you. See, Sumitra Devi and Laltu Babu are coming this way. I am on my way ... take care."

Sumitra Devi again stopped midway to talk to someone. The dinner had already started in the garden. It was not possible to listen to any conversation with the stereo blaring all over the garden. Still Kunti thought that it was better to join the melee of strangers. She prepared herself and started out.

Laltu Babu reached near her with lightning speed. A terrible smell was coming out of him. It seemed to be a mixture of alcohol and cigarettes. Kunti wanted to close her nose with the corner of her saree. A few more moments and she might vomit or perhaps she would faint. Sumitra Devi might be offended in high society because of the uneducated, rustic girl. Laltu Babu caught hold of her palm and said, "I have been waiting a long time for you. Nothing seems to be right because you are not there in the crowd. Now come with me to the garden."

The soft palm of Kunti was getting crushed inside the palm of Laltu Babu like the petals of a rose. His nails had perhaps ripped open the skin of her palm. As she somehow pulled out her palm and started walking towards the house, Sumitra Devi called her from behind and said, "Kunti, where are you going? I am totally famished. Let me take a bit of rest. You and Laltu supervise the dinner. No one would eat unless they get a bit of personal attention."

Sumitra Devi went inside absentmindedly. Before Laltu Babu could catch hold of her hand again, Kunti almost ran inside the garden. What could she say to anyone? Still she moved from one end of the crowd to the other. Wherever she went, she came across Laltu Babu. The same red, stabbing eyes. The arrogant demeanour. He had the same vulgar bearing as that of a hunter who plays around with the prey before finally capturing it. To whom could she talk about it? And who was going to bother about her rustic outbursts? Still she could not sacrifice herself knowingly.

Kunti somehow manoeurved her way inside the crowd. Luckily, the electricity had gone out for a couple of minutes. No one knew the map of that place better than her. Sumitra Devi, who was resting in the drawing room, was directing Tapan in a high-pitched voice to make arrangement for gas lights. It was all right. No one had seen her in that darkness.

Like an injured doe, she ran up the stairs to the first floor. As she crossed her bedroom, the lights came on suddenly. That was not anyone's bedroom. That was the prayer room of Sumitra Devi. There were images of numerous gods and goddesses. But there was no electric light in that room. Only a lamp kept burning like it had some personal affinity with the occupant of the room.

Kunti tried to recover her breath after closing the door behind her. Sweat was running down from her face and body. She was feeling absolutely exhausted. Kunti felt extremely helpless amid such a big crowd enjoying itself to the full. People examined her in detail wherever she went. As if she was some kind of a strange animal. Besides, the blue silk saree felt like a huge serpent embracing her. She had been running all her life to save herself in some impregnable, thorny forest. She could not continue doing it forever. She slept prostrate before the images of gods and goddesses while continuing to sweat as before. She had prayed so often in her childhood abiding by all the rituals. But her prayers had never been answered. Somebody seemed to be saying from deep inside her that however much she tried to seek asylum somewhere just to delude herself, no one was going to provide any shelter to her. She was as much afraid of others as she was of herself.

Suddenly, the sound coming from the garden increased in intensity. The city dwellers perhaps pushed each other back and forth a great deal more while eating. Perhaps they did not feel like eating if the stereo was not played at full blast. She felt like vomitting when the thought of dinner came to her mind. Only now she remembered that she had not eaten anything throughout the day.

Kunti looked at the images of the gods. They had all worn new clothes today. They were smiling benevolently pleased with the fragrance of fresh flowers and incense sticks. A streak of moonlight had fallen on the brass lamp through the opening in the window. Kunti sat down exhausted on the floor.

She looked at the skies for a while. She looked at the gods too. Suddenly, she thought of something and put out the lamp. And then she went to sleep there. Her eyelids were heavy. The melody of music from the garden had been increasing in intensity keeping pace with the progress of the night. Kunti was feeling terribly sleepy. She made a great effort to keep her eyes open. Finally, she closed her eyes. She had never been able to sleep peacefully as she could never abandon herself totally. Sleep seemed to fly away in the breeze whenever she tried to sleep. And when it came to Kunti to be caressed, she never had the time to take it into her lap fondly. She had walked her path throughout her life quarrelling with sleep. But she felt defeated at this moment. She simply surrendered herself. The streak of moonlight hid on the other side of the window.

She had no idea how long she had slept. Suddenly, there was a sound of something falling with a thud. Kunti was awakened from her deep sleep. A strong hand cut off any sound from her mouth before she could know anything or cry out 'Maa'. Who was it? Who was it? Kunti started groaning. A mountain seemed to press her down the next moment. She hit her head on the floor as she tried to get up. Kunti had been staring at the darkness in that trembling state. She was listening to the melody of the music which had got mingled with the voice of midnight. Her body and mind were gradually getting exhausted. Kunti could know who it was even though he could not be seen and it was pitch dark as she was being pressed down to hell. He was no ordinary person. He was the son of Sumitra Devi for whom the festivities had been arranged today.

Kunti tried her best so that some sound would come out of her mouth. It was futile ... it was a thousand times more cruel than the cruel bites of a hundred Manuas. The gods were never there for her. Even now they were not there. In spite of it, Kunti had thrown her left hand towards them. The gods, who were earlier dazzling in garlands, had gone into a deep sleep by this time.

Kunti had no idea how much time had passed. Not a sound could be heard by the time she recovered her senses. It was quiet everywhere. It was the time for the dawn to break. It was not possible to know whether it was evening or morning, village or city. She could not even know whether it was dream or sleep. In such a half-forgotten hour, there was neither any past nor any future! The future was always linked with the present. But those few moments? Kunti sat down slowly. Her body was aching all over. The head was reeling. God! What could she do now? How had the night passed with her in that room? Hadn't Sumitra Devi come to this room in the night? She should have come. If she would have asked for her ...! She looked at her body. No, no. The clothes were in place all right. A white bedsheet was on her as a covering. Who covered her? Had Laltu Babu tried to cover his crime in this manner? Or had Maa come here? Or had Tapan come looking for her? Who could answer this question? Kunti looked at the gods and laughed. The poor gods of this age remained only as stones or pictures on papers or images on wood!

A crow flew away making its caw, caw sound. The morning star was fading away on the dull sky on the other side of the window. There was no point in delaying things any more. She had to get ready before anyone could question her. How many more times was she going to be the victim of others, taking refuge under her incapacity? How many more times was she going to be the object of pity? Kunti somehow pulled herself together and went inside the bathroom. Sumitra Devi was in deep sleep in her own room.

As they sat down to lunch, Kunti could not look at Sumitra Devi straight in the eye. She was scared that she might ask something. What could she say if she asked why Kunti had slept in the prayer room? It was difficult for her even to gulp down her food. Where was Laltu Babu?

Kantha came and said, "Maa! Laltu Babu had telephoned."

"What did he say?"

"I told him that you were having lunch. He said that he was busy in some work. He could not return before the evening. There is a meeting somewhere. He might be delayed till late in the night." Sumitra Devi became grave. She indicated Kantha to leave without answering him. Then she asked gently, "Where did you eat yesterday? I could not see you. It was so late in the night that I did not have the patience to check out what was happening."

Kunti only looked on, a bit stricken.

"Why are you not eating anything? Aren't you well? Why is your face swollen up?"

"Why, no ...!"

"The season is changing. Had you switched on the fan at full speed?"

Kunti knew that Sumitra Devi had not seen her lying in the prayer room. She was somewhat reassured. Still she could not say anything. She only shook her head in the negative.

Sumitra Devi started out in her car before evening. Her face looked sad at the time of leaving. Kunti did not come out to talk to her. She was still scared.

The evening passed and the night came. The cook and Kantha asked her to eat. But she did not pay any heed to them. She locked her door from inside and lay down on the bed. She thought deeply about herself. But she could not find any way.

At long last Kunti could hear the sound of a car entering inside the gate. She sat up anxiously as if a bomb was going to go off near her. She opened the window a bit to see Sumitra Devi and Tapan coming out of the car. Oh! She exhaled a deep breath with a great deal of relief and came outside. Sumitra Devi was telling the cook loudly to serve dinner. There was something in her voice. Kunti went inside her room and closed the door.

Sumitra Devi was saying, "You know, Tapu. I don't like these strange ideas of Laltu. I have organised these meetings with such a lot of labour. You know everything. I cannot understand why he has gone away like this. What would people say?"

Tapan stammered, "He was very much worried about the telegram in his hand. He could not reach there at ten if he would not have left by the night flight."

"What did the telegram say? Who had sent it?"

"How can I know? How could I dare to read the telegram of Laltu Babu? You know how short-tempered ...."

"Still he could have waited till my arrival. I would have made some arrangements. Yesterday the party was going on. His friends were there. He vanished somewhere. He did not even eat anything feigning illness. He doesn't know what a shame it was to drink so much in public. I have some prestige! Some image!"

Tapan had been standing with bowed head. Kunti had been staring at them through the opening of the door. Without knowing it, she was trembling from head to toe. So Laltu Babu had left the place yesterday night. Perhaps that is why Sumitra Devi looked so sad and dejected. Hence, she had not bothered to find the whereabouts of Kunti. She had slept like a lump of clay being pressed down by her own sorrows. The bottle of sleeping pills was near her head. The cook had said so many times that she moved around the house like a mad woman because she could not sleep. At times, she slept for a day or two after gulping down the sleeping pills. She did not eat regularly because she did not feel well. But she had been eating and sleeping regularly since the arrival of Kunti. Kunti's eyes were filled with tears because yesterday night was the first exception to the rule. How unfortunate was she! She only spread the seeds of sorrow wherever she went. Sumitra Devi was unhappy because of her. Tapan was also not floating on any sea of happiness. She wiped her tears and locked the door to lie down on the bed. She had no courage to come face to face with Sumitra Devi and Tapan. There was no point in crying over split milk. But who had entered the prayer room in the quiet hour of the night and covered her violated, naked body with the bedsheet? It was definitely not Laltu Babu. Nor was it Sumitra Devi. So, was it Tapan? Had Tapan followed her or what? But Tapan would not have seen her come inside in the darkness. Apart from that, he had never taken liberties with Kunti until now. Then?

Someone was knocking on the door. Kunti did not answer. The footsteps moving away softly could be heard. The reign of silence started which did not have any definite circumference in the night. Sumitra Devi had not switched off the light in the room on the other side. Perhaps she was sitting quietly. Or may be she was reading or writing something. At times, she slept with her head over a book with the lights on. What was the point of thinking about all these?

The sound of the car going away could be heard a little later. Who went out at that hour of the night? Was it Tapan or Sumitra Devi? Perhaps both had left.

The wall clock indicated that it was 4 a.m. The day and the night were the same in the dark, closed room. Kunti closed her eyes. The darkness of the eyes was the only darkness. It was more deep, more black and more hideous.

Time waited for no one. Days passed on their own! Come sorrow, come happiness. Sometimes the living man jumped into it, swam and took dips to pick up pearls. Some other times, the same living man turned into a corpse, floated and fell prey to animals. No one was near him to offer a word of sympathy. Yet, the day was the same for all. The hand of the hour never stopped for anyone.

Tapan did not come near her any more. Kunti had no idea what had happened to him. He said that he had a lot of work even if he came at times. He asked Kunti to read by herself and refer to the dictionary in case of difficulties. Sumitra Devi too kept him engaged in some work or other the moment he arrived. Or else, she took him along with her when she went out. Earlier, he used to come home when Sumitra Devi would be out. But that did not happen any more. When they met, he only asked - Have you completed that book? Have you read this book or that magazine? Kunti sometimes nodded yes. Some other time she kept quiet. Time flew away. The history of the past floated away over the books in the library. The prayer room seemed to be the abode of Yama. Her own bed seemed like a bed of thorns. And yet the days and the nights did not wait for her.

What was Laltu Babu doing in Mumbai? When would he return? Who could say that? Asking anyone meant inviting problems for herself. But how long could she remain quiet?

Kunti's body seemed to have fragmented into pieces with utter hatred the day she had discovered the possibilities of motherhood after returning from the *Jhulan Jatra*. She had not been able to die even if she wanted to, carrying someone else's child in her womb for all of nine months. People had surrounded her on all sides. Ineffectual masculinity had waited in the wings to provide fatherhood to that child. That was an excuse for her helplessness in her unwanted motherhood indeed! Why did her heart get pierced even now when the face of that tiny girl floated before her eyes? But she had to ignore her cruelly one day! She did not even have the time to press her close to her chest and shed a few drops of tear.

But what about today? She had no way of ignoring it when motherhood came three months later - wanted or unwanted. She knew she could not the carry the burden for long. But who was going to provide support to her here? She had tried to speak about it to Sumitra Devi many a time. But every time she had stopped short. She had returned in silence. She had no idea whether she was going to admit the bad deed of her son. But she herself could not muster enough courage for that. These days, Sumitra Devi spent days at a stretch in the service of the people. There was hardly any scope to talk to her alone. One day Tapan was sitting alone in Sumitra Devi's library and typing. Sumitra Devi was meeting people in the drawing room and discussing their problems. Kunti went and stood quietly behind Tapan. Tapan stopped typing and asked, "What do you want to know? I don't have the time to breathe as Maa has asked me to do a lot of unnecessary work. You can concentrate on the dramas of Shakespeare ...."

Tapan stopped midway. Tears were rolling down Kunti's eyes and her saree was drenched. Tapan had never seen her crying.

"What has happened? Has Maa said anything? Look, Maa is there in the drawing room. She might come any moment."

Kunti still could not stop sobbing. All the water stored in the seven seas seemed to be in a hurry to open up through her eyes and rush on to the chest of the earth. Tapan was going to be drowned in that vast body of water. Tapan thought that someone had opened the locked door of his chest and was standing in front of her. The entire area was inundated ... there was only a tree shorn of all its branches in the middle ... the tree was likely to be uprooted or float away any time.

Shaking her by her arm, Tapan asked, "Tell me what has happened. Or else I will beat you with this scale. Women do not seem to have any other work except to weep. Stop crying, or else ...."

Kunti went on crying like that and said, "Beat me. Go ahead, beat me. Kill me. I do not want to live for another moment. I have no further desire to live. Why don't you do anything? Beat me up."

Kunti had been staring straight at Tapan. The corner of the white saree had slipped from her head. The hair on her head looked unkempt. There were deep black marks under her eyes. The cheeks were sunken ....Why? He had been too busy in the last two or three months to keep any news of Kunti. Laltu initiated talks about the factory and then vanished. So he had to give up teachership and look after it all the time. Not only that. Kunti had to prepare for her matriculation examination. Was that why Kunti felt peeved?

Hiding her face in the two palms of Tapan, Kunti again started crying. Her body was shaking like a straw being blown away in a strong breeze. What had happened to Kunti? Tapan lifted her face in his palms and asked in an agitated voice, "Tell me. What is the matter with you? Won't you tell me? Don't I mean anything to you? Have you ever tried to understand how terrible I feel when you cry?"

Kunti still could not say anything. She could hardly see anything in front of her with tears rolling down freely. Waves of sadness were running across her face. Tapan could not help but swim in that. Gradually, he got dissolved in that. Without knowing it, he had lost his existence in that stream. He clasped Kunti on to his chest with total abandon. The tear-filled eyes of Kunti had sought solace for a moment in the wide chest of Tapan in search of some deep intimacy. They were searching for each other within themselves. They had lost count of time.

All of a sudden, they separated from each other hearing a sound near them. Who was it? Who was it? Who was hiding there behind the screen? Someone seemed to hit on their chests with sledge hammers. She was none other than their saviour Sumitra Devi.

Kunti ran near Sumitra Devi and caught hold of her feet tightly. She wailed, "Maa, Maa! Forgive me, Maa! I could not tell you anything. Hence, I had come to tell Tapan Babu. I am not able to continue with my accursed life any more! Give me a bit of poison!" Sumitra Devi stopped short. She turned around and looked at Tapan once. He had bowed his head like a criminal. She looked at Kunti. Her eyes were tear-filled. She put down the cup of tea and said, "What kind of problem can be solved by Tapan and not by me? I feel like laughing when I think of it, Kala."

Tapan pushed ahead and said, "She hasn't told me anything. She is only crying. The more I ask her, the more she is crying. I … I …."

"You keep quiet, Tapu. I am an old woman. Can't I make a guess about the problem? Tell me what has happened."

Kunti sat up. She wiped the tears off her eyes with the corner of her saree and said, "Believe me, Maa. I have come many a time to tell you about it. But I have returned every time. No words would come out of my mouth. I have not been able to tell anything to Tapan Babu too. My chest seems to burst every time I want to tell it. I feel so ashamed …."

"I do not have the patience to listen to all this ornamental lecture. What matter could be so grave which you can tell Tapan but not me?"

"I have not been able to tell him anything, Maa. What Laltu Babu has done to me the other night… its fruits…."

Sumitra Devi stepped back, startled. Kunti had again sat like the silent bird at the end of the storm. Sumitra Devi shouted, "Tell me, what has Laltu done to you. He had come home for a day after twelve years. He had no idea who you were? Tell me. What has he done to you?"

"Maa... I ... I am like your daughter. You have given me a fresh lease of life. I would never lie to you. I ... I ... Maa...."

Sumitra Devi got up angrily. Her eyes seemed to be raining fire. She was going to burn the whole world with that fire. Kunti was only a piece of straw.

Tapan advanced a step and said, "Tell us, Kunti. What has happened? How can any one know if you don't come clean."

"Laltu Babu was drunk that day. He was not in his senses. I have to suffer for what he did to me that day."

"What did he do to you?" Sumitra Devi gave the appearance of a cobra with its hood raised.

"I am going to be a mother once again. His child is there in my womb."

"Kunti! Kunti! You shameless woman! Doesn't your tongue snap off when you say this? I will burn you alive if you say it again." Sumitra Devi kicked Kunti on her back, spitting fire. She fell down on the ground. Her head hit the floor.

As Tapan ran to pick up Kunti, Sumitra Devi said, "Watch out Tapan! You two cannot exist before my eyes with your dramatics. I have seen with my own eyes how she was embracing you in your love-act. You are trying to blame my son in order to hide your own misdeeds. Oh, no! What misfortune! I had fed the snakes with milk and bananas so that they could bite me!"

Kunti again held Sumitra Devi's feet tightly. She said, "No, Maa! I will not be able to repay your kindness even if you kill me. Do I have the strength to malign Laltu Babu? I have been dying every moment since that day because I have not been able to tell you anything. It would have been much better if I had died. But I never wanted to bring any kind of slur...."

Tapan sat down leaning against the wall with his hand over his head. He had no words to express himself. Sumitra Devi had provided a new lease of life to him too. He had received education, job, everything because of her. He could not show any kind of disrespect to her. But he could never tolerate the way she had tried to extend her circle of influence and amass wealth amid all her wildness and pretenses. It was unbearable for Tapan that she used service to the nation as an alibi for everything. He had stayed near her every moment of the day. In stead of developing any affection and respect for her after seeing her cruel wildness and her capacity to manoeuvre things to achieve her own ends, Tapan had lost all his respect and affection for her. He had no idea what to say to whom watching the pathetic condition of Kunti. Besides, it was quite natural for anyone to suspect Tapan considering the way Kunti had surrendered herself to him in utter grief. So he was in no position to do anything apart from staring at both Kunti and Sumitra Devi. There was no count of innocent people being sacrificed at the altar of expediency in this manner. The country was full of clever people who performed their misdeeds and went scot-free leaving others to take the blame. Tapan had been sitting without a word. There were any number of examples in history of such strange happenings.

Sumitra Devi came slowly near Kunti and lifted her by her hand. She wiped her tears with the corner of her own saree. She said, "You have still not been able to develop self-confidence. That is why, you are trying to cover up. I have watched your intimacy and love towards Tapan. If Tapan has done such a heinous work being emotional, I don't find any reason why you cannot marry him."

"No, Maa! Tapan Babu is blameless. I cannot hold him responsible ...."

Sumitra Devi pushed Kunti harshly by the neck. She somehow caught hold of the wall and checked herself as she was about to fall. Kunti said, "Yes, Maa! You kill me. But I cannot tell a lie. Tapan Babu is blameless. I cannot put blame on a godlike man."

"What did you say? Tapan is a god and Laltu is a devil? Do you mean to say that the drama that you two were enacting a little earlier was false? I don't want to ask you anything more. The black can take no other hue. I want to hear it from Tapan."

Tapan said, "I have nothing to say. I can only say this clearly that I am not responsible for the misfortune of Kunti. You know the nature of Laltu Babu. Why did he go overseas twelve years ago? As a mother, can you say with your hand on your chest that Laltu Babu was not responsible for the death of Madhumita? What could Madhumita do in that state? But the matter was shoved under the carpet. You paid money to the police and everything was hushed up. And that maid servant of yours, Sebati...?"

Sumitra Devi caught hold of Tapan's ears and slapped him hard. She roared, "I had reared you as more than a son. For this kind of reward? Now you go out of my presence. Never put your foot inside this house if you value your life ... go ... I say get out!"

Tapan smiled mildly, "My life is not all that valuable to me. I know that your goons will shred me to pieces within a moment. How many innocent people have lost their lives because of you ...?"

"Are you leaving now or shall I telephone the police?"

"You are making me laugh at the last moment. Where do I have the strength to take on your reputation, wealth and status? I am leaving. But let me say this. History will repeat itself. You will not even get a moment to finish yourself with your own hand. Fie! I hate you. I am not able to make peace with myself because I have been reared by you. Oh! I am free and independent from now on. I had never imagined that freedom was so close at hand ...!"

The agitated voice and body of Tapan melted behind the screen. The pigeon, caged since ages, seemed to run away frantically to be one with the golden chest of the blue horizon. The silent, sobbing voice of the exhausted, helpless female could not hold him back.

All the pent-up feelings of the encaged female pigeon seemed to create the illusion of music in the air when Kunti broke into a wail and said, "Maa! Maa! Don't drive out Tapan Babu from home for my sake. He hasn't done anything. I am the unfortunate one. There is no happiness in my fate."

"So you are admitting that Tapan is responsible for this misfortune?"

"No, Maa. He cannot be blamed for anything. You are holding him responsible wrongfully. He is as pure as the gods...."

"Fah! Love is blind indeed! You are trying to blame my son in order to save your lover! You have lost all your finer points. Now you are only trying to bite me like a cobra."

"Maa! Give me a bit of poison! I don't want to live any longer. I am not telling a lie as God is my witness!"

Sumitra Devi sat quietly for a while. The wailings of Kunti had got assimilated with the breeze. She had been thinking of all kinds of things. She was experiencing a terrible shiver all over her. In spite of her best efforts, she was losing control over herself.

After some time Sumitra Devi said softly, "You see, Kuntala. I have neither the will nor the desire to indulge in any further arguments, dramas or farces. I had given you a new life. But you have soiled it. You only say that God is your witness. You have something in you which would attract everyone towards you. Hence, I had made you wear white sarees and put you on a vegetarian diet. So that you would not lose control over yourself. I was not calling you to appear before other people. I had thought that you could control your evil instincts through your knowledge and conscience after getting a proper education. That was why, I had asked you to wear the blue saree that day and made you eat meat and fish. I had said...." Sumitra Devi gulped.

"Maa! Maa! Believe me, Maa!" Kunti again held her tightly by her feet.

Sumitra Devi seemed to be in a trance. She said, "I told you. Your own people turn into your biggest enemies. What else could you do? Ultimately, you blamed my blood! I know. You don't have a way out. I will not be desecrated whatever you might do. The world knows it, I know it, you know it yourself and that Heavenly Being also knows it that the poisonous germs of waywardness lie within yourself. How much of the charcoal can I wash? You are not the only one, Kunti. There are hundreds of women like you who are getting burnt in their own poison. I have made great sacrifices throughout my life. But I am beaten ...however much I have tried to lift this stupid womankind, the hunger of their bodies has been devouring them that much. You too blamed me finally?"

Kunti started crying loudly. "No, Maa! Believe me. I am not to be blamed for anything. I had absolutely no idea ... I was happy with your happiness until now ... I could not tell you anything that day, Maa! He is your son after all! The mother cannot believe her own eyes until now! But ... but the gods know everything, Maa."

Sumitra Devi seemed to come out of the trance. She was extremely angry. She leaned and slapped Kunti in both her cheeks. She went on shouting angrily. Most of what she was saying was incomprehensible. Kunti had only been staring like an idiot. As if she was dazed before her all-devouring figure.

After a while, she closed the door and went downstairs. Kunti looked around. Her chest and stomach were in a churn out of terrible sadness and hatred. She vomitted on the floor. She lay down there in an exhausted state.

The afternoon was about to pass. The sharp voice of time seemed to have vapourised inside the enclosed room. The moving earth outside had become even faster and seemed to be running ahead frantically. There was still a long way to go. How could it get exhausted and stop? The earth had been victim to many more heinous crimes than this. It has had a bloodbath on many nights only to get up from sleep with a smile in the morning. It had held greeneries, flowers and fruits in its bosom. True, it had died everyday with the sufferings of the body. But what strength it had! It had again taken birth with a smile. Was it going to stop on its way only because of a little oppression? It had seen the test by fire of Sita. It had felt the physical pain of Draupadi having to make love with a tired body with her five husbands. It had been victim to all kinds of humiliations throughout the life of the frivolous motherhood of Kunti. It had drowned in the silent tears of the crowned queens Mandodari and Tara. Yet it had freed itself every time. The arrow of values had hurt its body in every age. It had bled and suffered. But it had never got exhausted. It was the earth! It could take everything in its stride!

The earth moved fast to cross the day and knock on the night with Kunti in its bosom. The outside world had undergone many changes between the Kunti of *Mahabharata* and the Kunti of this age. But the utter darkness inside continued to be just as dark.

Kunti had sat up a number of times during this time. She had dragged herself near the door and knocked on that. But the door had not opened. It had been closed and locked from outside. No one responded also when she called. The cook and Kantha must have been given strict instructions. How did anything matter to them? Had Sumitra Devi turned into a woman of stone? Kunti had again gone back to sleep on the floor. At times the pictures of her parents floated before her. At other times, the hideous laughter of Radhu Mahajan and Manua was reverberating in her ears. The past that had been sleeping like a python was again rushing at her with its mouth open to gulp her down. There was no doubt that there would be no more future if this present was lost in the womb of the past. No one could live forgetting her past. It remained in hiding like fire under the ashes. It needed very little encouragement to raise its head again.

Suddenly, she thought that someone was calling her. Who was it? The lights had been switched on in the room in the meantime. Sumitra Devi and a gentleman were standing near her. Kunti sat up. The gentleman checked her pulse and palpated her abdomen. Then he said something to Sumitra Devi in English. Kunti could not understand anything. An injection was administered and the gentleman left.

She had no idea what time of the night it was. Sumitra Devi and the gentleman picked her by her arms and put her in the car. No one else seemed to be present in the house. No, perhaps someone was there. But Kunti could not see anyone. In spite of making an effort, her eyelids were dropping down.

It was not easy to identify the place in the dim of the night when the car stopped. But she could know as she entered inside that it was the clinic of Sumitra Devi's doctor-friend Pushpalata. Even in her subconscious state, it was not difficult on the part of Kunti to know what was going to happen next. Sumitra Devi was talking with someone very softly. Two nurses made her sleep on a table without asking any question. That was all. She was getting suffocated within herself when the entire place started dazzling with bright light. She had been running and running on some deserted road... who was that calling out to her shrieking wildly amid those broken earthen pots, stones and skulls of human beings? Pitch dark eyes, curly hair, body as soft as milk... who was it... who was it?

Kunti seemed to have jumped into the bottomless sea. Her past, present and future seemed to dissolve into deep darkness.

Kunti had returned to Sumitra Devi's house the very same night. The reputation and dignity of others were much larger than her life.

Kunti knew that her room always remained locked. Sumitra Devi even carried her food inside the room. Was there no one at home? It was strange that Sumitra Devi was spending almost all the time in her library. She was even sleeping there on an armchair. Kunti's room was adjacent to the library. The small prayer room was to its left. Sumitra Devi's bedroom was in front of that. Everything was open. And yet all the rooms had been locked from outside. There was food, medicines and reading materials near her reach. What else could be wanting?

Kunti could move around in two or three days. Whatever should have been destroyed had been destroyed. She felt no remorse for that. Her only sorrow was that she could not make anyone understand her. Her sorrow was that she could not die, try as she might. Why? What was there for her in this world? She could not be of any help to anyone. Finally, Tapan was blamed and insulted for her and he had to leave his shelter. Kunti had a lot of hope that Tapan would definitely do something for her. But all kinds of problems arose because of her carelessness before she could tell him anything. But if what Tapan told Sumitra Devi at the time of leaving was true, then Sumitra Devi was no better than Radhu Mahajan, Sadhu Parida or Manua. Her entire persona was filled with hatred. No, she might die. But she was not going to stay at that place. Living was never in any way attractive for her. So why the fear?

Sumitra Devi came inside the room and said, "You are not keeping well in either body or mind here. I considered things from all angles. I have come to the decision that you should go somewhere else for a few days for a change. Besides, I will be going out for about ten days. I would not like you to stay alone at this place."

She turned around to leave while saying this. She stopped near the door screen for a moment and said, "What did you say? I could not hear you."

Kunti shook her head in the negative. She had never talked back to Sumitra Devi until then. And that day she had nothing to say for herself anyway.

"I know you would remain quiet. That is your greatest faith." Kunti's body and mind had taken in so many poisoned arrows from birth that she did not feel anything any more these days.

Sumitra Devi again came in front of her and stood. Who knew how much poison was there in that raised hood?

"You may have some curiosity. You may not have any too. Tapan is not here. I have sent him to Nagpur on an errand. I would not be afraid to leave you alone if he was around...."

Kunti could see a smile of hatred and sarcasm knotted with the net of her words. She had no such faith on Tapan.

Kunti had not received any kind of commitment from Tapan that she could reject the entire world on the basis of that. All the typhoons of the earth blew her away when she had tried to open up helplessly before Tapan at a weak moment. Tapan also fell victim to that situation and left home for ever. Who knew whether Tapan was still alive with the body reared by Sumitra Devi! Her problems were going to be multiplied if she asked more questions about Tapan. How did she gain by that too? Her question to herself melted away within herself.

Kunti was moving around the room in an agitated manner. What deathly silence was there all around her! No, no. She could not live there any longer. Whatever be the sorrows or deprivations, she wanted to hear the voices of human beings. There was no point in even drinking nectar in a silent and deserted palace. Yes, she wanted to shout out aloud that she needed the contact of human beings. She wanted to live with human beings. She wanted to talk to human beings. She could not live by herself ... she wanted to go away from that place as soon as possible. Perhaps the people of other places might play treachery with her. They might cheat her. Even then she needed her freedom. She wanted her freedom from this heaven. Hell was a hundred times better than this. She did not want to stay even a moment longer in the place that was considered to be heaven by Sumitra Devi. If she would drop her in hell, she would consider herself lucky. Oh God! She had not heard the voices of either the cook or Kantha since the day of that accident. Where had everyone gone? There were not even ghosts in this house that they would startle her at lonely hours. Kunti was going around the house as if she was running, waiting for the untasted freedom. The unshackled breeze, the mango grove, the moonlit night, the lotus pond and the blue, blue water of the river from her village had created the magic of the rainbow in her eyes and mind after a long, long time. Swimming in the river with her friend, swinging from the trees during the Raja festival and spending the entire night singing on *Kumar Purnami**

* A festival celebrated by unmarried girls.

– the memories of all these came alive within her. That day she had not understood what life was. The complexities of family life were not known to her. That was why, her young, impetuous feet always hopped over the earth with the desire to touch the blue colour of the skies. The sun, the moon and the earth had remained the same even today. It was only Kunti who had changed. She had never been able to breathe peacefully, overtaken as she was by fright for a long, long time. And yet ...!

Sumitra Devi came and stood before her. Gravely, she said, "I have packed your clothes in the suitcase. One of my acquaintances is accompanying you. He will leave you there. The rickshaw is waiting."

Kunti looked at the four walls of the room. She looked at the windows, doors, screens and calendars. For the last time she looked at the floor. When she tried to touch Sumitra Devi's feet, she could know that she had already left for her study room. Still she made obeisance on the ground. How could her eyes not turn into a hot desert? How could her chest not burst?

Sumitra Devi had been walking in front. She got down in the staircase. Kunti was following her. There was a huge lock on the door of the drawing room. The tremendous heat of the sun seemed to have checked the speed of the afternoon breeze. However, the summer was still a long time away.

As she was about to sit in the rickshaw, Kunti suddenly looked back. Sumitra Devi had been looking at the skies bathed in sunlight. It was as if she did not even know who Kunti was. She was just another person. There was nothing strange about her leaving. Anyone would have been scared by her terrible grimness; Kunti was just a rustic woman.

Kunti sat down on the rickshaw. A middle-aged man was standing near her with a tin suitcase tied to the carrier of his cycle. Kunti looked at the road. What else was there to worry about!

The rickshaw had been going sometimes through the narrow streets and sometimes on the wide, pitch roads. Where was it going? What was the point of knowing how long it was going to take or what was the destination! She had no desire to learn too. That middle-aged man was following her with his head bowed. The tin suitcase was at times making a rattling sound when the wheel of the cycle hit a ditch. Who had arranged her clothes? She would never know.

The afternoon was gloomy. There were very few people on the road. Some good-for-nothing boys were playing marbles in one corner of the street. Some others were gossiping. Who was bothered about that? Kunti had been lost quite intimately within herself.

Some deep intimacy had developed between her and her life after enjoying it layer by layer. She had clasped on to it with great affection. Life was quenching its unending thirst by sucking her dry every moment. So much so that as Kunti went along on the unknown road with a stranger, she did not even ask a single question to the middle-aged man. She had never received a correct answer in her life whenever she had asked a question. She had been cheated by whatever answers she had received. She had bled in the process of playing merry-go-round with the illusion of pretensions. What was the point of repeating the process yet again today?

The hazy shape of a girl, who used to swim in the river, catch butterflies, munch nuts, sing in tune with the birds in the morning and evening , and run along the paddy fields suddenly danced before her eyes. The hair was unkempt. She was moving around the bank of the pond, the mango grove, the paddy fields and all the houses in the village. With two weeping eyes, the girl was running after the flying butterflies. They were flying away into the blue sky. The helpless girl was crying and rubbing her eyes. And again came floating before her eyes....the *pallu* of the beautiful, young bride in red saree...the bejewelled young bride and her tiny feet decorated with *alta*...the hesitant walk. Again the face of that stupid bride blocked her path. A fluttering mind of tender age which wanted to lose itself in the *Jhulan Jatra* wearing a deep red saree.

No, it was not possible to return to any of those times in the past. It was even difficult for her to imagine. Her boat was floating away in the foamy waves of the bottomless sea. She had no idea where it was going. Sitting on that boat, she was watching the scene of the sky and the sea coming face to face and embracing each other. But the boat was getting slowly submerged in the foamy chest of the bottomless sea. Kunti had never known what the sea looked like. She had read its description in the books. She had seen its wavy shape in picture books. That was enough. But her eyes did not close any more nor any shiver ran down her spine now when she watched the scene of the boat getting sunk.

She had no idea how far she had come or how long it had taken. The sun was going down beyond the distant houses. The crowd was getting bigger on the streets.

The rickshaw stopped. There was a big compound surrounded by bamboo fencing. There were mango, coconut and palm trees inside. She did not have to wait long. A group of women, holding the hands of a few children, surrounded her. They were looking at her amazed. The women wanted to ask her something. But they could not do it. The lips of the children seemed to have been sealed. Kunti thought something and alighted from the rickshaw. A signboard on a tin plate was hanging on the bamboo gate. "Sri Bhavan" had been written on the signboard in bold letters.

3
The Story of Shakuntala

One afternoon Kunti had sat quietly. There was so much of work to be done from morning till evening that many days passed when she never found a moment to think about herself. Kunti relaxed back with a book in hand if she did not have any work to do. Her past was going to take her toll if she sat alone doing nothing. Even if she did not think about some one else, she would become a burden unto herself.

Still "Kunti" and "Kuntala" pushed and shoved their way in to her mind through some character of a book or the *Puranas*. As if the afternoon had been designed to exhale deep breaths or shed tears quietly. The afternoons seemed to be getting longer these days in Sri Bhavan. Similarly, the women who lived there seemed to maintain a distance from her. The children stopped playing and sat quietly when they saw her. They talked in a hushed voice. They ran away if she called them near her.

She could not forget the memories of her first day at Sri Bhavan. The darkness of the dusk was about to cover the face of Sri Bhavan. Someone led her by her hand and made her sit on a cot inside a room. Someone else carried her tin suitcase and put it alongside her. Kunti had not bothered to find out whether that middle-aged man had stayed back or gone away. She had no idea how to conduct herself amid so many people. And yet, when she had been locked inside a room in Sumitra Devi's house that morning, her heart had cried out for the company of other human beings. There was an intense desire to talk to someone. Everyone had been staring at her as if she was an animal in some zoo. That day Kunti had not been able to understand. She was feeling ill at ease because everyone was staring intently at her. But now she could realize the difference between them and her. No one read any book or slept on the bed in Sri Bhavan in the afternoons. Yet, they had provided her with a cot even though she had not asked for one. The children were curious to know what was there in her tin suitcase. No one had a suitcase in this place. Ropes had been tied in each room. They kept their sarees, frocks and shirts on the ropes. The children opened her suitcase to check the contents when she herself was busy elsewhere. They ran away when they saw Kunti. She had been playing this game of hide and seek for quite a number of days. Kunti could not get close to them in spite of making every effort. They seemed to be somewhat respectful towards her. Why? Kunti had never sat down and talked with Sri Bhavan's Maa. Maa sometimes joined others for prayer in the mornings and evenings. She did not look at anyone. She made her way back to her room after the prayer. Sometimes, she moved in the garden with the children. She had never called Kunti near her to ask any question. Kunti too had never dared to go near her. Maa was a big question mark. She was thin and of small stature. The eyes were filled with kindness. Almost as if tears would roll down her eyes if someone stared hard at her. She did not talk much. Only smiled a bit when she saw someone. Kunti had also addressed Sumitra Devi as Maa. Because she could not legally address her as anything else. And yet, she had never got the opportunity as yet to address Sri Bhavan's Maa as Maa in a loud voice even though she wanted to do so. No one had the audacity here to talk to her. How could Kunti do that? Still her sight was always reassuring. The intimacy of that silence filled Kunti's mind with love and peace. There was no fear of Laltu Babu or the fiery anger of Sumitra Devi in this place. Everything was peaceful and quite.

A new human being or a new situation was fascinating for a few days only. Unless it was coloured afresh, it became jaded. The thrill of arriving at a new place had vanished from her mind. No one in Sri Bhavan, whether adult or child, had become intimate with her. Kunti had acquired the knowledge of becoming intimate with other people. She had become a victim of circumstances in her father's house, husband's house and Sumitra Devi's house bearing the burden of mountain loads of suspicion. Neither had she been able to explain herself to anyone nor understand any one else. Why had she not been successful in finding someone on whom she could rely? But no one could maintain her position only through belief and intimacy. In that case, Nima Bhai would not have gone away leaving home, her friend would not have poisoned herself or Kunti would not have abandoned her baby daughter and left home. And Tapan? Kunti had not disbelieved him. But he had no existence in this world. What solace could he provide to others? Had this world been going on only with pretensions in that case? Did it mean nothing at all to be a decent human being? All the books that she had read in Sumitra Devi's house concluded that truth always prevailed in the end. That there was nothing more desirable than to strive to be a decent human being! So why was everything an exception in the case of Kunti? Tapan was also punished without deserving it. Kunti's eyes closed automatically when she recalled the events of that day. The more Kunti tried to leave her past behind her and proceed ahead, the more the past came and stood in front of her like a ghost.

Kunti had no other option to while away her lonely moments except to stare at the roof with her eyes open or lose herself in the pages of the past with her eyes closed. The hours of the summer were long indeed!

Suddenly, two or three women opened her door and sat down on the floor startling her in the process. Kunti sat up on the bed when she saw them. Then she thought of something and sat down on the floor along with them. They had been looking intently at her from head to toe. She felt very uncomfortable. What were they looking for? She smiled at them to lighten the situation. Everyone had kept herself at a distance until now. If they had come near her, why couldn't Kunti smile a bit in order to make them her own?

One of the women stared at her with large, round eyes and asked, "Why did you come here? You look exactly like a queen. You could easily take care of yourself. You could even take care of another five families. Any number of princes would not mind serving you. The whole world would not have sufficient space to keep all your happiness together."

Kunti was startled out of her wits. Oh God! What had these people thought of her?

Another came near her and whispered, "You will not get happiness here if you have come like Goddess Sita on a *vanavasa*. You are not lame or blind. May be you do not have a husband. But does any one leave home and come here? And what kind of people live at your home? They pay your maintenance regularly every month. But no one ever shows up. Maa was saying...."

Another woman was picking her teeth at a distance. The aged woman said, "Everything is over for a woman once she loses the bangles from the wrist and vermilion from the head. What is the point of showing meaningless affection? You only eat a little bit in order to live. That is all. To hell with the life of a woman!"

Kunti had no other option except to continue to sit with a sad face. She was known as a widow even when her husband was still alive. Was it a blessing or a curse of Sumitra Devi towards her? But both had equal meaning for her. Nothing was to be gained by grieving.

The first woman shook Kunti out of her reverie and asked, "How is the woman who comes in a car to enquire about you related to you? She is handing over loads of money in the hands of Maa. But she never visits you. How cruel she is!"

Kunti did not answer. So Sumitra Devi was coming to enquire about her and paying money for her upkeep? Why? What other designs did she have in her mind? Perhaps that was why these people were respectful towards her. They were scared of her. They were serving food for her at a different place and placing a mat for her to sit on. They were collecting her clothes from outside and placing them in her room carefully. She was sleeping on a bed when everyone else slept on a mat. How could these people know that the donation for which she was revered by all had heaped so much of inequities on her! It had shorn her of her inner beauty. It had led her through loads of sufferings.

Again someone asked, "Did you feel bad about what we said? We could not control ourselves on seeing your beauty and demeanour. Please do not tell anything to Maa."

Kunti held the hand of the woman and said, "No, no. Please consider me as one of you. What beauty do I have? And how does that help? Just as you are unhappy because of lack of beauty, I am unhappy because I am beautiful. I could not get any place to live in this world because of that. I had thought that I would forget my grief living with you people. But you never consider me as one of your own. You don't even talk to me. How do I continue to live here? I have no one to call my own in this world."

Kunti's eyes were filled with tears as she said the last sentence.

A young girl put her hand on Kunti's feet and said. "Don't talk like that, sister. I cannot tell you in words how much better we feel since your arrival. You see, the children were not studying properly. They did not clean themselves properly at the time of bathing. Now they listen to you and do everything properly. We feel we are looking at a goddess when we look at you. That brat Mahani was asking me yesterday whether you were Goddess Durga. He is such a big boy. He was not sleeping peacefully since his arrival here. When you caressed his head yesterday and asked him to sleep, he slept like a log. You have magic in you. The children simply eat out of your hand...."

Kunti laughed so loudly when she heard this that all the children came and surrounded her. Her own daughter's talkative eyes seemed to stare at her in the simple, innocent eyes of the children. Kunti suddenly lost her equanimity. An earthquake seemed to shake her both inside her and outside. She held the children with her arms spread and started a never-ending wail. She had lost all control over herself. The aged women caressed her on the back and the cheek and also started sobbing. Some started to reason with her. But the tears in her eyes could not be held back. It was as if the darling daughter was crying after her favourite toy had broken. The stream of tears was not going to be checked until the new toy arrived. The kids surrounding her broke into a loud wail. They did not only cry. They rubbed themselves against Kunti and embraced her. It was as if the mother had left home for a long time and was narrating her sorrows and deprivations before her children after coming back.

At this time, an extremely grave voice could be heard, "Who is it? Why are all crying?"

The children dispersed hearing that voice all of a sudden. There was a lull in the storm of Kunti's sobbings.

"Stop crying, Shakuntala. You are educated. I had not expected this kind of behaviour from you. Don't insult your education. Control yourself and stop sobbing. You will find that your mind will be free of all evil thoughts and ignorance. Happiness and sorrow in this world are transitory. The only truth is God. Have faith on Him.

Kunti was amazed.

Shakuntala!

The reared child of the Puranic saint Kanwa. Shakuntala!

Who was this Shakuntala at this place?

Draped in white dress from head to toe and with silver hair, Sri Bhavan's Maa was standing before her. Kunti might have seen her once or twice since her arrival. She had always been busy with either prayers or the accounts. She had never imagined that she was going to confront her at a time like this.

But who was Shakuntala?

Maa had been talking to her!

So, had she gone through another metamorphosis! From Kuntala to Shankuntala?

Had Kunti heard all right? Someone seemed to have done some magic because of which her tears had dried up. Was there so much of strength in a name?

She opened her eyes and looked straight at Maa. She was over seventy, wheatish in complexion and had silver hair. The eyes were filled with kindness. And yet there was some kind of agony writ large in those eyes. Kunti did not know who Maa was, about her past, and about the kind of burden she had been carrying. How could she judge her only through her naked eyes? She was ashamed at the expression of her own weakness. She was sad to some extent too. The women and children sitting there were looking at her and Maa alternately. She was filled with a sense of uneasiness.

Maa could perhaps read her mind. She said, "There is nothing to worry, my dear. The world is full of sorrows, pains and sufferings. One has to seek refuge in God if she has to free herself from the ties of the world. Only He can provide you with peace. You can understand what is the real joy in life when you rid your body and mind of all kinds of pretensions."

She said this and left. The children ran after her shouting 'Maa,' 'Maa'. She turned around to caress someone on the head or someone on the cheek. She picked up someone and kissed her. The verandah was noisy for some time. After a while, the children went away with her to work in the garden.

The girl sitting near her again said emotionally, "Look, sister. Your name is just as beautiful as you are. Tcha! My name is Puni. Maa fondly calls me Punei. The others are called Kamali, Shukuti, Moti, Champa, Gedi, Jhara and Malati."

Kunti could not hold her curiosity in check. She asked, "Did you know my name today?"

Puni came near her and said like a grown-up person, "No, I just said like that. Maa had told us on the day of your arrival that Shakuntala was not to be asked any questions... that she would get better if she took enough rest. You fainted the moment you got down from the rickshaw and came inside to sit on this cot. The doctor came and administered an injection to make you sleep. Maa had been sitting near you throughout that night. She was crying.... All of us felt very bad. You won't believe it, but even the children did not drink a drop of water.

Kunti was amazed. She did not remember when she had lost consciousness. But she had slept very deeply that night. She had opened her eyes only in the morning. She had remembered that Maa had slept near her in an armchair. Maa had never said anything nor Kunti had ever asked her anything afterwards.

Kunti laughed and said, "Puni! I did not know that all of you would love me so much. Come, let us go and do some gardening. The sun is about to go down."

All of them walked behind Kunti. Everyone seemed to be happy. There was a sense of belongingness. How starved these thin, naked children were for a bit of love! These uneducated, old, middle-aged and young girls were also extremely simple. The rays of the last sun were fading over the plants and flowers of the garden. Kunti's mind again felt damp after a long time at the touch of the human heart.

With her hands folded, she made obeisance to the last ray of the setting sun. Of course, it was out of habit only. Every work was done out of habit. One got deliverance when all the doors were closed and consciousness turned to subconsciousness. Sumitra Devi might have told this to her a number of times. How anxiously she had run to taste the fruit called 'Deliverance'! How many people had that experience! Yet, the not-so-easily available thing was pushing away to the distance. The lotus was going further and further away. From knee-deep water it had now become as deep as her neck.

Again, she remembered her new name. Kuntala from Kunti, Kala from Kuntala and again Shakuntala from Kuntala. Strange was her life indeed! Layers of slime caught on as easily as they came off. And again they caught on. Kunti, however, continued to exist as before.

Kunti could not accept the name 'Shakuntala'. She had read the story of Shakuntala. Her entire life became accursed because of a little bit of absentmindedness. Finally, she felt humiliated and insulted not being able to establish her identity in the King's court. What terrible punishment for a simple mistake! What misuse was being made of prayers and *mantras* in that age! Were the gods mute then! Not only in that age, even in this age they were cruel and heartless. Why else would her life be accursed time and again? Who was cursing her like this ever since her birth? Kunti was going to cut that invisible power into a hundred pieces and throw it into the sea if she ever came face to face with it. She had no further patience to bear the decision of the invisible power. She did not want immortality. Nor did she want someone's pity and handouts. She only wanted to live like a human being of flesh and blood. She wished she could live as per her own wish, work as she wished and after that she wanted that her earthly body would turn into ashes and dust as that of an unknown person. She had no illusions about her next birth or about heaven or hell. Kunti wanted deliverance, the liberty of body and mind so she could breathe a little more peacefully.

Today she felt that she had everyone with her even though no one was with her. The young orphans, the handicapped old people and women more unfortunate than her had bound her with love and affection. She did not desire any greater happiness than that. Why couldn't she find her deliverance in serving and taking care of these people? No, she was no longer going to look at either her past or her future.

Somehow she had arrived near the front gate while watering the plants. Maa had forbidden all inmates to go near the gate without any valid reason. There were two dense jackfruit trees in the front. Tall deodar trees were on the other side. Lightning struck in the sight of Kunti's thoughts. A car was standing near the gate. It was Sumitra Devi's car! She hid herself behind the car. Oh God! Let her never meet Sumitra Devi again. A huge explosion might take place if their eyes met. She won't say anything in deference to the quiet and dignified face of Sri Bhavan's Maa. She would only watch and hear.

As she talked to her, Sumitra Devi extended a packet to Maa's hand. What could it be? Was it the money needed for Kunti's maintenance? Or did she want to be known as a philanthropic person with the money gathered through evil ways? Couldn't Maa understand Sumitra Devi's evil intentions? Kunti was going to tell her everything about Sumitra Devi if she had not been able to understand. Let everyone die of hunger in Sri Bhavan....

The car vanished from sight blowing its horn. Maa proceeded towards her room seeming to be a bit absentminded and worried. She had a small office room adjacent to her bedroom. There were two chairs, a table and a broken wooden almirah there. Maa read, wrote and kept accounts bending over the table. At times, she went outside for a walk wearing a white saree. She returned the same way, sweating a bit. No one bothered about no one in this place. Yet no one felt good if Maa was not there. Everyone kept waiting expectantly for her return. No one again bothered about her once she was back.

Who had the guts to face that peaceful and quiet image? She lived in everyone's heart. The spring flew bursting the cruel chest of the hills. Not for its own sake, but for the happiness of others. Kunti bowed her head towards Maa in her mind's eye.

Kunti's feet again stopped near Maa's room. The screen of the window was fluttering against the wind. The lights were on. Maa was taking out the money from the yellow packet and counting it. Perhaps Sumitra Devi had given some of the money. But Maa was counting the money and laughing. She was folding her hands and praying God. Again...what was this? What kind of scene was Kunti witnessing? There were tears in the eyes of Maa. She immediately wiped her eyes with her handkerchief. Then she left her chair and came so fast near the window that Kunti did not have a chance of moving even a step. She was embarrassed and lowered her head.

Maa's voice could be heard, "Shakuntala, why are you standing there? Come inside. I have been waiting a long time for you."

She had heard the invitation of such sweet voice many a time. She had only drunk poison to the brim whenever she had taken a dip in that honey. Was it again to be repeated today? Let it. Kunti had nothing more to fear. The man floating in the mid-sea in heavy storm could not afford to be afraid of the depth of the sea. He could never reach the shore if he was afraid. True, she had the desire to reach the shore. But she was not going to back out from confronting the storm for the sake of other people.

Maa again said with a soft voice, "What do you want to say? Ask any question. You must search for an answer if there is a question raised in your mind."

Kunti did not have any question. She only had curiosity. Hence, she bowed her head as if she was ashamed. Maa again said in an emotional voice, "I have heard your history. Your silent eyes are telling me that you have been exhausted, having fallen victim to wealth, selfishness and greed. What you consider to be your sin is not in fact a sin. Don't hold yourself responsible for a sin which had not been intended by you. Release yourself from all ties. Deliverance is in your own hands. What are you searching so much for? Now tell me, what did you want to speak about."

In the faint darkness, a shiver ran through the entire system of Kunti. Her voice was full of apprehension. Shaking from head to toe, she asked, "You are not going to send me away from this place, are you? I do not want to go anywhere else."

"You are insane! How little understanding you have of this world! Measuring the entire mankind by the yardstick of one or two persons is a great sin, my dear! You are my daughter! May be not by blood, but by soul! You cannot be infected by any sin, Shakuntala! I have finally found you after a long, long wait. How could I throw you out? Who would take care of these children, old people and the helpless women in that case? You only are going to rear them like your own children. You have that strength in you, my dear! I have discovered that divine power only in you...."

Somehow Kunti stopped herself from breaking down and said, "You have got it wrong, Maa! I have no other wealth with me except infamy. I am... I am...."

Maa pulled Kunti's head to her bosom with some deep emotion and said, "What is infamy, my dear? If there is art, there would be infamy. As time changes, infamy again turns into art. That infamy might turn out to be your biggest asset one day. Don't think that you are going to have your run of bad luck for ever."

The prayer song of Sri Bhavan could be heard. Maa proceeded quietly towards the place holding Kunti's hand. Hearts were searching for other hearts in the evening's breeze to lose their individual identities. Everyone's eyes were closed with some deep emotion. Kunti knelt down to pray with Maa.

Days passed. Layers of moss formed on the mind. The sun of the morning, the moon of the night, the butterflies flying over the flowers and the unknown birds of the blue sky again started making rounds in the mind. Kunti surrendered herself to the service of mankind with a great deal of enthusiasm. She fed the children every morning with breakfast and then gave them a bath. Then she taught them the alphabets and told them stories. Again she fed them lunch in the afternoons. The routine was again repeated in the evening. The small children did not know who their parents were, where they belonged and what was their future. They never asked any questions. But Puni, Kamali, Shukuti, Jhara, etc. sometimes cried for a long time. Only one of them never lost her cool. She was Padi Apa. She was old and a widow. She did all the cooking. She served everyone. That seemed to be her only pleasure in life. She did not talk much. Kunti thought many a time in her lonesome hours about the ways in which she could bring a smile to the sad faces of these women. It was not an easy thing to make something out of the children or weave dreams in the lives of unfortunate creatures like Puni, Kamali and Shukuti. She herself had age in her favour. She had some education even though it did not amount to much. She could take care of herself by putting in a bit of hard labour. But what about these people? They could not turn to anyone except Maa. What kind of dreams could she weave for these people? Kunti sometimes felt totally exhausted. The past visited her in waves. What had happened to those days when she used to dream? Tapan had sown a few dreams in her mind and eyes. Poor man! Sumitra Devi wanted to pass the misdeeds of her son on to Tapan because he had stood by her through thick and thin. He had never crossed swords with Sumitra Devi because he had been reared by her. Where was he? Kunti had no way of knowing where he was. She was sure that they were not going to meet again. But only one person had been able to understand her amid all the storms of her life. He was the only person who could pour his heart out before her. That was perhaps the only saving grace of her unwanted life. Sumitra Devi could not tolerate it. The gods too perhaps could not tolerate it. The inability to talk openly with Tapan had suffocated her. She wanted to die at such times! But she could not. She had to go on living again for everyone. There was no greater pretension on earth than to go around with a dry smile on the face while burning inside oneself all the time.

One evening she heard the terrible stories of Shukuti, Kamali and others from themselves. Someone's husband had kicked her out of the house after beating her up. Someone else had come out into the open after losing her chastity. Someone had perhaps married; but she had not been able to stay at home being continuously oppressed by the mother-in-law or the sister-in-law or the brother-in-law. The only thought of a girl's parents was to somehow get the girl off their hands. All of them had gathered here propelled by the cruel hand of fate. Everyone had a sea of tears in her eyes. Who was going to wipe whose eyes? The extended hand of Kunti had again come back to her own lap. When she heard all those stories, she started thinking that she had no grief. She never even had any kind of grief. Kunti came awake when she sometime heard some child hallucinating in her sleep in the night. She could not sleep any more. The face of a baby girl floated before her eyes. Curly hair, fair in complexion and tear-filled eyes. Why such bad thoughts came to her mind?

Had Radhu Mahajan married again? He would have killed the girl by throttling her if a son was born this time by the grace of Manua. Why should he spend money to keep the girl alive? The girl was not related to him by blood. So there would be no hesitation on his part to throttle the girl. But what about Gunduri Apa? Was she not going to look after the girl?

Tears rolled down from her eyes without her being aware of it. She wiped the tears when she found others coming her way. They were even more unfortunate than her. What people had to do just for a bowl of rice! As if life meant only to eat a handful of rice and somehow keep breathing in order to live. Hence, she had no desire to go through with this life. Whatever she was going to do had to be for the welfare of others. It was enough if she got some peace out of it. Kunti thought that everyone in Sri Bhavan including Maa was unhappy. Her grief was much less in comparison. One lost directions in this world submerged in her own problems and sufferings as long as one had not understood others or discovered others. Once she started weighing herself by the scales of others, she began to understand how insignificant her own problems were. One might tire out in the process of sorting out her own problems. But she had to pick up the cudgels for others. Otherwise, the world might have been destroyed since long. Everyone would die when some terrible event occurred. The world would be destroyed; mankind would be annihilated. Mankind had been going through incidents and accidents since the primitive times. Its dharma was to forge ahead. There were so many books in the library of Sumitra Devi to acquire knowledge. The memory of some of those books was still fresh in Kunti's mind. The characters and incidents of those books popped up when she was exhausted. They provided her with courage. They wiped the tears from her eyes. A lamp of hope again started flickering inside her chest. Kunti wiped her tears again. She broke into a smile and concentrated on her work once again.

One morning Puni came running to Kunti and shook her awake. She shouted, "Didi! Didi! Get up quickly. There is something gravely wrong with Maa. She is not able to speak up. She was singing bhajans. Suddenly, a groaning sound came out of her throat. It seems her tongue has been sucked inside. Maa has lost consciousness at the place where she was sitting."

Kunti got up rubbing her eyes. She could not attend the prayer session every morning. Maa had left strict directions that no one was to disturb Kunti if she was asleep.

As she made the effort to get up, she sat down again. Tremors were going through her body. What had happened to Maa? She was quite jolly the day before. She was reciting the *Ramayana* flawlessly the night before. She had her dinner of bread and milk like every other night. There were no signs of any sadness or suffering on her face.

Trembling with some unknown apprehension, Kunti came near Maa. Maa had been staring ahead with her eyes open. But her sight seemed to have been fixed on some distant horizon. Her body was thin and frail. The nose was straight. There were sweat beads on her wide forehead. Twenty to thirty handicapped children had been sitting near her with tear-filled eyes. The elderly people had been sitting with their eyes closed as if they were praying. Silent tears were rolling down everyone's cheeks. A long breath of hopelessness escaped Kunti tearing her chest to shreds in the process. She broke into a loud wail and fell down near Maa's feet.

Somehow Maa managed to lift her hand and put it on Kunti's head. She whispered something to Kunti. Kunti could not understand anything. Everything looked dark to Kunti. She had no idea how she could go on living in the absence of Maa. Hence, she kept on banging her head near Maa's feet, wailing loudly. Maa was trying to say something to calm her. But her words were not even audible. But she had to say many things. She had tried to talk to Kunti many times. But somehow the opportunity had eluded her. Kunti had come back and waited again to hear those unsaid words. But.... Kunti had lost herself in her loud wails, placing her head on Maa's feet. Kunti could not even think how poisonous the earth was likely to be and how unbearable her life would be in the absence of Maa. It was dark everywhere for her.

Many people had gathered there by that time. The message of sadness and death spread very fast even though there were no immediate neighbours. Someone had telephoned and informed everyone.

The doctor arrived. The ambulance was summoned as per his advice. Kunti was none too worried on seeing the doctor. It was the same doctor to whom Sumitra Devi had taken her at midnight a few days ago. The doctor might not recognize her. But how could she forget her features? She had a premonition that Sumitra Devi might also arrive. But she did not come.

Maa returned from the hospital at 4 p.m. Her eyes were closed just as they were when she had left for the hospital. The closed eyes did not open any more. She did not ask even once whether the children had finished their supper. She went away suddenly without giving any indication about the history of Sri Bhavan or the accounts or her vision of the future. Was this then the fruit of one's *Karma?* Or was it fate? Or was it the will of God? Kunti had become unconscious for a long time.

Maa took leave of Sri Bhavan forever that evening. Many social workers, capable administrators and experienced journalists had come running for a last *darshan*. The ordinary public had also arrived in large number. Even though there were many women social workers present in the crowd like Sumitra Devi, she herself was absent. The middle-aged man, who had dropped Kunti in Sri Bhavan, had laid a wreath near the feet of Maa. He had perhaps come as a representative of Sumitra Devi. This intentional absence of Sumitra Devi had amazed Kunti and made her speechless about the direction of life.

A huge condolence meeting was organized for Maa within the compound of Sri Bhavan. No one had been able to keep count of the people who had gathered. Everyone shed tears. Everyone praised Maa's sacrifices effusively. The strangest thing was that everyone made commitment to help financially for the smooth running of Sri Bhavan. Some donations were collected at the place of the meeting. Puni was making a long list of people giving donations and making commitments. Kunti could neither hear nor see anything. The sad and benevolent eyes of Maa seemed to be everywhere. Maa seemed to be alive in the trees and plants, in the white walls of the houses and in the faces of all the people who had gathered there. She seemed to be calling Kunti and saying, "Your infamy is your wealth, my dear. I have seen traces of divine power inside you. Only you can show the path of living to these unfortunate creatures. Shakuntala, I am leaving this world relying on you."

But to whom could she say this? What power had she that she could carry the burden? She had received many commitments and assurances in her life. But everything had come to nought. She was herself floating in the middle of the bottomless sea. What commitment could she give to anyone that she would hold him by the hand and take him to the shore?

The *shraadh* ceremony of Maa passed in sadness, a sense of loss and singing of bhajans. No one knew who sent the food all those days. No one asked any question. The pang of hunger heard music only in its own voice. It seemed as if everyone in Sri Bhavan was eager to eat. Good food and heart-touching promises had created an illusion in the minds of Sri Bhavan's inmates. Only Kunti was moving around restlessly. Her eyes had run out of tears. She had lost all feelings of hunger and thirst.

She had missed her steps and fallen down a number of times in the process of trying to seize the time. There was no end to making efforts. There was no limit to losing either. She had been continuously in search of someone with a ravaged heart. Who was it? Where was that divine power within her? Maa had seen that. But she herself could not discover it!

Time did not wait for anyone.

The crowd of people turned into a thin trickle. After a few more days, no one was to be seen coming. Sri Bhavan had run out of all kinds of provisions. Even the shadows of the people who had promised to make donations could not be seen. Padi Apa had exhausted everything that was available. Even the vegetables from Sri Bhavan's gardens had been exhausted. Kunti was very much aware of the situation. But she had been lying on the bed as if she did not know anything. The grown-ups managed somehow on half empty stomaches. But what about the children?

One afternoon, a kid came near Kunti and started howling. She did not want to face the unpalatable truth. Puni came and said, "Apa! He is crying because he is very hungry. Padi Apa has been giving us a handful of rice and a bowl of water since the death of Maa. She is locking the storeroom and the kitchen. The elderly people can go without food. But children cannot manage to stay that way. You tell Padi Apa to feed the children properly."

Kunti looked at Puni. She was hardly thirteen or fourteen. Her fleshy limbs had become thin. There were black marks below her eyes. The hair was unkempt. It seemed that she had not applied oil to her hair since long. She too must be terribly hungry. She had come to fight for the small children.

Kunti had never asked Padi Apa about the supply of rice and dal. Padi Apa had also never volunteered any information. Maa was not there today. Hence, these people had run to her to complain against Padi Apa. But what could she do? She had herself seen that there was nothing in the storeroom. There was only some rice in the bag. Padi Apa was quietly crying with her hand inside the rice bag. She had seen that Padi Apa was herself going without any food. How could she console anyone? What could she say?

The people who had shed tears and made commitments at the condolence meeting were nowhere to be seen. Padi Apa had made the rounds of their houses. No one was available. Hence, Padi Apa had been crying round the clock. Padi Apa and Kunti had put their heads together on many sleepless nights without finding a way out.

As she was moving around in this kind of helpless manner, the unshakeable love and faith of these stupid people had shaken her. It was not just a question of her survival. The survival of others also depended on her.

The kid had gone to sleep sucking his finger in Kunti's lap by that time. Kunti knew that others would also come crying after that. The women would gather at one place with sad faces. Raghu and Madhav were going to beat on their chests and cry in the room in the corner. They were here since ages. One could not move his hands and legs. The other was blind. No one could tell them anything. They were worse than children. They did not understand anything.

Puni walked away angrily without getting any answer. As she walked away, Kunti recalled that Maa had once said that a lot of donations came to her. The donors did not want their names known for different reasons. But no one came to this place even to take a round these days ...!

Padi Apa came and stood before Kunti with a sad face and a pale look. Kunti was even more disturbed. Before Kunti could ask anything, she said, "There is not even a grain of rice at home for tomorrow. Kamali, Shukuti and Puni had brought some money working as day labourers. I managed with that. Puni did not go to work today. That contractor is a drunkard. He pulled Puni's saree. No one is going to work from tomorrow. It is difficult to bear the wailings of the children."

Kunti asked like an idiot, "Why have you come to me to tell all these things? I don't have a dime with me. You have seen my tin suitcase lying open."

"How can we manage to run this place if you break down so soon? You must leave this place and go outside to make some arrangement. Maa had so much faith on you. She loved you!"

Kunti stared outside. She saw no need to cross words with her. What was the point? Padi Apa was beyond fifty. She knew how to cook. But she had no idea where the rice came from. Padi Apa moved near Kunti and said, "Are you getting exhausted,

Didi? Don't read any meaning in my words. You are still young. You are educated. You can meet people outside and talk to them to find some food for this place. I am an old woman. On top of that I am illiterate. I become mute when I see strangers."

Kunti laughed with great difficulty recalling her past. Padi Apa moved closer to Kunti, encouraged by her laugh. She said, "This house seemed to be a den of ghosts when Maa brought me here initially. Then I found four to five kids shouting and running around one day. I thought that perhaps they were related to her. Later, I came to know that she had picked them up from the gutters. But Maa was showering all the affections on them. She even put them on her lap and cried at times. There was no earning member in the house. Maa sold her ornaments and managed somehow. Many people came and stayed here of their own accord. The number of orphans and women increased gradually. Then Maa started stepping out of the house. She met officers and other people. She begged for their help. She never spent anything for her own comforts. The children who grew up here and made something of their lives forgot this place after leaving it. No one ever helped out. Whatever you may say, Didi, but there is a difference between one's own children and other children."

"Does this house belong to Maa or is this a rented house? Rent must be piling up if this is a rented house."

"Ha! Don't you even know that? This is her own house. The landlord would have thrown us out since long had this been a rented house. Maa had sacrificed everything she had to us orphans. I have seen everything with my own eyes!"

Kunti asked eagerly, "Padi Apa! How did you come here? Don't you have anyone?"

Padi Apa's face turned crimson. The eyes seemed to be in some distant past. She started saying, "It seems like ages now. Maa's husband was a high-ranking officer. But destiny was against her ... a huge truck hit her husband's car in such a way that he and his four children died on the spot. Maa's leg had broken.

She spent six months in the hospital. I have seen with my own eyes. She was losing her consciousness all the time. She survived with a great deal of difficulty. I was lying on the hospital floor at that time. I was suffering from peptic ulcer. The doctor wanted to operate on me. But I had no relation worth the name. Who would take care of things? I was a child widow. I worked as a daily labourer. I had one saree, a silver bowl and a mug to call my own. When I felt a little better, I pressed Maa's legs or gave her a drink of water. Maa recovered gradually. When she heard about my ulcer, she spent money and got me cured. I came here with Maa. But she went away leaving me all alone here. I am an unfortunate character. One cannot quarrel with destiny."

Padi Apa pressed the corner of her saree to her mouth and burst into a wail.

Kunti picked up the child from her lap and made her sleep on the floor. Then she said, "Why are you crying, Padi Apa? Wait for a day or two. The gods will provide some help definitely."

Kunti was startled by her own words. Where were the gods? She had never seen any of them. Kunti had cried in her childhood for her failure to catch butterflies. She had been a prisoner in her house when all her friends were splashing around in the river. She had gone into Radhu Mahajan's house not knowing what was waiting for her there. She was reminded of Manua and his friends taking her apart at the time of the *Jhulan Jatra*. Laltu Babu, the son of Sumitra Devi, had devastated her. And she still believed in the gods? Wouldn't the gods have come to her rescue if they were there? She had cried for days lying near their feet. And yet they had not even extended a little finger to take her to safety. Kunti would never understand why they always came to mind first when the going was tough! Was it because she could not see them? Or was there anything else?

Kunti opened the almirah and boxes of Maa that night in Maa's room after everyone had gone to sleep. There was a notebook in one of the boxes in which only the names of the children had been written. Their addresses or the names of the parents were even missing. Maa had written something in her own handwriting below that list. She had written, "I know the names of the parents of these innocent children. But there is no need to mention their names or addresses here. They are not going to provide these children with any social recognition nor are they likely to take them home. So why should I create any disquiet in the minds of the children? Donations are coming for them. They can get proper education and take care of themselves. They will be recognized in the society by their own deeds. The donations still continue to come. They will still come after my death. I have no doubt that God will help these unfortunate people."

Maa had left no other indications except this. There were only books of scriptures in the wooden racks around her room. The photographs of great persons like Gandhi, Nehru, Mother Theresa. Sri Maa, etc. were hanging from the wall. But there were no photographs of gods anywhere. So, was her god inside her mind? Or did she write like this because it would provide some solace for these unfortunate people? Why? Who was going to provide the answers to these questions?

The screen was fluttering because of the breeze. The beliefs held in the mind of Kunti for a long time also swung along with that. Wherever she looked, there were only storms ... and storms ....

Kunti saw in the morning that the children were moving here and there with sad faces. Kamali, Shukuti and Padi Apa were whispering something to each other leaning against the wall. Padi Apa came near Kunti and said, "Puni has run away. She has left a letter ... she could not die in hunger when she was still young. It was better to live in that contractor's house ...."

"Could no one stop her? Why didn't you call me?"

"No one knew. She has gone away in the night. She is a grown-up girl. Anything might happen."

The proverbial last straw on the camel's back came in the form of Kamali. She said, "Do you know, Didi? The children had decided to go out for begging today. I have held them in check. You tell us what is to be done."

The children were standing in a queue and looking at Kunti. Their stomachs were sunk. There were tears in their eyes.

Kunti stood up and said, "No, no, Kamali. They won't go to beg. Maa has put their responsibilities on my shoulders. I will definitely do something. I am going out now. I will return in an hour or two after making some arrangements. There is nothing to worry about."

As she said this with a loud voice to hide her helplessness, she started trembling from head to toe. She sat down again for a while. Padi Apa held her by the hand and shouted, "Maa, your legs are unsteady as you have not eaten anything in days. You have a high temperature. Where can you go? But there does not seem to be any way out ... you have to go ... wait, I have saved a bit of *chura* in my box. You eat that first. Then you can think of going out."

That was true! She had not eaten anything for the last three, four days. As she came back after washing her face, Padi Apa had put the *chura* in a bowl before her with a pinch of salt. One or two insects were walking on the *chura*. It was perhaps lying since long. Kunti removed the insects with her fingers. Her head was reeling. With her hand inside the bowl, she looked around her. All of them were looking intently at the bowl. The *chura* slipped out of her hand. She could not eat even one grain of the insect-infected *chura* ignoring so many hungry stomachs and eyes. Kunti pushed the bowl away and got up after drinking a glass of water. Immediately, the children rolled over each other to snatch the bowl away. The *chura* fell on the floor. The bowl rolled away towards the drain. Padi Apa and Kamali caught hold of a stick each to beat the children. The children were rolling on the floor at that time to collect the *chura*. Kunti's hunger and thirst vanished on seeing that scene.

The earth had not created a greater demon than hunger until now.

She recalled the household of Sumitra Devi. Pots of rice were thrown away at that place. Sweets and fruits were thrown away in the drain after a while. Again, new stuff piled up from somewhere every morning. There was no one to eat there. Even no one had the time there to give something away to the beggars.

Should Kunti go there? She would say that she had not come for her sake. She had come for the sake of feeding orphan children. Throwing her own life to the wind, she had come to beg for a handful of rice for others. Should she say ...?

There were only question after question in her mind. What right had she at that place that she could extend her hand there and beg? Were there no other rich men in the city? No other organization? Was there only the house of Sumitra Devi? Was she only the limits of the city? Why didn't she put a few rupees in her tin box if she were all that philanthropic? She was also saying that she was depositing some money every month in her name in the bank. She was signing on a revenue stamp pasted on a register every month. But she had no idea about the amount of money involved. The amount was never written on the register. What happened to that money? Of course, she had not earned the money through any kind of labour. But didn't she have a right to that since it was ascribed to her? Yes, she had a right. She would not open her mouth even if she and her womanhood was insulted. But today she was going to claim that amount for these orphans. She would remind Sumitra Devi of what was rightfully due to her. She would go there first. Then she would see how things turn out.

What apprehension could be there once she had understood what life was and when she had realised the significance of handouts? Her persona had been exhausted having got burnt thrice in terrible fire. But she was going to make one last effort.... She would not hesitate to have blood on her mouth to achieve that.

Why should she be afraid? Her parents were calling her Kunti. But she did not have the dedication of Kunti. In stead of giving her a new life, Kuntala had again pushed her towards death. To be free of the curse with the patience of Shakuntala or to wait indefinitely to receive divine succour was not her cup of tea any more. Neither the Sun nor Dushmanta had ever come to her life; nor were they ever likely to come. There was only the roars of a hundred Dushashana around Kunti. But there was not a single Bhima who could uproot the arm of Dushashana. And where was Sri Krishna after all? She was terribly tired of seeing Him either in the temples or in the calendar of the bedroom. Would Kunti keep waiting for Him to cast a glance of sympathy or to pick up his *chakra* to kill!

She entered inside Maa's room and made obeisance before her image. She took out one of Maa's white sarees from the suitcase and wore it. She felt that her hand of love was applying a layer of sandalwood paste all over Kunti. Ah! What a wonderful feeling it was!

Everyone in Sri Bhavan had gathered near the gate and looked at her with tear-filled eyes. As Kunti sat down on the rickshaw, Padi Apa said, "Come back soon, Didi. We will be sitting here waiting for you. Don't leave the rickshaw. The rickshaw puller is known to us. I have told him that we have no money. The rich never bothered for us. But the heart of the poor rickshaw puller melted for us. Don't you worry at all!"

Kunti went outside seated on the rickshaw. She was looking at the city again after a long *vanavasa*. The external beauty of the city would dazzle the eyes. And yet the internal poverty had no bounds. There would only be tremors in the chest.

The rickshaw puller asked for directions. She asked her to drive on. A chill wind from the Himalayas seemed to have rendered her speechless. The rickshaw puller said, "Padi Apa was saying that you would go to that grey house. Everyone knows that house. It is a big house. The lady of the house is very well known. She is loved by everyone. God is kind to her...."

Kunti did not say anything. The rickshaw puller may jump to some uncalled-for conclusions.

The rickshaw stopped near that grey building. So Padi Apa knew Sumitra Devi. She would also know that Kunti does not know anyone else in town. Did she know something more than that? She was extremely close to Maa. Kunti had no idea what kind of description Sumitra Devi might have given about her to Maa.

She recovered her senses when the rickshaw puller called her. She got down hurriedly and walked inside the house like it was familiar territory. If Sumitra Devi would not be there? If she refused to recognise her? If she kicked her out of the house even if she recognized her? What would she do ...?

Kunti stopped short. Someone answered from within her – she was going to introduce herself if no one recognized her. They would recognise Kuntala even if they did not recognise Kunti. Even if they did not recognise Kuntala, there was always 'Kala'. Couldn't they recognise Kala? If they could not recognise Kala, there was still Shakuntala. She was not the Shakuntala of the *Puranas*. She was the Shakuntala of this age. She had come here with the right of claiming her rightful share. She was not going to be scared by any adverse circumstances. She was going to meet them head on. There was nothing to be afraid of any more. She was not extending her hand for her own sake!

Kunti placed her feet on the steps and looked up. Oh yes. It was the same house where Kunti had spent long three years of her life. She had also dreamt of a new life in this place. Yet, this house had shattered all her dreams and had kicked her on the backside. And yet ... the passage of time had again landed her at the doorsteps of this house. She had arrived with some hope in her eyes and some claims in her mind. She hadn't come here with nothing.

The drawing room was located downstairs. The green-coloured screen was fluttering in the breeze. Someone was seriously reading a book sitting on the sofa. Who was he? The long moustache was swelling up like that of a tiger. Oh God! It was ... it was Laltu Babu! She had only thought of talking with Sumitra Devi when she was on her way here. She had not imagined that she would run in to Laltu Babu. The scene of that night danced before her eyes. She shrank into herself with fear when she recalled his demonic appearance. Suddenly, she stopped on her way holding on to the screen. The door swung and made a sound. Laltu Babu lifted his head from the book and looked at her.

Laltu Babu seemed to have fallen from the skies! Then he stretched his legs and asked with a smile, "So you remembered us after a long time! How are you?"

His voice was full of intimacy. As if he had no other motive in mind except wishing her well.

The senses of human beings were inexplicable. They made you get angry when there was laughter around you. And they made you cry when you wanted to get angry. And waves of fun were created when you were crying. Kunti could not succeed even if she wanted to become soft. She wanted to throw a large stone at Laltu Babu to shatter his smiling face. But that was impossible. Somehow she controlled the anger welling up inside her and asked, "Is Maa at home? I have come to meet her on an important work." There was a tremor in her voice. Even her body was shaking.

Laltu Babu stood up and came near Kunti. He put his hand on her shoulder and said, "Why are you trembling like this? Am I some kind of a wild animal?"

Kunti moved his hand from her shoulder and said, "Is Maa at home? I have important ...."

Laltu Babu said in a respectful voice, "Maa has gone to the village. She may not be there. But I am present here. You tell me. I may be able to help. I have waited a long time to make penance for my sin."

Penance? Sin? What could be the sin of a person like Laltu Babu? And he was interested in making penance? What kind of illusion was this? Kunti took two steps back in fright. The rickshaw puller was fanning himself with his towel sitting on the verandah. Kunti felt a bit reassured when she saw him.

Laltu Babu said, "There is every reason for you not to believe me. Still, I would like you to believe that I want to do penance for my small mistake. Don't deprive me of that chance. Come inside. The servants are all new. No one can recognize you. What is there to be scared of even if they recognize you?"

Kunti was in no condition to stand for a long time. She was getting weaker by the minute. Finding no other way, she sat down on the sofa. She had never thought that she would have to beg before a man who had taken away everything in life from her.

Laltu Babu came back and sat on the sofa. Then he asked in a grave voice, "You are perhaps not feeling well. What has happened?"

"Nothing. I am all right. When would Maa return?"

"This is your stupidity! I am my mother's son. Can't I do her work? Of course, you have many reasons to be suspicious of me. You have suffered a great deal because of me. I am prepared to do anything because of that. I have always prayed God that I should meet you again so I can free myself from the burden."

His throat seemed to be parched and his face turned crimson towards the end. He came near Kunti and held her feet lying prostrate before her.

Kunti was not at all prepared for this kind of situation. Surely she was not dreaming? She shouted, "What are you doing? Please leave my feet. I am ill-fated. Otherwise...."

"No, I am not going to release your feet. Tell me. Will you forgive me or not?"

Was Laltu Babu really crying? How did her feet feel wet? Something gave way somewhere. Tears again welled up in her dead eyes. A few drops rolled down her cheeks. Somehow she controlled herself and said like a shameless woman, "What is the point in discussing the past? I was doing a job when I was with Maa. I do not remember the name of the bank where Maa had deposited my salary. I need that money urgently today.

Some women and children will die of hunger if I don't get that money today."

Laltu Babu seemed to be absentminded. He had been staring at the almirah of books. Kunti had no idea what was going on in his mind. Seeming to be lost somewhere, he said, "I am really sorry. I have met you only for a few hours. I have never dared to ask Maa anything about you. I do not know anything about your job and salary. But you take some money if you are in any kind of trouble. I will personally hand over the rest of the money when Maa returns. Of course, I do not know your address... otherwise...."

Laltu Babu extended a bundle of currency notes towards Kunti as he said this. The bundle of currency notes seemed like the hood of a snake to Kunti. She stopped for a while as she was about to extend her hand. Sadhu Parida had handed over a bundle of notes in this manner. Radhu Mahajan had done the same with Manua ... she had been dying every moment with the poisons of many snakes. Someone was whispering in her ears that this hand was also going to bite her. The serpent will do its deed anyway. It will pour poison.

"Take it. What is the hesitation? I am giving this to you because you need it. Apart from that, you have earned this money."

Kunti accepted the money. She did not count it. There was no need for that. The snake did not bite every time. There were times when the snake charmer had done away with the poisonous fangs. There was no point in thinking about what had happened and what might happen. There was no further fear of getting bitten by the serpent. That time was over and done with. She herself was about to transform into a female cobra. What poison could affect her?

Holding the bundle of notes in her hand, Kunti said, "I am not asking for any accounts. Your mother had rescued me when there was no one else for me. I will never be able to repay her kindness. It is a crime on my part to ask her for any money. But

I would have a bit of peace of mind if I can feed hungry children for a couple of days. I have one request to make. I hope you will not disappoint me."

Laltu Babu got up from the sofa and sat down again. He said earnestly, "Tell me. Tell me what I can do. I will do it even if I have to part with my life for that, Kuntala."

Kuntala! Kuntala!

Laltu Babu had no idea that that quiet, respectful woman had died since long. He did not know that the Shakuntala, who had taken birth from Kuntala, was a female cobra.

"Please find a job for me, Sir! Not a leaf would fall from the trees if I drop dead. But how would the children continue to live? Maa has put their responsibility on my shoulders. I am talking about the children of Sri Bhavan."

"Oh, you are at Sri Bhavan? I did not know that … this is sad indeed. How many people are there?"

Kunti lowered her eyes and said, "About thirty persons. The able-bodied left after the death of Maa. No further donations came. I do not know who were the people who helped Maa out. Now we are about thirty people consisting of ten helpless women, two grown-up girls, two handicapped old men and a few children. No one has the capacity to earn a dime. Everyone is looking up to me … there has been no cooking done at the place for the last four days."

The crying faces of the children danced before her eyes as she said this. Everyone would be standing near the front gate waiting for her return. Unruly tears dropped down from her eyes. Laltu Babu seemed to be disturbed. He said, "Don't cry, Kuntala. I cannot see tears in your eyes any more. I remember that Maa used to call you 'Kala' fondly. I will call you by that name. You are indeed full of arts. Your heart is clean. I have rarely seen such sacrifices to save the lives of other people. Of course, I cannot find you a job overnight. But I will find something for you in a few days. But don't be scared to meet someone for getting a job. I will be there by your side. What do you say, Kala?"

"I will do whatever you say. There is no further shame once a woman puts her foot outside home. That looks good on rich men's daughters and daughters-in-law. It would be a great boon if I can manage the children for a few days."

With his hands in his pockets, Laltu Babu was moving around the room. He said, "Not just for a few days, Kala! You will take care of them for all time to come. I will make foolproof arrangement of that. I don't like half-baked things. I may be a sinner. But I don't like to play with the lives of poor people. It has happened once ...."

"Please don't talk about it again, Sir."

"Yes, Kala. Let the past be buried in the earth. I want that a new world should be created where there would be no distinction between the rich and the poor. Everyone would be the same."

"Let the children survive first. Then we will do whatever has to be done."

Laltu Babu said equally gravely, "No, survival alone is not a big thing. This country has become immobile because of meaningless living. Hence, I want that each child there would get the facility to study. Everyone must get medical facilities. Then we have to find ways to provide them with social recognition. Drastic changes are needed in the laws of the country...."

Kunti said, "I have to leave now. The children would be waiting for me."

"Oh yes! I had forgotten that! Shall I drop you in the car?"

Startled, Kunti said, "No, no! I have a rickshaw waiting for me. I will go on my own. You don't have to take any trouble. I have to buy some provisions on the way too."

Without waiting for an answer, Kunti went outside. The rickshaw puller seemed to be worried about her by that time. As the rickshaw moved away, Kunti turned around. Laltu Babu had been staring at her - who knew what was there in that stare?

The rickshaw moved ahead. Kunti pulled the corner of the saree as a veil over her head and sat. Hunger and tiredness seemed to have vanished. The money was there in her waistband. It was as if a huge stone had been put on her waist. The poisonous snake had coiled itself all around her body. Who knew when it was going to strike? Today, she was no longer afraid of that. She herself was now the storehouse of poison. But could Kunti save Sri Bhavan?

There was no difference between believing or disbelieving Laltu Babu. The snake and the frog found the same shelter in the branch of a tree during a flood. She would know that her life was worth living if she could provide succour to other people by putting her life at stake.

Was there a real change in Laltu Babu? It could be true. He might have burnt in the process of blaming himself. She had been a victim of treachery all her life. She could not accept anything on its face value. She could see nothing else except demons inside gods. Kunti could not understand anything. How insignificant was her life after all! How could she understand everything so easily! How could she get behind the masks?

How old was she? Twenty two ... twenty three or twenty five? More or less? Her mother was crying because Radhu Mahajan was two and half times as old as she. Lest Kunti should feel bad about the old bridegroom, she seemed to be telling the walls aloud, "How does age matter for a male? The more you rub a brass pot, the brighter it becomes. You only have to know how to rub it." Kunti burst into laughter when she was reminded of her mother. Poor woman!

Man could never understand how time flew. If you dug under the manure heap, a bit of fire would definitely come out. That fire would definitely burn your fingers. How old would be the embryo now that had germinated during the *Jhulan Jatra*? Would Gunduri Apa still be loving her? And if there would be a stepmother at home now? Poor kid! She didn't have either a father or a mother! How would she survive? How would she make something of herself? A long breath escaped her and melted in the air. Why did a three and half year old beautiful girl look at her at the wrong time like a ball of fire from under a heap of ash? The minds of human beings were indeed strange!

Sri Bhavan was just ahead of her. Kunti wiped her eyes. The children were running towards her happily.... Their faces were full of joy!

She got down from the rickshaw and embraced the children with both hands. She thought - let the past be gone. She had found many today in the place of one. Many lives, many hearts.

Seven days passed away without anyone being aware of it.

She had not counted the money she had brought along with her. It was enough consolation for Kunti that that money was going to drag everyone along for some days. That it would provide rest for a moment so they could think about their future course of action. But what was going to happen after that? Yes, what would happen when she ran out of the money? There was no way of knowing what arrangement was going to be made by Laltu Babu. She was also ashamed to go to him again to beg for more. It was as if there was no other person in this world to turn to for help except the one person who was an anathema to her. There seemed to be no other soul who could stand near her in this crisis. What irony of fate indeed!

Kunti did not find any solution to the problem even though she was deep in thought.

A car arrived from nowhere in the evening. Kunti had run out of patience after her long wait. She could not hold herself back. She ran outside with the exuberance of a young girl. There was no rice at home for the day after.

Laltu Babu and a few other people were sitting inside the car. As he saw Kunti, Laltu Babu said, "I have taken a long time in coming here. I may please be forgiven for that. It also took me a long time to find a job for you. My close friends were amazed to learn about your sense of responsibility and awareness. Hence, they wanted to meet you personally. That is why, they have come running to this place."

Kunti rearranged the *pallu* over her head which had slipped. She looked around her carefully. Hopefully, no one was watching her.

Laltu Babu smiled and said, "You are indeed very shy, Kala. All these people are extremely close to me. They are also highly respected people. You must have heard about Janapriya Babu, the eminent social worker. And this gentleman here is Gananath Babu, the local M.L.A. Shethji Raghavananda is sitting in front. The man in the driver's seat is a top officer in the police department. Many other people will also come to your help. You keep some money as advance towards your salary. There is no dearth of money for the purpose of serving poor people... whatever amount of money you need will come near your feet ... yes, Kala ... unlimited amount of money will come."

A breeze of spring seemed to caress her. She was no longer afraid. All the stored up fear seemed to have vanished by the magical touch of some god. Only now she understood that her body was as much her wealth as it was a handicap. Otherwise, why the human beings made of flesh and blood, however rich or influential they may be, would stare at her like hunting dogs? Didn't they find any other place to serve the people and donate money? Or, were these people really so kindhearted...? In that case, why were they examining her from head to toe in such great detail? She had seen that kind of look on the face of Radhu Mahajan. But he had not touched her. He had seen that kind of hungry looks in the eyes of Manua and his friends. This blood-thirsty look was also there that night in the eyes of Laltu Babu. But he seemed to be a great deal more quiet and innocent right then.

So was this the fate of Kunti? Was it ordained for her that she should keep on suffering in this manner for all time to come? Couldn't she ever talk with another human being comfortably? Why? She was no longer going to be scared if this was what was known as fate. She was going to fight before she was captured. It only remained to be seen who was going to win the fight.

"What are you thinking about, Kala? We have a great deal of work at other places."

"Won't you come inside and have a look at the children? The orphans would feel a great deal reassured."

One of the guests said, "Don't feel depressed. Everything will be okay. We only value your opinion. We have nothing else to worry about if we have a comrade like you with us. Please say something, Kala Devi."

Kunti answered softly, "People like you have come forward to feed orphans and helpless women and make something out of them. What could I say ...?

Shethji was suddenly overcome with emotion. Holding the hand of Kunti, he said, "No, no, Kala Devi. Don't talk like that. We know what sacrifices you are making. One should go ahead and perform public service whenever opportunity presents itself. How many people of your age have left their homes to perform public service? I have heard everything from Laltu Babu. This is the fate of our country. No one can put his fingertip on you. We will also make that provision."

Kunti knew that her palm had remained a prisoner under the pressure of the thick fingers of Shethji.

Laltu Babu removed the hand of Shethji and said, "Shethji, Kala Devi is new in this field. Hence, it is natural that she would be a bit nervous. She will understand everything gradually."

Kunti had been staring at the face of Laltu Babu. It was not possible to understand the expression in those eyes.

They talked among themselves partly in Hindi and partly in English. After a while, Shethji extended a bundle of currency notes. The police officer was smiling. Others were also smiling. Kunti too joined them and smiled. Everything seemed too inexplicable to her. The M.L.A. reassured her that he was going to send groceries the next day in a truck.

Without waiting for any definite answer from Kunti, they drove away. Her eyes turned hazy in the dust. She was able to see a few leering eyes even in that dust. She had no affection at all for her youth, beauty and body. She had never done anything for herself. It was not always possible to dedicate oneself for the sake of others. No one else would understand the sufferings one had to undergo in sacrificing herself knowingly.

From somewhere the children came running and held her tightly. A car had come after such a long time. Big people had come. They would definitely get a great deal of food to eat. They were breaking into a dance with that knowledge. There was the sign of happiness in the eyes of everyone after such a long time. What fantastic desires human beings had just to live!

Kunti knew that the fly had been caught in the web of the spider and that there was no way out.

The children shouted in unison, "Didi! We will sit in the car. Won't you take us for a ride in a car some day?"

Kunti did not answer. There was no end to the greed of human beings. Who did not want more and more of everything? They were children. They would never try to stand on their own legs once they got the habit of begging. How could she solve this critical situation? The time for that test had arrived.

Somehow she dragged herself inside her room. She saw that Padi Apa was sitting on her cot. She had put a *paan* in her mouth after a long time. The oil she had applied on her head was glistening. When she saw Kunti, she said, "Who were they, Didi? Why did you talk with them outside for such a long time? Menfolk did not ordinarily come here when Maa was there. Whenever they came, they talked with Maa sitting in her office. You get them inside from now onwards. You are still new here. How would you know everything?"

Kunti kept quiet. There was no point in having an argument. Padi Apa spat through the window and came near her. She wanted to say something.

Happiness was quite apparent on the face of Padi Apa. It was natural. The passage of life would continue. She had great satisfaction even in living for one more day. The people who had come in the car were rich people. They would dazzle their eyes. They never imagined sufferings and the agony of fire even in their dreams. Forget about feeling them ....

Padi Apa whispered, "Puni has been back home since the afternoon. She is sitting under the mango tree in a hungry stomach. The contractor has beaten her up and broken her wrist. What could I do? I could not bear the scene. I have given her some rice to eat. But the idiotic girl didn't eat that. She will stay here only if you permit it. Otherwise, let her go anywhere ... I can't take it any more."

Puni had come back. That was a foregone conclusion. How could Padi Apa even think that Puni would go elsewhere leaving this place? If she left this place, she would go to the side of the street or to the branch of a tree or at the most it would be to a pond or a river. Kunti had left home because she could not get a handful of rice. She had thought she could not die while she was still young. But she could not do it. Age was her undoing. But once she was beyond the age, there would be nothing left of her. All this drama was for that handful of rice. Someone was the hunter, someone was the hunted.

But couldn't the hunted ever become the hunter? From which book or person could she get this information? She looked at Padi Apa and said, "Where else would Puni go when we are there?"

Her eyes moved towards the photograph of Maa. How sad and yet how kind she looked! The still, unmoving image seemed to give the impression that she would drink all the evils of the world at one go.

Kunti had not been able to know when Padi Apa had gone outside and brought Puni inside the room. As she looked at Puni, she said with tear-filled eyes, "Forgive me, Didi. I went away because I could not bear hunger any more. But I could not cope with the beating and the insults. I might die here. But I am not going to step outside again. I am holding your feet, Didi...."

Kunti had tried one day like this to reason with Sumitra Devi holding on to her feet. But she had cast her away like so much dust beneath her feet. When she saw Puni, Kunti thought that she was Kuntala - one more image of Kunti. She had been seeing the scene of that woman falling on the floor and suffering for a long time. She had been burning with the pangs of hunger. She had been crying because she had been kicked around in the process of searching for a bit of security. But she was not able to surrender herself.

Satiating hunger and security, security and hunger – these were the major problems in the life of a woman. Would she go on selling her body for these generation after generation? Her body had turned into a commodity. But neither had she been able to satiate her hunger nor had she got security. All that she had got in return was falsehood, infamy and illusion.

Kunti pulled the crying face of Puni on to her bosom. She had a feeling that she had clasped Kuntala to her chest after a long time. Could she free the fly which was in its last stage in the spider's web? Where was that prince in this age who was going to run in to free her by opening the door of the temple which was sealed from all sides?

Kunti had attended many important meetings when she was in Sumitra Devi's house. She had listened to lectures sitting in the company of famous people. She had seen dreams within herself listening to the various proposals for the emancipation of women. Many books and magazines were coming to Sumitra Devi's house. She had the opportunity of reading all those. But the earth had continued to remain the same old, rusted place in spite of all that.

She could recall her childhood days. She was playing wearing a frock. Women's committees were organised in the village under the aegis of the block office. Some women came and made her mother a member. When her mother had gone to attend the committee meeting once, her father had broken the rice pot with a wooden stick when she returned and shouted under the influence of *ganja*, "The women of the village cannot hold any congregation in my house. Nor are you going to those meetings again. I will bash you up if you ever again step outside the house."

Mother was angry. She slept for two days without eating anything. Father was unfazed. Some old woman had come and made the peace. She fed her mother and said, "Hey, Nima *Bou*, all good things are being planned for the benefit of the women all right. But nothing will come out of it. You would only get new problems. You would be knocking everyone's door for no good reason. Remain as you are now. The gods have provided the males with the horns. Would the women dig the ground with their fingers? All these meetings are hogwash. They would amount to nothing. You only will be exposed everywhere. Would you fight with those males when you have no strength of your own? The gods were partial when they gave us life. Otherwise, women would not be bashed up and suffering like this over the ages."

That day Kunti had laughed aloud hearing the old woman talk. But she was understanding the meaning of those words thoroughly today. There were strict rules for women everywhere–from the village till the city, from the temple to the streetside. Even if they were educated and employed, they were bogged down by security and an easy life. Neither there was any security nor was it an easy life. And finding both of these was simply inconceivable.

Wiping the tears off Puni's eyes, Kunti came outside. It was a moonlit night. Different kinds of flowers were swaying in the gentle breeze. But her chest seemed to burst in sadness. There was a sense of uneasiness all the time. Why did she again get entwined in illusions? Who knew what sorrows and sufferings were in store for her in the future. A small boy came running to her and embraced her. He said, "Didi, Didi, you teach us English! You had promised to do that. Come, we are all sitting with slates in hand."

Kunti was amazed to see Mahani's eyes which were dazzling with happiness. How did so much of happiness and eagerness come to the minds of the children? Who provided them with so much of security? Yesterday, they had started out to beg for a handful of rice. But today they had thought of studying and making something of themselves! Who was it? For whom all the impossible things have become possible? Was Kunti capable of keeping this dream alive till the end?

Time fled. It did not wait for anyone. Something or other kept arriving everyday, be it groceries or school books or clothes. Money too arrived regularly from different people. Now there was neither hunger nor any other kind of deprivation. The children enrolled in schools. Kunti also made arrangement for different kinds of training so that they could earn a livelihood on their own. No one knew when things might turn bad again. Everyone should become capable by that time. No one would go out to beg. This was the basic purpose of Kunti. Two old men were lying in a room. Finally, both of them passed away within a couple of days of each other. One was a blind person. The other was paralysed. There was no end of a helpless person. God finally delivered them. How long would they have continued to live on the handouts of other people? Still Kunti had taken the responsibility of their treatment like they were her own people. Everyone in Sri Bhavan had joined in the last rites. The ties of the heart were stronger than that of blood!

Every two or three days, either Laltu Babu or one of his friends made a round of Sri Bhavan. They gave chocolates and sweets to the children. Nothing seemed to be strange any more.

Some days they sat down and talked. They questioned about Maa. They read her books. They discussed many things with Kunti too. At times, Kunti showed a lot of eagerness to know about the outside world. These days a newspaper also arrived free of cost courtesy Gananatha Babu, the M.L.A.

One day Laltu Babu stopped there at about 4 p.m. while going on that way. There was a foreigner lady with him. She was aged. Quiet too.

Laltu Babu showed her around Sri Bhavan. The lady chatted with the children. She gave them flowers and chocolates. She also left a box of vitamin tablets in the care of Kunti. She took many photographs of the children, Padi, Kamali and Shukuti.

She also took a few photographs of Kunti. There were tremors within Kunti's chest. She had never had the opportunity of being photographed. If anyone saw it outside, they would come here and take her away. By force! Radhu Mahajan, Manua....

"You seem to be worried, Kala?" Laltu Babu asked.

"Why, no. Nothing like that...."

"She has asked you a number of times to smile. But you are not listening. You know a bit of English."

Kunti smiled. She wanted to say that not only did she understand a bit of English, she also knew how to read and write English. She had been able to get a hold on the English language in the meanwhile. But she had not been able to accept a bohemian culture. She wanted to ask why all those photographs were being taken and where they would go. But she stopped short. When the body and mind had turned to ashes, what was the point in fretting about a photograph?

Laltu Babu said as he was leaving, "Kala! You will go mad if you continue to stay indoors all the time. You step outside at times .... You come to the place where we hold discussions about various things and decide on our courses of action. Many ladies come to that place. Besides, it is worth listening how discussions are carried on about the problems of the country."

Kunti said, "No, Sir. Please don't call me to that place. This house is the place where I find peace."

"Kala! Can you see how single women like you are crossing the seven seas to come to our country? They are dedicating their lives for rendering service. Yet ... you Oriya women are so shy that you are afraid to venture out even inside the city!"

"It is not that! Has Maa returned from the village? I haven't seen her since a long time ...."

"You are scared of Maa, Kala. But she loves you a great deal. She will be very happy if you dedicate yourself for the service of the nation."

Kunti knew that Laltu Babu was not willing to give a clear-cut answer to her question. Still she persisted, "When would Maa return from the village?"

"I will definitely inform you when she returns from the village. Don't you worry."

A long breath tried to escape her tearing her chest. But it stopped near the throat.

While taking leave, the lady shook hands with Kunti and requested her to attend that day's meeting. Laltu Babu said, "You get ready. I will come and take you there. I will be back in half an hour."

They left. Padi Apa came to her and said, "Didi, why are you scared? You take a round. You will know many things when you move around. Only education will not do. We are illiterate people. We will feel happy to listen to various things from you."

Laltu Babu actually arrived after half an hour. There were two other women also with him. Kunti heaved a sigh of relief when she saw them.

About twenty to twenty five people were present at the place where the meeting was scheduled. Everyone's eyes seemed to be riveted on Kunti. Some people advanced towards Kunti to converse with her. But Laltu Babu intercepted them and took them away from Kunti.

Lectures were delivered at the meeting. Many people praised the lady from overseas. A sumptuous dinner had been arranged for everyone. The driver dropped Kunti in a car at Sri Bhavan after that. Everyone had finished dinner and gone to sleep at Sri Bhavan by that time. Only Padi Apa had waited for Kunti with her dinner. Kunti said that she did not want to eat. She was ashamed to say that she had eaten outside.

These days the car came for Kunti at intervals of one or two days. Either there was a meeting somewhere or there was an exhibition or there was a health camp or sometimes relief work was on for the flood-affected people. Rich men were coming to all these places. They were throwing away loads of money by way of donation. Kunti had already come to know a lot of people in the meantime. Many people were also aware of Sri Bhavan. They were anxious to donate money to enable the helpless people to stand on their own feet.

Laltu Babu had kept on whispering in her ears, "Don't let go of the opportunities, Kala. You have to try all the tricks so that enough money is available for the organisation. The future has to be taken care of. Do you think that the large organisations of the country have sustained themselves because of the ordinary men? The edifice of service to the humanity has been built because of the sacrifice and dedication of individuals. The ordinary people showed interest only after that. They want to buy a bit of virtue by making some donations. There are many people in our country. But no one is there to work ...."

Kunti was startled. Whose language was this? Laltu Babu was talking like Sumitra Devi.

Kunti prepared herself mentally for the plunge. There was no other aspiration. She would find some peace if she could make some penance by serving people. There was no point in arguments any more.

She had started feeling a bit self-conscious these days when she returned in the nights. Padi Apa always came near the gate when she heard the sound of the car. Some inmates opened their windows and looked at her from inside their rooms. Their faces were not visible. But there was no doubt that they were the grown-up girls or Sri Bhavan. Padi Apa always left chapattis and curry in Kunti's room. She did not ask whether she would eat or not. How many nights could she wait up for Kunti?

One day Laltu Babu sent a message. A noted educationist and businessman was to be felicitated that evening. Kunti had to reach before the evening to take care of all the arrangements. The businessman had agreed to donate five thousand rupees to Sri Bhavan. Hence, Kunti had been reminded to carry a bouquet. Kunti prepared herself finding no other way. When she started out from Sri Bhavan everyday, she felt as if she was going towards the jaws of death. Her eyes had the same expression as that of a goat about to be slaughtered. Was she the surety? For whom? She was dying every moment against her own wishes. Again she was looking up raising her head. She was staring at death. She was feeling it inside her. Who knew when that last moment would arrive?

It seemed that a hundred eyes were examining her in detail from behind at the time of leaving Sri Bhavan. They seemed to be analysing her movements. And yet, she had been running so that the people behind her could live decently. Strange thoughts perhaps came to the mind once someone was free of hunger. The human being did not kill oneself burning in that thought. She burnt other people.

The car raced away raising dust after it. Kunti saw that Puni had been staring at her standing near the jackfruit tree. Someone else was also standing near her. As Kunti's gaze fell on that person, the figure moved behind the tree. Should she turn the car around and check? No, let it go. Many events like this were likely to happen. She could not even sense any of them. Forget about finding solutions for them.

She found that there were many people at the meeting. Many people had surrounded the businessman. The Superintendent of Police, the M.L.A., engineers, social workers, etc. had surrounded him. A discussion was going on about education and its proliferation. The businessman was not only known in this city. He was well-known in many cities in India and even at many places abroad. A few photographs were taken when Kunti offered the bouquet. Everyone seemed to be staring at her with leering eyes. Kunti was introduced to many people present there. Laltu Babu was whispering something in the ears of the businessman. Then he called Kunti near him and asked her to sit. A discussion started about Sri Bhavan and its problems. The businessman promised to send some money every month regularly. A plan was prepared to establish a school near Sri Bhavan and appoint Kunti as its headmistress. In the midst of all these discussions, a lot of drinks were being served. Everyone went on downing them without a care in the world.

Four or five large tables had been arranged in a row. There were chairs all around them. Men and women were sitting there and talking to each other. They also kept on drinking from their glasses. Some drunk extended a glass towards Kunti. Laltu Babu removed that glass and placed a glass of sorbet in front of her. Overtaken by fear and sadness, Kunti had only been staring at everyone like an injured pigeon. A deep sense of loneliness had got hold of her amid that crowd. Luckily, Laltu Babu had reformed himself. Otherwise, she might have been in big trouble.

Kunti was startled out of her reverie all of a sudden. The hot palm of the businessman-cum-educationist had clasped the soft palm of Kunti tightly. He had been saying something in Hindi in a guttural voice. Kunti could not understand anything. Even she did not have the courage to free her palm forcefully. Others had been sitting there as if nothing untoward had happened. Laltu Babu came near them and said, "All of you sit straight, please. Banaja Devi will sing." As he said this, he freed the palm of Kunti from the grasp of the businessman. Everyone looked at Banaja Devi who was present in the middle of the room. She had a very good voice. But she was elderly and not at all good-looking. Still she was a woman and that had an attraction in all ages. Man could not free himself of that.

Kunti was watching everyone in a strange way. Some ladies and gentlemen had picked up the tune of the song and started singing. Some people had started dancing. Arrangements for dinner were going on in the adjacent room. Kunti had also been smiling along with others. The lives of orphans and handicapped could not be saved otherwise. She would perhaps have committed suicide by this time if she were called upon to do this for her own sake. Who knew when there would be an end to all these? When would that never-ending, cold death would come? Who knew?

The light had become dimmer by the time Banaja Devi's song was coming to an end. As the environment was turning cosy and comfortable, a lady pulled the curtains on that and rushed inside the room with the speed of a storm. Her clothes were in a dishevelled state, her hair was loose and her eyes were flashing in anger. Tears were rolling down. The people present there had been so drunk by that time that it was not possible to understand what was happening there. But Kunti was terribly disturbed to see her in that state.

She thought that she had seen her earlier somewhere. But where? She could not recall that.

Suddenly, the lady let out a shriek. Tears continued to roll down her eyes. Her body was shaking in anger. As if she was going to burn everything down in one moment. The murmuring in the room came to a sudden halt. Someone came and tried to pull her away by the hand. She shouted, "Watch it! Don't you dare touch me. You are doing a farce here with wine and women in the name of service to the nation. You have beautiful, educated and earning wives at home. And yet you are having fun here with a group of whores! I will meet the minister tomorrow. I will see that all of you lose your jobs. See here, I am tying a knot in the corner of my saree."

Many people burst into laughter at the same time on hearing this. Kunti felt extremely uneasy in that surrounding. Eight or ten elderly, top-ranking officers were laughing together without a care in the world with dinner plates in their hands. One of them said while chewing on a piece of chicken pakoda, "She has gone totally mad. It gets worse with the onset of evening. Where is Mr. Raysingh?"

Another person pointed in one direction with his finger. A gentleman was sitting in one corner of the room. He was fully drunk and dozing. All that noise had not been able to disturb him in his sleep.

The lady stopped near Kunti's table. As her eyes fell on Kunti, she pulled a corner of her saree and shouted, "Aren't you through yet? You chewed off the head of Sumitra. Finally, you have started sucking on the blood of so many people! And you are looking after orphans? Why have you taken such a fancy to others' children? Just tell me!"

The *aanchal* of the saree was slipping from her shoulders. Kunti had pressed both of her hands to keep it in place. The lady was quite strong. The people around them were enjoying the scene.

Laltu Babu rushed at them from inside the crowd. He freed the *aanchal* of Kunti's saree from the grip of the lady and pulled her outside. But the lady was not finished yet. She slapped Laltu Babu hard on the cheek and said, "Hey Laltu! You have finally come down to this? Who bothers about these old haggards? But even you...?"

"Quiet, Aunty! Don't shout here like this. What would people say? Many gentlemen have come from outside...."

"What did you say? Gentlemen? Where has that bastard Raysingh gone? I have to settle things with him today. Leave me. I am not going away so easily."

Raysingh opened his eyes only a wee bit in that noise. Again he went to sleep on the armchair. The lady smashed a glass bottle on the floor at this time. She again shouted, "Die! All of you die after cutting each other up with this glass. I will throw all of you in the burial ground. Die ... Die...!"

Laltu Babu explained things in English to the businessman. The lady was mad. She went stark, raving mad as the night progressed. Especially when her husband Raysingh went out in the evenings ....

The lady shouted again. She held Laltu Babu by his ears and said, "What did you say? I am mad? You think I do not understand English? Who is that womanizer? He is having a farce here. You have brought all these women here for his benefit! Laltu ... Your mother died drinking poison because of you! But you are still not bothered? Finally you have gone into trafficking of women! All the reputation of Sumitra has vanished because of you. Oh, my sister! Where are you? Why did you leave me behind to see this scene?"

The lady sat down on the floor and started wailing towards the end. This time Raysingh came near her and slapped her hard. Two persons lifted the lady physically and took her outside.

The incident occurred in a flash. The next moment Kunti discovered Raysingh picking up a bottle and starting to drink straight from it. Then he started dozing again. What a horrible, scandalous situation!

Kunti had been standing amazed. Tears were running down her eyes without her being aware of it. Everyone stopped eating and came near her. They advised her not to lose patience because of the unwarranted situation. Laltu Babu came and said softly, "Why are you crying, Kala? This does not look good. The lady is absolutely cuckoo. She had to be taken to the mental hospital of Ranchi twice. She was all right for a few days. Her madness has again manifested today. How could she know that Raysingh has come here beats me!"

Kunti sat down with her head resting on the table. Someone from the melee said, "It is indeed sad. Kala Devi must be feeling hurt and humiliated. We will forbid Raysingh to come to this place if Sushama Devi behaves in this manner once again. All of us have some prestige in society after all! If some young journalist colours the matter and publishes it in the newspaper, then ...."

Laltu Babu seemed to be angry. He said, "Gananatha Babu, you are just too much. How much more experience do you need to have to know the ways of the world? You have to digest a lot of nonsense if you get involved in service to the nation. Especially, there are no end to hurdles when you try to do some noble work. Does that mean that you will dissociate yourself from work which you consider right?"

Another person interjected, "This country is like that. This is the country of ungrateful people. Gandhi and Nehru sacrificed their lives for this country. Has this country been able to properly honour them? Now people are trying to find what kind of weaknesses they had ... with which women they were romantically involved and so on. Fie! This country will never come to anything!"

Yet another person said, "Stop all these discussions! The night was progressing wonderfully well. It took one mad woman to spoil everything."

Kunti was turning into a statue hearing all these. The strong palm of the businessman was gently caressing her back. Had Kunti turned into a mad woman upon seeing another mad woman? Why else couldn't she say anything in spite of hearing and seeing everything? Was she all right?

Yes, she had seen the lady in the house of Sumitra Devi. She came and talked with Sumitra Devi sitting in the drawing room. She had never seen any sign of madness in her. But she told Laltu Babu that her sister had committed suicide because of the misdeeds of her son! How much truth was there in that statement? When they had met for the first time, Laltu Babu had said that Maa had gone to the village. Another time he had said that things were delayed because she was busy in solving some disputes over landed property. When Kunti asked yet again about a month back, Laltu Babu had said that Maa was getting strange ideas these days. She built a pucca house in the village even though no one was likely to stay there. She established a girls' school in the village even though there was no one from the family who could either study or work there. Even then she insisted on doing it. Now she was planning to go around the entire country. She was too busy in serving the people for a very, very long time... Kunti did not think it fit to ask any other question. If Kunti would have asked anything more, Laltu Babu would perhaps said that Maa had started out on a world tour. But there was some mystery somewhere in what the lady said today even if she might be mad. Who knew how Sumitra Devi was! There was a dampness in her eyes. She had given her shelter one day when she had nowhere to go. It was not just shelter. She wanted to make something out of Kunti in real earnest. It was her misfortune that she was accursed. She had fallen down into some abyss.

Laltu Babu held her by the hand and made her stand. Kunti could not eat anything in spite of all the persuasions. She feigned a headache and wanted to leave early. The businessman-cum-educationist expressed his sorrow. Others too did likewise. Gananatha Babu extended a cheque for five thousand rupees to

Kunti as she was about to leave. The businessman also promised to send some more money when he got back to Varanasi.

Laltu Babu himself came with the car to drop her. It was quite late in the night. The roads were almost deserted. Very few people could be seen. Laltu Babu was doing his best to reassure Kunti. Laltu Babu begged forgiveness of Kunti for his crime on that fateful night. He seemed to be burning in the fire of remorsefulness to correct his ways and turn into a decent man. He had never touched her till today. What misdeed did he perform in that case for Sumitra Devi to commit suicide or stay in the village for all time? Should she ask about it? There was no point in that. The car stopped near the gate of Sri Bhavan. Electric lights had been provided in front of Sri Bhavan courtesy the Chairman of the Municipality. The gate and people walking on the main road could be clearly seen from inside Sri Bhavan.

As Kunti alighted from the car quietly, Laltu Babu said, "Kala! Forget the entire past. I am sorry that I have violated a goddess like you. I have behaved like a fiend. I cannot absolve myself even if I do penance for the rest of my life. I am also not eager for deliverance. I am prepared to take any punishment for my misdeed. But my life would amount to nothing if you don't forgive me. Tell me, Kala, tell me."

With some deep emotion stirring inside him, Laltu Babu caught hold of Kunti's hand. Why was his hand shaking like this? What new pretence was this? What illusion was this, O God?

Kunti said agitatedly, "Your mother had provided me shelter once. I have not forgotten that. I will never forget as long as I live the kind of courage you have provided when I was going through the wringer. I can never forget the way you have stood by me. My body is full of poisonous germs. Just give me the word. You will take the responsibility of the children of Sri Bhavan should anything happen to me."

Laltu Babu shivered with some emotion stirring within himself and bowed down to kiss Kunti's palm. With tear-filled eyes, he said, "Don't speak like that, Kala. I am filled with grief.

I am always there near you. I will consider my life to be well-spent if I can do anything for Sri Bhavan."

Were some people standing on the verandah? She pulled away her hand hurriedly and came away. If you kept the snake alive by giving it milk, did the snake forget its nature? There was the snake in front of her. There was the snake behind her. There were snakes all around her. Could Kunti go through her life drinking poison to the brim? She might die any moment after getting bitten by the snake.

It was true. Puni was standing leaning against the wall. There was curiosity on her face. Primal thirst in her eyes. What kind of poison had taken hold of her that she had not been able to sleep until now? As she came near her, she asked, "Puni! Why haven't you slept until now? Why are you moving outside? Call Padi Apa. She will lock the gate."

Without answering that Puni asked, "Didi, you have taken liquor, no? Don't you feel like vomiting? One day that contractor made me drink country liquor. I could not get up from the floor. I lay down on the floor vomitting throughout the night. But you seem to be quite composed."

Kunti stared at Puni. Such a young girl. But her thought process was amazing. And she was talking like an extremely experienced person. What cheek she had. Kunti had not touched anything till today even though she had attended enough number of parties where drinks were served. Besides, she was a widow as far as other people were concerned. Her life was continuously burning in the pyre even with a white saree and a white blouse. Sri Bhavan would have already turned into a desert if she would be involved with alcohol, meat, clothes and ornaments.

Puni came near Kunti and looked at her with round eyes. As if she needed an answer to her question. She shook Kunti and asked, "Why don't you say anything? Don't you feel intoxicated when you drink?"

Kunti slapped her hard. Puni rubbed her left hand on her cheek and said, "Why are you getting angry, Didi? I didn't say anything bad."

"No, you are saying nice things. I am asking you why you are moving outside in stead of sleeping in your room."

Puni was not cowed down. She looked straight at Kunti's face and said, "Why are you getting angry, Didi? There is a vacuum inside me just as there is a vacuum inside you. What is the point of living like this? There is something called the mind and the heart. I get restless, sitting at home always. Why don't you take me along with you when you go out? If you could persuade Laltu Babu to find a job for me, I would no longer be a burden on you. I could even help you at times. I don't like to only sit at home. I only think of different things. I am not even able to sleep in the night. Today you are with us. But...."

Casting all the pent-up anger and humiliation of the evening on to Puni, Kunti roared, "Okay! You want to die? Go ahead and die. I don't want to keep you for a moment longer. Get lost in the morning. Otherwise ... you have me to reckon with."

Puni shouted back angrily, "Do you think I do not know you?"

"What did you say? Could you repeat that?" Kunti shook in anger.

Puni shot back, "Why once, I will tell it a hundred times. Who does not know about you here? We are not getting a proper meal here even if you are getting lots of money in our name. How are you concerned in keeping us alive in this manner? You earn money in our name and then save it in your own account. We don't have to say anything. God has endowed you with beauty. You are also educated. We are fit for nothing. But Didi ...."

Puni stopped short when she looked at the face of Kunti. Kunti was listening to Puni in amazement. She could not reconcile with the fact that the people for whom she was dying every moment could criticise her so cruelly. Was she not fated to hear one decent word?

Shaking Kunti by her arm, Puni said, "I am telling you the truth. I have nothing against you. I just want you to think about it. Jhara, Kati, Suni and me could set up home only if you want it. Padi Apa and Kama Nani have become old. They have no other option except staying here. But why should we waste away at this place?"

Kunti became speechless looking at Puni in the bright light of the verandah. Youth was running amok in the body of that girl. There was thirst in her eyes. There was a huge storm of hunger in her mind and body. But Kunti lost her anger when she realised the helplessness of Puni. It was indeed true! Youth had its own hunger, spice and expectations. There was no point in living without these. Nothing was to be gained from getting angry with the children. The eternal truth could not be ignored. But Puni's words seemed unbearable. Why?

If she could not get Puni married off as a guardian, why couldn't she bear her desire to fulfil her primal hunger? Why was she trying to injure Puni for the sake of cheap and artificial culture? Why was she trying to keep others chaste when she herself had failed that test? That was why they were taking digs at her. And she had borne all the indignities with a bowed head. She would perhaps die like that throughout her life.

When she raised her eyes again, Puni was nowhere to be seen. It was as if she knew that Kunti could not provide the answer to her question. She had known nothing else except that. Puni wanted to get married and set up a home. Yet she did not know how insignificant was the value of her youth in today's society. First, she was black in complexion. Second, her parentage was unknown. And thirdly, she had no capability to fend for herself. What was the worth of her body? The stupid girl did not know that bodies of attractive women were available cheaply and without any reservation in this country. Who would bother for her pitch-dark, shapeless features? No one will hesitate to use her for his momentary pleasure. Someone even might marry her if he took pity on her. She might even become a mother. She might get the right to offer *pinda* to the ancestors. But would her womanhood and wifehood get any recognition? A woman was not only a mother or a person wearing bangles and vermilion. A live human being kept struggling within her. For the sake of liberty. For the sake of living with dignity. She is a human being first. Only then she is a woman. Where was that weapon with her with which she could earn the pride of womanhood? She was not the only one. Millions of women were burning in this kind of fire throughout the world. Even though they were established in various walks of life, they were still ignored in their private lives. They kept shedding tear silently. A woman's right and respect were not established only if she got married and put a lot of vermilion on her head. In the past few days, Kunti had thought about the women of villages and cities. It was the same state everywhere. The only difference lay in the clothes they wore.

Kunti had no wish to continue any further discussion with Puni on this matter. Kunti went and lay down on her bed. No one asked her these days whether she had eaten or not. Padi Apa did not put chapattis and curry in her room as she did earlier. She preferred going without food in the night. So she too did not bother much about this.

The huge oil portrait of Maa hanging on the wall seemed to be silently watching her. At times, she was scared to look at those eyes. Padi Apa said that Maa moved around Sri Bhavan in the quiet nights. She caressed the heads of the sick children…she cried silently with tears rolling down her eyes. She watered the plants in the middle of the night. She woke up Padi Apa from sleep if she was late in rising. Her body had died. But her soul had not got peace. It was moving in this place. Ah … Kunti would never let her go if she would come near her once. She would bare her heart before her. The eyes of Maa seemed to be filled with kindness. Kunti would have loved to jump on to her lap for all time. She would say that she had been defeated. She was tired in the body and mind. She was exhausted, totally exhausted …. She could not even bear herself any more.

No one was happy with Kunti ever since her birth. She had been looked down upon because she was a girl. She had cried before her mother requesting that she should be allowed to study. Father and Brother had severely reprimanded her if she ever went out to move in the mango grove in her childhood. She had not been able to catch a butterfly or build a house of sand sitting on the riverbed. She had an irrepressible desire to do all these. But someone had killed all her feelings.

Her parents had considered her to be a burden and had turned restless because of her. Radhu Mahajan, the man she had married, had taken all kinds of liberties with her. In order to save his dynasty, he had left his own wife near another man without any inhibitions. And Sumitra Devi? She could not understand the mind of another woman even though she was a woman herself. Yet she kept beating her drums in large meetings that her heart always bled for emancipation of women. The weaknesses of men did not mean anything to her. But she was very conscious about how a woman conducted herself. Otherwise, Kunti would not be facing this kind of situation today. Where was she? Was it not possible to trace her any more? She had rescued her from inside mud in order to turn her into a lotus. But she became the victim of her own superstition and self glory and pushed her inside the mud yet again. There was no more fear today. She was going to unmask her if ever the opportunity presented itself. The person who was not scared of death and who had been waiting for death never felt any fear. And then there were Laltu Babu and his gentlemen social workers. Had Laltu Babu really changed? Did he really repent for his past deeds? It might be true. She had read many stories. Even a demon could become a god. Kunti had not seen any kind of depravity in him until now. He carried a grave face. He always looked worried and repentant. And he was all alone at home. Kunti could not understand anything. Everything turned into a puzzle. She recalled that first meeting with him. Besides, he had become so respectful these days that it was difficult to use any rough word while talking to him. Sri Bhavan might already have been razed to the ground if he would not have come to the rescue. He was not able to know that Kunti was dying everyday because of his friends even if he caused no harm. No, no one could understand that. Even Kunti herself could not understand that.

Tapan had entered inside her dark house holding a bit of light in his hand. That lamp went out in a sudden storm. How weak Tapan was! He could not fight against wealth and aristocracy even though he was a male. Yet he might have lectured Kunti a number of times against the misdeeds of Sumitra Devi. She had thought at that time that Tapan was going to remove all the darkness of the earth by radiating his light. But it did not even take a moment for all such thoughts to go up in smoke. So where had Tapan gone? Whom could she ask about it? There was no doubt that Laltu Babu was not going to give her his correct address. Why should she ask him in that case and create questions in his mind? Things were okay now. Let Tapan be well wherever he might be. Poor man! He did not have any parents or family. The insides of her chest seemed to get torn by pieces of sharp glass when she thought about the past. There was no doubt that the people for whom she had dedicated every bit of her life and had burnt like an incense stick to turn to ashes had never given her the prestige due to a woman.

And this Sri Bhavan! Kunti had been running for it rising from her death. In stead of giving her any respect, it was not even willing to smile at her. She was not able to make anyone happy. The more she ran ahead, the more she came back. The demand made by everyone was so heavy that it was not possible to fulfil them. Puni wanted to fly away like a bird in the open skies. Padi Apa and Shukuti craved for security in their old age. And the children wanted the promise of a secure future. But she could not provide anything to anyone. She knew one thing that she had to somehow arrange a handful of rice as long as there was strength in her body. Apart from that, she could not do anything else. Puni was right. Was there nothing else to life except living? It was better to die than live like that.

The year of the women and the year of the children were celebrated recently throughout the world. All kinds of festivities were organised. Meetings were held everywhere. Government and non-government organisations became active. Single women and orphaned children were invited to attend the meetings.

Everyone in Sri Bhavan attended those meetings. They were amazed hearing the lectures and discussions. The rich and famous people spun innumerable dreams in the minds of young children.

The women thought that their deliverance was at hand. Someone suddenly seemed to have opened the door of some inner store room laced with cobwebs. The entire world dazzled with lights. But the dreams were soon over. There was a lot of talk about the implementation of the new plans. But not even a hand of kindness was extended towards them. The year went on its own way creating ripples in history, literature and the social system. Human rights, equality and peace only remained as slogans. Kunti had moved around throughout the year. She had explained things to children. She had sown the dreams of a New World. But everything looked dark to her once she closed her eyes. That was why she felt that tears were welling up in the portrait of Maa.

Kunti sat up on the bed. The sound of a street dog barking was coming from a distance. A bird fluttered away in the distant sky. The children were sleeping in a huddle on a mat in the courtyard. Kamali, Padi Apa and the others were lying here and there. It was extremely hot. A child started crying in his sleep. He went back to sleep again on his own. The older people continued to sleep. Why should they wake up... Ah ... poor child!

Her own daughter might be crying like this sleeping in the lap of Gunduri Apa in a quiet night like this. Who knew whether Radhu Mahajan had kept the girl alive? Kunti's vitals were in a churn. She tried to compose herself. She tried to say that the girl was not hers. She was the daughter of Kunti. Shakuntala was even free of the shyness and fear of Kuntala. Kala was her recognition in the outside world. Shakuntala knew that giving birth to children was a biological phenomenon. A child would be born out of the union of a man and a woman. The child might be desirable or undesirable. Why should the gods be responsible for her child in the king's court and be humiliated like Shakuntala in the process. She would rather bear the curse of Durbasa on her head for all time to come.

Her body again felt tortured in the unspoken sufferings of Kunti, Kuntala and Shakuntala. Her womanhood was frightened from her birth. She had lost her own motherhood. And yet she was searching for some peace in the process of sacrificing herself by way of showing affection towards the unwanted motherhood of other accursed women. Was she searching for her own child among those children? She was startled by her own thoughts. Why had she been running like this all day and night? Could she continue to live in this manner by ignoring the time and the change of seasons while laughingly admitting infamy? Could she keep hundreds of girls like Puni alive who lived only through dreams? She felt very weak these days when she thought of these things. From the children to the elderly, everyone in Sri Bhavan seemed to be asking her this question silently. She marvelled at Puni's courage. That was why she could question the person who provided her with the daily bread. And she had no qualms while doing it. She even had the cheek to castigate her.

Kunti had taken a great deal of trouble to build up the world around her. She had seen many dreams about that world which had kept her enchanted. But all those dreams had vanished like clouds that floated away. The fluttering wings had got exhausted and had dragged her down to some bottomless pit. The boat that was floating on the sea until now was mesmerised by the beauty of the shore in stead of measuring the depth of the sea. She alone had to suffer the consequences of her shortsightedness. Apart from that, could anyone live with the leftover, sarcasm and arrogance of others? She was no accursed Shakuntala. Bharatavarsha was today a cripple and a coward because of the infamous legacy of numerous Bharatas who were the sons of millions of Shakuntalas like her. Dushmanta, the king, had perhaps lost his memory because he was cursed. But who was going to challenge the hundreds of Dushmantas who had been indulging in mortal sins while being fully aware of them? These Bharatas might some day cause destruction all around in an effort to avenge themselves. But Kunti could not wait that long. She had been getting terribly exhausted .... Suddenly she could hear Maa's voice – Shakuntala! You cannot get exhausted in this manner. This is not your individual struggle. This is self-immolation on your part for the entire mankind.

Kunti looked around her. An agitation again rose in her mind. A quiver ran through her from head to toe. She was ashamed at the thought that she could be tired so soon. Why did she think that her life was so valuable? Why did she turn so selfish clasping on to the valueless, nameless life? Fie on her! She had made so many promises. That she would make something out of these orphan children and put a smile on their faces. That she was going to bring Maa's dreams to fruition. But she felt down and out because she was always busy with her own thoughts. She was as selfish as the others. She was trying to quench her personal thirst in the garb of serving the country. Fie! Fie!!

Kunti could not look at the photograph of Maa. What would she be thinking of her if she would be aware of all this! Maa was saying that nothing was impossible. But what dedication, what sacrifices, what bloodbaths ....

The birds started chirping in unison. The sky was getting lighter. It was morning. Still ....

Someone had been looking at her through the window. Who was it? Kunti's chest fluttered in the hazy darkness.

This time she could hear a clear voice –

"Didi, Didi! Have you gone to sleep again? It is morning already."

Padi Apa was calling her. Why? She never called her in the morning. She got angry if anyone else called her. There was fear and a sense of urgency in her voice.

"Padi Apa! What's the matter? Come inside. I am opening the door... is someone sick?"

Padi Apa brought her mouth near Kunti's ears. She said, "Quiet, Didi! The children have got up from sleep. If the word spreads...."

"What has happened, Padi Apa?"

"You came and closed your door to sleep. Have I been able to sleep even a wink throughout the night? Puni had been behaving like a bitch in heat. Someone who knows the taste of meat is not likely to settle for fruits. Just see …."

Kunti knew that Padi Apa could never come straight to a point. Who would have the patience to hear the last word!

"Don't be in a hurry, Didi. How would you understand things if I don't explain properly? Puni has been going near the jackfruit tree and coming back since last evening. She seemed to be very, very scared. I was serving food to the children. I saw her talking to someone near that rose plant. I will roast in hell, Didi, if I am telling a lie. A kid like that… and she told me straightaway that there was no one there. But I don't give up that easily. I went to the bed when everyone else slept. Puni was restless throughout the night. I was just lying like that. The girl got up and went outside for a while. I followed her. She jumped over the fence and went outside. The contractor was waiting for her. He took her away lifting her by her left hand. I was only staring at them …."

Kunti put her hand on the mouth of Padi Apa. She could not take any more of that stuff.

"What should we do now? Tell me." Padi Apa groaned.

Looking towards the morning sky, Kunti said, "You are unnecessarily worried for her, Padi Apa. Go and take some rest. You have remained awake throughout the night. Tell Kamali to start cooking. Don't worry about Puni. She would return in her own time."

Padi Apa stared at Kunti with uncomprehending eyes. Anyone would be shaken by such an event. But she was quiet and at peace with herself. Padi Apa slipped away.

The hunger of Puni's body, the mental agonies of Kunti, the personal problems of all others – everything belonged to a class of its own. Nothing was to be gained or lost from blaming anyone.

Kunti raised the screen of the window. The morning was almost in the offing. The morning star was dazzling. At such times, she had tried many a time to forget all her woes and become one with the Lord. But she had failed every time. Why hadn't she ever succeeded? What was her crime? Who had blocked her path? Kunti had lost out every time that she had questioned herself.

Still, she closed her eyes out of habit and tried to touch the image of God. Where was that eternal loving image in whom she was going to lose her identity? Whose thought had sustained Sita in the midst of demons in the Ashoka Bana? And Panchali? She was disrobed in the King's court even though she was the wife of five husbands. Nothing untoward had happened only because Sri Krishna was present. Where was that strength and determination which had resulted in Sabitri defeating Death. She could hold Time in her grip. And, in the process, she has been respected and remembered in all ages. There were tears in Kunti's eyes. She thought about Ahalya. For a small mistake, she had to wait for ages in the shape of an accursed stone only to be released by the touch of God. And her namesake – that Queen Kunti, who had to face numerous misfortunes and tests throughout her life. Even when God was always present near her as the closest friend. So was it Fate?

Kunti closed her eyes. Darkness. There was only darkness. There was darkness inside and outside. The only light inside was her existence.

So God was not there in this age! The world, with all its living beings, was an illusion! The *Puranas*, the *Shastras*, literature and history were only the bare imagination of man! God was not there. Even if He was there, man had defeated Him in battle today and had kept Him in an inanimate state! So, the name of the animal who was the god of this territory was man! The animal without a thinking faculty and without a conscience! But the soul which had been creating all that magic of light and shade within the man seems to be lost in its own illusion. It made as much effort to destroy itself as it had to make itself whole in all spheres. On whom could she rely to conduct herself in a world like this? On herself?

The prayer song of the children floated in and hit her hard on her ears.

For the first time, Kunti could not even hum the song under her breath to join the children.

The day's chores had started everywhere. It was the daily habit of mankind. It had to push itself somehow through all the sorrows and troubles.

Kunti came outside as if nothing untoward had happened. The oppressive atmosphere seemed to be playing hide and seek everywhere. Everyone was busy in her work. But the enthusiasm seemed to have gone out of everything. The children did not come running to her shouting 'Didi', 'Didi' as they did everyday. Kamali did not come to ask what curry should she prepare that day. Padi Apa was quietly busy in cutting vegetables. Shukuti was wiping her tears while cleaning the rice of the impurities. That was because Puni slept with her during the nights and ate with her. At times, she embraced Shukuti saying that she was her mother.

Kunti spoke in a voice that was meant for the benefit of everyone, "Padi Apa! I have not slept throughout the night. I am feeling feverish. I am going to sleep for a while. I do not want anyone to disturb me."

Kunti banged her door shut. She closed the window too. That was it! The room was dark and closed from all sides. Only she was with herself. That was good. There was no information here. There was no wish either to do high quality research in order to understand life. She could only pick up her loss like a pearl and caress it with an open mind. She had done nothing else for days except to ignore her. No one had come near her to speak a word with love. The only thing that had kept her busy was money....

She had actually fallen into a deep sleep. Someone was banging hard on the door. Who was it? She tried to get up. But again she went to sleep. No, these people were not going to allow her to sleep in peace.

As the door opened, Padi Apa said, “The car has come. I told the man that you are sick and I was not going to call you. But he wouldn’t listen. The children are running towards the car.”

“Who has come?”

“How do I know? He said that that Laltu Babu has sent the car.”

Kunti was amazed. Why would Laltu Babu ask her to come at this odd hour? He was quite scared of the light of the day. Still ... there was no way she dared ask any question. If she was asked, she had to go. If she was asked to return, she would return. What power Kunti had to refuse? She had already surrendered her willingness as well as unwillingness. She was someone who lived on pity. All hell would be let loose if she started thinking about her rights. She changed clothes and went near the car without any protest. It was strange. There was no one in the car except the driver. Kunti stood with questioning eyes. The driver said while combing his hair, “Come home. There is urgent work.”

Kunti did not feel like arguing. The driver was talking a lot of nonsense on the way. Kunti knew that a man’s mind ran away with all kinds of imaginations when he found a single woman at a lonely place. He talked incoherently. That man did not bother about education, riches or aristocracy.

Laltu Babu was indeed waiting for her at home. Many cars were parked outside. The place was quite crowded. What was the matter? Laltu Babu had given no indication of any such thing last night.

Kunti got down from the car pulling the corner of her saree over her head. Laltu Babu took her to a corner room and said, “There is nothing to worry about. You sit here, Kala. I am saying this because you do not like a crowd. I will be with you in a minute.”

Kunti looked at the photograph hanging from the wall. It was the photograph of Sumitra Devi's cook and that servant boy Kantha. Oh yes. Now she could recall that they were staying in this room. They had taken this photograph together and shown it to her one day. That photograph was hanging. It was a symbol of the days gone by. But where had they gone? Where was Sumitra Devi?

The other day Laltu Babu was saying that Maa had gone on a *tirth*. It was difficult to believe that. Had she vanished throwing away all her plans, work and service to the people? Or was there some other mystery to it?

The staircase was visible when the small window of the small room was opened. The bedroom of Sumitra Devi was in the first floor. The library was adjacent to the bedroom. The prayer room was next to the library. The old wound started opening up when she thought of the prayer room. The helpless condition of that day had remained hidden somewhere inside her chest. It seemed to have found the opportunity to grab Kunti with its claws. She sat down on the floor with her hand on her head.

Many people had gathered in the other room and were discussing something. Why had Laltu Babu called her if he was not willing to take her before the public? She had not only fasted yesterday. She had hardly slept in the night. She felt exhausted.

Something fell on the first floor with a metallic sound. Kunti stood up and opened the window. Who was it? Who was standing near the window of the prayer room? Maa? Sumitra Devi? Unkempt hair had spread on the face. The cheeks were sunken. The gaze was perhaps fixed on the sun in the sky. Her jaws were moving. She seemed to be speaking something like a mad woman. Kunti was not sure whether it was true or she was dreaming. She got ready to somehow look at her with straight eyes so that she could know her identity.

Some kind of puja was going on in a nearby room. *Mantras* were being chanted. There was the smell of incense sticks in the air.

Again there was that still image in front of her. Should she go upstairs and embrace Sumitra Devi? She would definitely recognise her. She would wash her feet with the tears flowing from her eyes and beg her forgiveness. What was the point in holding a grudge even today? Apart from that, she did not seek any largesse from Sumitra Devi. But how could she go there? The door was locked from outside. It was not just that either. Laltu Babu might not appreciate her unnecessary curiosity. In that case ...?

There was a writing pad on the small table in that room. There was a paperweight on that. If she threw that paperweight on to some heavy object in the courtyard, Sumitra Devi's gaze would definitely fall on her. She might not get this opportunity if the crowd thinned out on the other side.

Kunti picked up the paperweight and threw it at the bucket standing near the water tap in the courtyard. The entire house reverberated with that sound. Sumitra Devi's gaze turned and fell on her. She stopped short for a second. Then she again went on talking to herself. She was throwing her right hand towards Kunti. There was a framed photograph laced with sandalwood paste. It had to be the photograph of some deity. Kunti closed her eyes out of fear. She saw clearly that Sumitra Devi was uprooting the hair from her head with her bare hands. She was spitting time and again on the floor. Oh God! What was this! Why did this happen to a healthy and respected woman like Sumitra Devi?

There was the sound of someone opening the lock from outside. Kunti put her head down on the table feigning a headache. Of course, she had closed the window before that. Laltu Babu entered inside the room. Someone else was also with him. Kunti stood up.

Laltu Babu said, "You must be tired of sitting alone, Kala. But I had not imagined that so many people would come. I had only called my well-wishers. But I had to treat everyone. You are getting late perhaps. Hey Banu! Keep the *bhog* here and get a glass of water."

The closed window suddenly opened in the breeze just as Banu left the room. Kunti's eyes moved automatically to the upper storey. Sumitra Devi was laughing loudly exposing all her teeth. Laltu Babu closed and locked the window. Then he said, "You know, Kala. I am in great trouble. Maa has gone to the village to build a house there. She is staying there. No one knows when she would return. But she has left her mad sister here…."

Laltu Babu became absentminded. Kunti had never seen the sister of Sumitra Devi! What kind of game was this again! Laltu Babu smiled and said, "You must be amazed, Kala! Her sister looks exactly like Maa…. Besides, there are many reasons for her to go mad. The menfolk in our country are extremely arrogant. My uncle tortured Suchitra Devi a great deal … it is a long story."

Something fell on the floor in the upper storey making a metallic sound. Kunti asked as if she had not heard anything, "Why had you called me?"

"Oh yes. I am forgetting the real thing. How would you know the kind of pressure under which I am working! Nothing had been settled until yesterday night. That apart, another mad woman spoiled the party yesterday night. I am not able to remember anything amid all these."

Laltu Babu wiped the sweat dripping from his brow. He said as if he was worried, "You take a bit of *prasad* first. I will tell you what happened after that."

Kunti took a bit of *bhog* reluctantly. Laltu Babu said, "I could not ignore the people. Maa is also not there. I am not able to consult anyone. Finally, I am forced …."

"What has happened?"

"I am going to contest the election. I have to stand for MLA from this city. There are enemies everywhere. I am scared…."

Sumitra Devi too had contested some election. Oh yes. It was the municipality election. Getting elected as MLA was even a tougher job. Kunti had not been able to understand anything at that time. Everything had gone beyond her. But she was no longer so inexperienced about the ways of politics. She knew that Laltu Babu was going to follow in the footsteps of his mother.

"You seem to be so worried, Kala?"

"No. It's good. Everyone in Sri Bhavan will be happy if you are happy. Tell me what I have to do."

"No, no. There are many people to do all types of work. Besides, I do not want to use lady workers. The opposition will use it for character assassination. Many people have volunteered to work. I only hope that they don't cheat me. I had called you ...."

He stopped for a while as if something got stuck in his throat. Perhaps he was hesitant.

"I need your goodwill, Kala. My opposition is likely to beg you for help. They may try to donate a lot of money for Sri Bhavan. I just want that neither you nor anyone else in Sri Bhavan should be ensnared or influenced by that. I can tolerate everything. But I cannot accept any double cross."

Kunti hurriedly said, "Believe me. I do not involve myself in politics. And how many people know me after all? And why should anyone come to help me without expecting anything in return. Not everyone would be willing to spend money. That apart, who can give so much money for poor orphans?"

Laltu Babu said, "It's not that, Kala. You haven't been able to understand the many mysteries of politics. I will tell you all about that some other day. You will only pray God for me from today."

Was someone laughing somewhere? Oh no ... how ghastly was that laughter! Laltu Babu said, "Come. The driver will drop you back. I have got a lot of work to do here. I have to make arrangement of food for that mad woman upstairs also."

Kunti thought something and said, "I would like to visit Aunty for a while if you are not inconvenienced in any way."

"No, no, Kala! Never think of going there. She is so violent that she is capable of doing anything. What would people say about me ...?"

Kunti understood that Laltu Babu was extremely worried. Without saying anything else, she moved towards the door. Laltu Babu was following her.

She looked at the upper story of the house through the windshield of the car. It looked like an abode of ghosts.

The touch of the afternoon was in the air. The city seemed to have turned lifeless in the terrible heat of the summer. All the live existence had died down inside her. Kunti could not make a mistake in making an identification. When Sumitra Devi waved her hand, a huge black mole under her right wrist shone on her fair body. That black mole was still there today. The woman she saw could not be Sumitra Devi's sister. But how could this happen to her? Such an intelligent woman she was! She had handled so many adverse situations in her life. What was it that could turn her into a mad woman? There was no denying the fact that Laltu Babu had said a blatant lie. Laltu Babu should be ashamed of this. But he seemed to be hiding certain things from her....

The car stopped near Sri Bhavan. A thick silence reigned there too. No one had waited today for her to return. Even the naughty boys were asleep.

Kunti went inside the house feeling totally suffocated. Small matters disturbed her terribly these days. She took to the bed in a tired frame of mind at such times. She had left just before the noontime. The afternoon was almost over now. Why should anyone have waited for her? She also never took her lunch or dinner on returning to Sri Bhavan when she went out. But where were the children? There seemed to be a vacuum ever since Puni had left.

Kamali ran into the room wailing loudly as Kunti was about to take a siesta. She caught hold of Kunti's feet and cried, "It's all over for me, Didi. I cannot live any longer."

Kunti no longer felt startled at every small thing. She had been staring at Kamali with expressionless eyes. Kamali looked quite healthy Her age did not show. She was the mother of three children. But her husband and mother-in-law threw her out of the house before her youngest daughter Timi was born. Her husband married another woman and ran away to Jamshedpur. Where else could she have gone? Finally, she came running to Sri Bhavan. That daughter of Kamali was now fourteen years old. Padi Apa was saying that she had fever and head-reeling for the past two days. She hadn't also eaten anything since yesterday. Had her illness aggravated? Things were getting so complex that Kunti did not have the energy to solve all the problems. There were obstacles everywhere. There was absolutely no peace. Kamali again fell on Kunti's feet and said, "Didi, I cannot live any longer. Please give me a bit of poison."

Kunti pulled her feet away and said angrily, "Are you trying to threaten me? Die if you want to die that badly. You would never have given birth to Timi and come here to live if you really wanted to die."

Banging her head loudly on the ground, Kamali said, "Didi! How can you talk like this? I am ill-fated. Neither you nor God can save me. The bloody Yama has also forgotten me. It's my fate! What is going to happen to me ...?

Kunti could not hear anything. She had not addressed Kamali. Without being aware of it, she had addressed her own unfortunate existence. She too had given birth to a daughter and run away. Kamali was more fortunate than Kunti. Her daughter was with her. Still no one asked any question to Kunti because she could arrange a handful of rice for them. But her conscience was not allowing her to live in peace.

Kunti had been sitting as if she understood nothing. She knew that Kamali worried about every silly thing. If she was served less rice in her plate, she started wailing reminding everyone about Maa. Maa had brought her to Sri Bhavan when she was bleeding profusely and lying unconscious after giving birth to Timi near a tree. Kamali even sometimes chided Maa, asking her why she had brought her there. Hence, everyone thought that Kamali was a bit of a cuckoo.

Kunti did not want any more farce. Dhania and Gobi had their ears pricked at a distance. The children of Sri Bhavan were growing up quite fast. Everyone wanted to hear all the secrets. Without finding any other way, Kunti said, "Kamali! Don't put your head on my feet. You are older than me. You must first tell me what has happened. Don't cry like that. Everyone is thinking that something serious has happened or I have severely scolded you. Just look at Gobi and Dhania. They are eager to know what is happening."

Kamali shouted in a loud voice, "Those are the two rascals I wanted to talk about. They are getting too big for their pants. Either one or both of them are involved in this. Only the Lord knows everything. That Timi too is not telling me anything. She is moving around with those two brats all the time. She goes to school with them. She studies along with them. All three of them laugh together. I had tried to dissuade Timi many times. But she would not listen. I had also told you about it a number of times. You told me that children will be children. They will laugh and play together. Now you have to deal with this. Those two brats have destroyed my poor suckling baby. Just see how things have turned out. Where do I go from here?"

Kunti became still on hearing Kamali. She had no time for anyone else since she was totally exhausted in the process of carrying her own burden. These people could not stay together at this place. There was no blood relationship among them. There was no strength either to manage things by taking everyone along. It was not possible to know whether they had any faith on any person or religion. Just as there was no caste or creed in hunger, similarly, these people had been living together only to quench their animal thirst. Life and youth had gone on asserting their license without any apprehension. They did not understand what was acceptable and what was not. Maa took leave of this world in the process of making everyone understand. Many like Maa had passed away. Many like her would come again. But numerous Dhania, Gobi, Timi, Puni and even Laltu Babu, Sumitra Devi and Kunti were there in the country. Everyone was silently questioning Shakuntala. No one had ever been freed of the animal hunger of the body. Nor was anyone likely to be freed in future. It was immaterial whether it was the house or the ashram or the footpath. It was immaterial whether it was the temple, mosque or church. Where was that freedom?

Asking Kamali to be quiet, she went inside the house with a great deal of disquiet. She did not join the prayer as on other days. She lay down on the bed. She did not switch the light on. The hazy neon light of the street seemed to be playing hide and seek with the breeze. The light entered through the dirty screen of the window to illuminate the photographs hanging from the wall. Kunti passed into sleep while thinking of all these.

She did not have to go out that night. That was the only solace. The Shethji from Banaras was scheduled to lecture at Puri today. Laltu Babu and others were supposed to accompany him. It was not just that. They were going to partake of *Mahaprasad* in the premises of the Jagannath temple flushed with the dreams of winning the election. What was the necessity of Kunti and other women of low morals like her at a place like that?

Padi Apa came and shook her awake. She spat out the *paan* through the window and said, "You are at home today. Come and have some dinner. You never have a full meal in the nights. You have become thin. What is this ... do you have a fever?"

The rough palm of Padi Apa moved around Kunti's forehead. Kunti thought of getting up. But she again went back to sleep. Her head reeled quite a bit these days. Kunti looked at Padi Apa and said, "No, it is nothing. I just have a malaise. I won't have any dinner. Just let me sleep."

"No, you cannot sleep without eating anything. Let me make a couple of *chapattis* for you."

"No, I will get a fever if I eat anything now."

Padi Apa went away with a sour face. Perhaps she was not able to appreciate Kunti's words.

Kunti struggled throughout the night in hunger and fatigue. She was mortally scared of remaining awake in the nights. The past always grabbed her like a huge tiger in the silent nights. It sucked away all the blood from her body and mind. She felt very lonely and helpless. She was always scared to face herself in lonely nights. It was just as difficult to see oneself as it was to show oneself to others. The latter was perhaps less so. She had seen Sumitra Devi from close quarters – fight with some inner turmoil throughout the night, lie prostrate before the gods for hours with no trace of any such thing the morning after. She looked as cheerful as a fresh flower by the time Kunti was up. And yet what had happened today to that strong-willed, influential lady? She had been defeated and taken prisoner by her own son. Laltu Babu was also aware that Kunti knew his game. He was quite unhappy about it too.

No, she could not sleep. The floating clouds in the sky had crystallised at one place. The breeze was perhaps taking a rest somewhere. It was extremely sultry. She was feeling extremely uneasy having been drenched in sweat all over.

Kunti slept with her door left open everyday. She was no longer afraid of anything. Besides, everyone in Sri Bhavan slept either on the verandah or the courtyard. What fear was there?

Her feet stopped near the door screen. She could clearly hear someone whispering. Many a time, she had a feeling that some kind of conversation was going on somewhere in the dead of the night. But she had never even imagined that anyone could discuss her at midnight.

Kunti came outside stealthily. Padi Apa had been sleeping on the verandah on the right side. The sound of snoring was audible. The conversation could be heard from the left hand side. Kunti walked on her tiptoes and stood to a side. She was one with the white pillar. Shukuti had been sitting on the other side of the wide pillar. Kamali had been sleeping with her face turned towards the courtyard. The children had been sleeping in a huddle next to her. Shukuti started whispering suddenly. She said something. Kamali said angrily, "Why don't you speak louder? Everyone is asleep. The one we are most afraid of always drops off to sleep the moment she hits the bed. She sleeps without any worry. Does she die every minute out of worry as we do ...?

"Quiet! There is a sound from somewhere. Don't underestimate these children. They will go near her and tell her everything."

"No, don't speak like that. We should not criticise someone who has done a good deed to us once. It is all our fate," said Kamali.

Shukuti cleared her throat and spat out. She said, "You are not willing to believe, Kami. How would you do that too? But I have already experienced it. Everything is going wrong since the day this witch has landed here. Maa never fell sick earlier. She took to the bed after the arrival of this woman. She started worrying continuously. Finally, she dropped dead. We have never seen for a day what was there in Maa's almirah and suitcase. Oh God! Oh God!"

Kamali said in a sobbing voice, "Who knows? The sins committed by one hand are not accepted by the other."

"That's it. There was an increase in wrongdoings and sins. The donations stopped coming. No decent person put his foot here any more. The woman turned into a bloody whore finally. She is enjoying herself. And she is throwing a handful of rice towards us. You may not believe me....

Kamali asked, "What do you want to say?"

"Padi Apa was telling me ... you may not believe me. But ask Padi Apa."

"You tell me. What was Padi Apa saying?"

"I know. I know. You don't like my tongue."

"Please tell me. Padi Apa is like our mother. Would she tell a lie?"

Shukuti coughed again. She looked around. Then she said, "Don't quote me. Padi Apa will kill me. She is no less. She has already had two abortions since coming here. And she is taking the excuse of rendering service to the country. If money earned that way goes into our stomachs, our children will also follow in her footsteps. The fruit will grow from the seed. It is not going to fall from the skies. You tell me. We have never seen such things earlier, have we?"

"You are very right. I wonder how my daughter could go astray like this having been born out of my womb. When my mother-in-law kicked me out of the house, my distantly related brother-in-law came and begged me to stay as second wife in his house. But I refused. I would prefer to die. But I won't look at another man's face in my life. I have made up my mind since that day. I will beg on the streets. But I am not ever selling my body. My stomach is in a churn thinking about that."

"And why should it not? This is no small matter!"

"Get me some poison. Let me drink it and die! I had such high hopes that I will get the girl married off. My grandson will light my pyre some day. But it is all my fate!" And Shukuti really started wailing putting the corner of her saree in her mouth. The same musical sound was in her voice which had risen in Kunti when the butterfly had flown away eluding her palm.

While grinding lime with *khaini*, Shukuti said, "Come on! I will call that contractor tomorrow. You will see your daughter will be as good as new again. Of course, it will cost money. I will find the money from somewhere."

"Wherefrom would you get money? We will be dead meat if Didi comes to know of it. Won't Padi Apa have some money with her?"

"Why? I will get the money from that Didi. Do you have any idea how much money she has put away? She has collected all that money because of us. You will see. I will open her box and get the money. And why shouldn't she give it? All kinds of sins have overtaken this place since the day her shadow has fallen here."

Kamali seemed to be scared. She said, "Why are you shouting like that? There would be trouble in case anyone overhears us."

Shukuti was always obstinate. She asked others to talk softly. But she herself always shouted at the top of her voice. Kamali was also like that. Shukuti shouted in an even louder voice, "Who do you think I am afraid of? I am not saying anything unjust. The money has come for us. It's our money. She would herself eat meat and fish while our children starve. She would move around in motor cars. And we won't say anything? I will bring everything out in the open. Let everything burn down. There is no difference whether these children remain alive or drop dead."

Kunti turned into a statue holding on to the pillar. The slightest of grief that was within her melted away in the open breeze like water bubbles.

Why? What for? Why should she slog away like this day after day? Why had she been bleeding from the heart all these days? Who could she call her own? Hadn't Kunti known from her birth that strangers could never turn out to be your own people? Even if someone was accepted as your own, she turned into a stranger at the most opportune time. The dagger that one carried around in the waist for her own safety would chop off her own neck first.

Relations were established in this world only for selfish reasons. Arrogance and influence were the monopoly of only the rich people. Selflessness, humility and a life full of poverty had no value here. Humility in the other person was considered to be her cowardice. Selflessness was looked upon as pretension. And conspiracies were hatched in relation to poverty. What could Kunti explain to whom in a world like this? She herself had been the victim of all these. Shukuti and Kamali! What did they know of this world that Kunti would get angry with them! Or drive them out of Sri Bhavan!

There was no need to hear anything more. Someone again decimated the humane feelings that was sprouting inside her.

But there were no tears in her eyes as on other days. She went inside her bedroom without making any noise.

The harsh sunlight had spread throughout the room. No one had called her. She had slept quite peacefully. Everyone was busy in her work. Only Kamali had been staring towards the distant sky like an idiot leaning against the wall. No one knew the history of Kamali. She too did not volunteer any information. She just cursed her own fate. She believed that the Lord had been watching her every movement. She walked with a bowed head thinking that she was suffering the consequences of the deeds done in her earlier life. And finally, Timi, her daughter and her only hope had turned unchaste because of the sins committed in her earlier life. Why else would evil thoughts have entered into the mind of a fourteen year old girl?

Kunti felt like laughing after hearing everything. What language could she use to explain things to a quiet and innocent woman like that? Indeed, it was no use explaining things to her. It was sheer stupidity and a waste of time to ask her to identify the person responsible for the misfortune of Timi.

All responsibilities fell on her after the demise of Maa. She could not understand why she accepted that responsibility. Her only duty was to pull everyone out of trouble. That was not a very difficult job. After rubbing shoulders with people like Laltu Babu and his wealthy friends, she had come to the conclusion that if one had money, he had respect in society too. If there was money, all problems could be solved in no time. She could not ignore the importance of money. She was a prisoner to the illusion of money throughout her life. She writhed and died like a fish lying on the ground once it jumped out of water.

Perhaps Kamali knew that. Padi Apa, Shukuti and others also perhaps knew. She had tried to explain things to Kamali. But she had not succeeded. She was not mentally prepared to listen to anything. What could Kunti say? She had thought that either Kamali or Shukuti would come to her and tell her something. But everyone was moving around oblivious of her presence there.

Finally, Kunti started out with Timi. She informed Kamali that Timi had to stay in a hospital for a couple of days. If the matter was leaked, it would have a bad influence on the other children. Besides, one never knew. She could not call a doctor to this place. There would be a great deal more gossip in that case.

How much time would it take in a hospital after all? Timi seemed to be nervous. She had been sitting on the rickshaw with Timi on her lap. But she had promised Kamali that she would keep Timi somewhere outside for two days to save her from getting any disrepute. But where could she keep her? Did she have anyone exclusively her own who could drink all her infamy at one go? Someone who would say that he had been waiting for her till the last frontier of the earth! Oh, hell! How could she think of all that crap! Once Laltu Babu had assured her in an emotional state that he would be willing to help Kunti out whenever she needed help. Laltu Babu could never do enough penance for his deed notwithstanding the amount of money he spent for her. He had reminded her again and again that Kunti should keep helping him in doing his penance.

There was no more helpless situation in Kunti's life than the present one. So there was no reason why she should not ask for help. She had never needed anything for her own sake. She could see no difference between wealth and penury these days. But she badly needed help to keep this young girl hidden for two days. Otherwise, Kamali would look down upon her. Timi might have been Kunti's own daughter. She was not able to distinguish whether she was holding Timi on her lap or clasping her own cute daughter to her bosom. A time came in a person's life when she found herself in others and others within her. She became mesmerised and stupid at such times. There was no count of the number of times Kunti had turned stupid like that. Still, she was turning stupid over and over again. Even if there were enough preparations within herself to present herself as a capable and strong person. However, she lost out because of the curse of some evil spirit. She could not understand when she turned still and motionless.

She directed the rickshaw puller to go towards the residence of Laltu Babu. They had many rooms in that house. Timi could stay in any of the rooms quietly for a couple of days. Kunti could drop in sometime when she felt like it. She could even spend a night there. But .... Oh, yes. There was Sumitra Devi. But how did things matter any more for her? It did not matter whether she recognised her or not. She was known before everyone either as a mad woman or an old woman out on a *tirth*.

The afternoon sun was beating down. It was terribly hot. The summer always extended as it willed.

It was strange! There was an extravagant arrangement in front of Laltu Babu's house to feed the poor. Hundreds of lame, blind, hunchback children and women had gathered. The queue was just too long. Good food was being distributed. Everyone was busy in eating. Some of them were even tying up food in towels and any other thing that they managed. There was joy and happiness in the air.

For the past few days, Laltu Babu seemed to be worried a great deal. He seemed to be lost in worries even yesterday. But what had happened today? How come he seemed to have been overtaken by a great deal of joy? He was busy himself in serving food to the poor people. Even his friends had joined him in that. The photographers were clicking away. There was a festive feeling everywhere.

She had sent the rickshaw puller to call Laltu Babu. Where had he vanished? She had pulled a screen in front of the rickshaw like Muslim women did. Of course, she did not particularly fancy it. But she did not want to advertise her presence either. Timi could not take it surely.

What was this? Kunti looked through the gap in the screen. The rickshaw puller had sat down to eat. Who knew when he would finish eating! Kunti moved Timi to a side and got down. For some reason, she pulled the *pallu* of her sari over her head when she saw a crowd.

She looked inside the house leaning against the gate. It was a huge garden. There were people everywhere. The elaborate arrangement for feeding the poor seemed to be a farce in a place which was more famous for parties and drinking bouts. There was the arrogance of the plenty on one side. The sustained effort of Laltu Babu for self propaganda and aggrandizement was on the other side. Everything was crystal clear to Kunti. As he was serving food to the poor, Laltu Babu's gaze fell on Kunti. He was busy in serving food covering his bare body only with a towel. He acted coy when he saw Kunti. Wiping his face with the towel, he came near the gate with a bowed head. As if he was some kind of a criminal. The sickening route adopted by him to win in the election seemed to have become common knowledge. He had stood with a bowed head as if he had been caught unawares. He had perhaps not imagined that Kunti would come at this hour and catch him in the act.

Was it his aim to create an illusion in the minds of the people in order to win the election?

Kunti came to her senses. She was aware that people had been staring at her and discussing her on all sides. She could not hide her youth even in the garb of a widow!

What could Kunti say in that state? How could she apprise Laltu Babu of her poor situation? But there was no other way. Kunti explained everything briefly. After hearing everything, Laltu Babu said, "To err is human. But no one carries the guilt throughout the life. And children of this age are more prone to this kind of mistake. Intelligent women like you should not fret over a small thing like this."

Kunti did not answer. It was natural for Laltu Babu to be verbose at election times.

"You need money, Kala! I will send money through someone by the evening. Now you get back to Sri Bhavan. The journalists are looking at us from all sides."

"No, I don't need money. I need some place where I can keep this girl for two days. Can you render this help to me? I will come and collect her after that. I will be grateful to you for ever. You had promised ...."

Laltu Babu stepped two steps forward and whispered, "Please, Kala. Don't talk like that. I am helpless today. I am not able to help you out. The election is just ahead. The opposition is in search of something with which to malign me. Even one or two newspapers have published some defamatory articles linking you with me. I am totally helpless."

The rickshaw puller shouted, "Maa, your daughter is calling you."

Kala ran near the rickshaw to find Timi in an almost unconscious state. She was always an extremely weak girl. She asked the rickshaw puller to stand guard and returned to Laltu Babu. She said, "I have come running to you because there is nowhere else I can go. If you could take care of things for just a couple of days ...."

"Please, Kala. The journalists are everywhere. You please leave this place immediately. I will make sure that the money reaches you as soon as possible. You take Timi to a hotel or a lodge. I will send my personal physician to that place. Don't spoil my image before the public, please!"

Startled, Kala asked, "What did you say? You would send the money! And I will ensure that your image in public remains intact!"

"Yes, Kala. If you have money with you ...."

Laltu Babu was going on a ramble. He had never valued anything except money. Even now it was so. It was not possible to explain to him that all kinds of situations could not be tackled through money alone. She had to face the police and the public if anything went wrong at the lodging house. Who knew whether Timi was going to live or not? Her condition had deteriorated following her treatment by some quack. There would be a pandemonium in Sri Bhavan. It would no longer be possible to show their faces to the children.

Laltu Babu was impatient with the silence of Kunti. There was disapproval in his voice.

"Can't you see how people are staring at you? It is not possible to escape from the press and the photographers. All my efforts would go in vain if someone clicks a photograph and makes a poster of it. Still I have no hesitation in helping you. The reason is my duty is to help people in trouble. But why do you forget that I have a future? The election is in the offing. All the money and service might go down the drain for the slightest of mistakes. You know how delicate these things are …."

As she moved away from the gate, Kunti said, "The girl has become extremely weak. The matter will get a lot of publicity if I take her to a hospital for treatment. Who else is there to take this kind of responsibility? I had a lot of hope on you because you try to help people in distress."

"Oh Kala! This is awful! Why do you compare yourself with everyone else? The girls of poor families have congregated in Sri Bhavan. No one knows their parentage. Who knows them? This is their profession. Anyway, forget it. I have to help out when you are interested. Just for your sake. I am writing down the address of a doctor. Call him anytime you want. All expenses would be paid by me. Now go away quickly …. When people see you at this place … do you understand me? Don't take offense. People start thinking of weird things when they see women. Besides, the election is ahead … my future … you go away quickly for the sake of Sri Bhavan."

Laltu Babu lost himself in the crowd as he said this. As if he did not know who Kunti was.

Kunti returned to the rickshaw. She was not able to imagine that man could stoop so low when his own interest or image was at stake. Was this the Laltu Babu she thought she knew so well? What had happened to his promises? Of course, it was not as if Kunti had not known him. Even if that knowledge was temporary, still it was his real identification. Now there was only a mask on his face. The expert actor did not waste much time in removing and wearing the mask.

Timi had passed out into a weary sleep. Where had the rickshaw puller gone? Strange, that fellow was still eating. It would have been difficult to recognise him without the red towel tied to his head. What was his fault after all? What compensation could Kunti give him for making him wait for such a long time? Hence, he had perhaps taken the opportunity to make the most of the time at his disposal ....

Kunti observed that the thin, emaciated, handicapped people had been collecting the foodstuff with their hands extended. Perhaps they would vote for Laltu Babu in the coming election. They would hope to get food of this kind everyday without having to slog for it. They were cheering for Laltu Babu. They would perhaps get to eat this kind of food for some days at different places and start dreaming about a new country, new human beings and a new establishment. Their eyes were dazzling with happiness. A small present of money along with the food seemed to have wiped out all their miseries.

There was nothing more to worry about once you turn into a beggar after being in a helpless state. There was no more shame left in you when you start thinking that you could do anything for a square meal. Otherwise, these people would not cheer for people who had been sucking their blood for ages. The bloodsuckers too did not derive satisfaction only by feeding the poor, recitations of *Ramayana*, holding of *Ashtapraharis*, etc. in spite of indulging in all kinds of wrongdoings. They also got people to call them a pundit or a religious person. Of course, they did not mind spending money to get such accolade. They even did not balk at putting a plaque of their names in the compounds of temples, street squares or in government documents. And these helpless, handicapped, poor beggars cheered them in exchange of a handful of rice. Who had actually given birth to others as the fortunate rich? He, who had been playing with the fates of others, who had been trying to establish himself, who had been getting fatter by the day by sucking on the blood of others? Who? Who was he? Was it god or man or some other invisible person or existence? Kunti's system had turned poisonous out of hatred. When would such farces of service to the people and selflessness stop? Who could stop that? Kunti's palms were drenched in sweat and were trembling.

Kunti sat on the rickshaw asking Timi to sleep on her lap. The rickshaw puller said happily, "You know, Maa. I haven't eaten such wonderful food ever before. What a big man he is! He has so many cars, servants, properties. But he served us with his own hand. *Palau*, *kheer*, sweets .... I have eaten to the brim today. God will fulfil all his wishes."

Kunti did not answer. She opened the screen hanging in front out of sheer disgust. The sun was behind her. There was nothing to worry. Timi was sleeping. It felt nice to have a feel of the breeze. There was no point in hiding herself any more. Let everyone know. She was called a thief by the people for whom she stole. Why should she cover herself any more? She did not need to explain herself before anyone!

Suddenly, the rickshaw stopped at a crossing. A lot of people were coming her way. They had huge flags in their hands. They were also holding many placards. They were shouting slogans. What had happened? The crowd was swelling every moment in that narrow road. Someone was singing a song with a microphone in hand standing on truck. Cars and jeeps were following the procession.

Wiping away the sweat, the rickshaw puller said, "Maa, this is a political party. They would keep on like this until the voting is over. The traffic would come to a standstill once they take to the roads. After a few days, everything would become normal yet again. Wait for a while. Let them pass."

Kunti was worried. She exhorted, "No, the girl is suffering from fever. Your take the rickshaw through another way."

"People would also be coming from that direction. You can see that yourself."

Kunti fell quiet. There were people everywhere. She had only been staring. She had never seen an election procession earlier. She had only heard that posters were pasted on walls. She hadn't even seen them. She had read the lectures of Sumitra

Devi on the sly. She had heard them on the radio. But she had neither seen a procession not heard lectures and promises standing in a crowd. She had never had the desire to do so either.

"Kuntala! Kuntala!"

Someone was calling her somewhere. And that too as Kuntala …the name that had been lost under a heap of ashes since long. Who was digging under the ash to fan the fire!

"Kuntala!"

A very familiar voice was coming out of the crowd. An ill-tuned song of a forgotten past or the fragrance of some coveted flower led to a shiver in her body at the wrong time. Wherefrom was that sound coming? Wherefrom did that fragrance come? Kunti was thinking to wake up Timi and make her sit up. Then she would jump down. No, she would take a leap into the sky. From there she was going to jump to the earth. She would hold the wings of the butterfly in flight. She would steal away the pollen from its lips. She would hold the blueness of the blue sky in one hand and the greenery of the all-enduring earth in the other. Only then … Only then ….

"Kuntala."

Who was it? Where? Whose voice was it? That voice was creating a never-before-felt sensation in the blood. She had turned mute in silent sleep for a long time like the accursed Ahalya. Who had touched her and woken her up from that sleep?

"Kuntala …."

Kunti raised her head and looked. Someone was smiling at her mildly with a sweating body and tired eyes. Who was it standing before her having churned the seven seas and holding the pot of nectar? Was it god or demon? Kunti was blinded by the rays of a hundred suns. She lowered her eyes again. She could not believe that such a thing could happen in as insignificant a life as hers.

"Kuntala! Can't you recognise me? I am … I am Tapan. Of course, you cannot recognise me in these clothes. Besides, we are meeting after such a long time. I had never thought that we would meet under these circumstances."

Tapan was wearing a dhoti and a *panjabi*. There was a bag hanging from his shoulder. There was a placard in his right hand. There was a light of hope in his eyes. There was an unintelligible dialect in his tongue. Kunti was recalling those long-lost days. Tapan's promise to expose all the pretensions and misdeeds of Sumitra Devi. Finally, there was disaster in his life the day he had come forward to rescue Kunti from the machinations of Sumitra Devi without as much as understanding her. Where was Tapan since that day?

Tapan could perhaps understand the question lurking in Kunti's eyes. The procession had already moved ahead. The crowd had thinned. He had to move ahead.

"Where and when could we meet, Kuntala? I have a great deal to talk to you."

Kunti understood that Tapan had joined the party opposing Laltu Babu. He might have had some information about her relationship with Laltu Babu. Caressing the head of Timi, she asked, "Do you have any work with me? Your hand will burn if you try to dig out the past which is already buried. Why should you take all the trouble? You have already borne a lot of insult and humiliation because of me. I cannot repay even a fraction of that. Why do you again want to spoil your future prospects because of me?"

Tapan said in an exasperated voice, "I do not have the time now to answer all those sentimental questions. But let me tell you, Kuntala. I had waited for you for a long time. Of course, I did not want to create any disturbance in your life by going to Sri Bhavan. Even now I am a pauper. And that is all the capital I have gathered for my fight. What could I have gained by bringing more trouble for you?"

In an angry voice, Kunti asked, "In that case, why are you blocking my path today?"

"Kuntala! There is no meaning in being harsh without a sound reason. I had not known it that day. But there are no obstacles before me today. I know that one's conscience will punish him for every deed done. Sumitra Devi is suffering the consequence today. She kept waiting for the return of Laltu Babu after you left that place. God only knows what happened to her. And finally ...."

"What happened after that? After the return of Laltu Babu ...? Tell me."

Tapan was quiet.

"Why have you stopped? What happened? Did Laltu Babu say anything?"

"I do not know anything more. But everyone was told that Sumitra Devi had gone away to her village once Laltu Babu returned. I came to know recently that she has gone mad and is a prisoner of her own son. I feel really sorry for her ... you have yourself seen what a workaholic she was!"

"Are you holding Laltu Babu responsible for all this? It could be something else too."

"I don't disagree. But it is a truth that Sumitra Devi is mad; stark, raving mad. I wanted to show her the real truth in life. But I did not succeed."

Kunti did not ask any further questions. As if she had no desire to know anything. A young boy suddenly came near them in a bicycle and said, "You please come quickly. We have to make a phone call to the police. The goondas of Satyabrata Babu have started throwing stones on our procession at the main road crossing. Many have been hit on their heads and bleeding ...."

"I am leaving, Kuntala. We will meet again. Oh God...!"

Before Kuntala could say anything, Tapan had vanished sitting behind the bicycle. The rickshaw puller chided her, "I warned you. Still you went on talking. All these people in politics are of the same ilk. They only know hooliganism. There would be no way to go if the police arrives. Let us go through this narrow street."

Kunti thought that a farce was going on before her very eyes. The spectator wiped his eyes and came back to his own world once the game was over. Kunti too returned to herself likewise. Was she going to play hide and seek with games and pretensions until the end of her life? What kind of illusion was this? As she tried to grab one truth, yet another chimera unfolded before her. Was this what was known as life? Her hand spread the screen without being aware of it. It was not always possible to bear the harshness of light. Darkness was better than that. Ignorance was indeed a bliss!

Sri Bhavan seemed to have come alive again when it beheld Kunti. Kamali embraced Timi and wailed for a long time. The children too joined Kamali and started wailing. Padi Apa always scolded anyone who cried at other times. But she herself was wiping her tears leaning against the wall. After many days, Kunti sat on her bed and also joined others in crying her heart out. The face of the girl she had left behind in the house of Radhu Mahajan floated before her eyes. Who knew what might have happened to her? Her womb had been torn in the process of giving birth to her. She had given her life with her own blood. But why didn't she think about her future? Why?

Kamali's tears seemed to be bubbling inside the chest of Kunti. Kunti was floating away in those waves. The lost motherhood was wailing inside her chest, inside the whole of Sri Bhavan. How could she explain things to anyone? The complaint of Shukuti was no falsehood. The suspicious allusions of others were also not without any basis. Her conscience and mind would punish her even if no one else punished her for each of her deed. How many people could face the truth to admit all their deeds?

Had Kunti of the *Mahabharata* age been able to acknowledge Karna? She always grieved for Karna in spite of being the mother of the five Pandavas. The battle of *Mahabharata* perhaps might have taken a totally different turn if she would have acknowledged Karna as her son before everyone. But Kunti had not been able to do it ... the queen adorned in all kinds of wealth had only been able to sigh. Even Krishna himself had backed out from providing her with divine sight or power. Why? Why had society and the so-called intellectuals of the society been doing this kind of injustice towards women over the ages?

Kunti wiped tears from her eyes and looked skywards. The part of the sky visible through the window was enough. She could no longer bear hardships arising out of the greed to see the entire sky.

Was she actually the harbinger of destruction? What adjectives could she use for herself in order to find some peace? Tapan had perhaps said the right thing that the conscience and mind of a person were going to punish her even if no one else did. So was she undergoing punishment?

What else could it be? Where was Tapan all these days? He came and stood in the middle of the street turning her thought process topsy-turvy! Why? What right had he on Kunti? She tried to burn within herself in anger thinking about her own stupidity. She could not understand why she became so inexplicable before herself in spite of knowing everything every time.

When was she going to meet Tapan again? Where was he all these days? What was he doing? She had not been able to ask him anything. Everything seemed to have turned upside down the moment she laid her eyes on her. There was, of course, no doubt that there was a hidden desire within herself to meet Tapan sometime. She forgot the sufferings of the past two days, the behaviour of Laltu Babu and the ungratefulness of each of the inmates of Sri Bhavan. She seemed to have washed away all her agonies while crying and thinking about the daughter that she had abandoned. Now only Tapan and his unwritten promises kept dancing before her eyes.

What would be the time now? The terrible sun had mellowed and was taking leave in the western sky. A streak of the dim sunlight had fallen on the verandah. A corner of Kunti's saree was shining with the light falling on it. Her eyes closed in fatigue as she sat back in the armchair and thought of different things.

"Didi! Didi!"

Who was calling? Let her call. No one was going to allow her a shuteye in this place.

"Didi! The tea is getting cold. One should not sleep as the day comes to a close. Get up." It was not possible to get angry with Padi Apa. Nothing could be said even if she got angry with her. Such a quiet and decent person! Kunti opened her eyes. She said, "Padi Apa! Can you tell me what is the best time for me to sleep? What is good and what is bad for me?"

"Are you angry because of what I said? You are the guardian of the house. Do I look after you or do I look after these rumour-mongers Shukuti and Kamali? Come, drink this tea. You will feel much better. I will tell you after that."

Kunti looked at the face of Padi Apa as she picked up the cup of tea. Why had Padi Apa come running to her? Was there a new problem again? She was not going to be left in peace. This time ….

"You know, Didi. I am not able to concentrate on anything. You have been running to the hospital and various meetings throughout the day. You haven't even eaten properly. Where was the time to tell you anything?"

"Tell me now. I might go out in half an hour. I don't know when I will return. I have to get medicines for Timi too. I have to call the doctor …."

"I have told the same thing to that fellow. But does he listen to me? He has been coming here for the past two days the moment you are off. But he is a decent fellow. He is quite handsome. He also talks very decently."

"Oh … Padi Apa! I am scared. Why don't you tell everything clearly?"

"What shall I tell you? He comes looking for you. He does not bother to listen to me. He does not give his antecedents if I ask him. He arrived at the gate just as you entered inside with Timi. You were busy because of the drama that is going on. He was not willing to take no for an answer. He said that he was going to wait. He has been sitting all afternoon near that jackfruit tree."

"What did you say, Padi Apa? The boy is sitting near the tree in this hot sun? Had Maa taught this to us? Will her soul rest in peace?"

Padi Apa bit her tongue. She said, "I was just testing you. I provided a cane chair for him to sit. He sat neat the tree of his own accord. A good breeze blows there, you know."

"The boy must be terribly hungry ...."

Padi Apa wiped the corner of her eyes. She said, "You said this because I don't have any children. But I can never eat if any child is hungry around me. I gave him some snacks and tea. I have come to inform you about it only after that."

Kunti had been looking at Padi Apa, amazed. An indescribable joy had lit up her face. Even if she had no idea about the boy or his intentions. No one could exist on this earth being as credulous as that. How could Padi Apa not understand that no young man would enter the premises of Sri Bhavan without any purpose?

Putting down the tea cup, Kunti said gravely, "You have shown enough hospitality, Padi Apa. Now you tell him that I do not have any time. Ask him to come some other day."

"What did you say? The poor boy sat in the sun for such a long time. You talk to him for a moment and then dispose him of. Why should I keep running from one place to another?"

No. It could not be done. No one had been successful in getting rid of Padi Apa so easily.

Kunti moved towards the garden finding no other way. Padi Apa carried a chair and moved ahead of her.

He was not a boy. He was a man of around twenty four or twenty five. He had a couple of days' beard on his face. He had spectacles on his eyes. He had a thick diary and a pen in hand. Padi Apa told him something quickly and retraced her steps. The man moved forward and wished Kunti with folded hands.

Kunti wanted to say something. But she stopped short. The man was looking at her awestruck. He was not even batting his eyelids. As if he had lost his senses upon discovering the latest wonder of the earth. Kunti knew. She knew that her exquisite beauty was the cause of his wonder. Anyone, who had set eyes on her since her birth, had stopped for a while mesmerised. The man was no exception.

In order to reassure the young man, Kunti spoke in as soft a voice as possible. She said, "I heard that you have come two or three times to meet me. I am sorry about that. I have no time with me today either. Please tell me how I can help you."

Without being able to look Kunti straight in the eye, the young man lowered his gaze and said, "No, no. It is nothing important. I know that you are extremely busy. I apologise for wasting your time, But I do not have an option. I am a researcher. I am tired of moving around different places for more than a year. My guide is also unhappy with me. My scholarship will cease in another two months. I will be put into big trouble if you do not help me, Madam."

"I am asking you what you want of me. What is the purpose of beating around the bush? Students should learn how to talk briefly."

A class five girl student seemed to be ragging a class three boy. She wanted to burst out laughing. But she maintained her composure.

The young man was scared out of his wits. Gulping several times and rubbing his palms together, he said, "Yes Madam. I am doing research on women ... er ... I mean ... on the problems faced by women ... er ... about the women living in organisations like this. I would like to know more about the inmates of Sri Bhavan. I will also be extremely obliged if you kindly enlighten me on your personal experience in running this place. I hope you will not disappoint me. Please help me in my endeavour."

So the young man had come to learn about her personal experience and with such curiosity! What audacity! No one would dare speak like this if he was not utterly stupid. Didn't he get any other topic for his research?

"Madam! Perhaps you are angry with me. Please, Madam."

In a sharp voice, Kunti retorted, "Why? Why do you want to know more about us? Is there no other problem in the country?"

"It's not that, Madam. Not much analysis has been made of a problem like this. Hence ...!"

"What do you mean by that? You are going to amaze everyone by opening a storehouse of knowledge? You think that you can create a stir? Is that all there is to it?"

The young man started biting his nails. In a frightened voice, he blurted out, "Please do not misunderstand me, Madam. I have no ill intention. I want ... I just want ...."

"You are wasting your time and my time. Just remember that we do not have a history which is worth recounting. The present does not make any sense. And we see no dreams for the future."

The young man took a few steps near Kunti and said, "How can you talk like this? I was told that no one had ever heard a harsh word from you. Hence, I had come to you with a great deal of hope. Apart from this, you are an educated woman ...."

"I find you to be extremely adamant. There are many educated, knowledgeable and noble women in this country. They might be able to help you more than me. I know nothing. I am not even highly educated."

"You are perhaps annoyed with me, Madam. If you reflect on it for a while, you would know that the so-called educated and aristocratic women might provide me with bookish knowledge. I have enough books with me. What I need is the personal experiences of women who are directly involved in the battle. I might be able to find some way to solve the problem only when I am able to complete my research work on that."

Solution! Way to solve the problem! Who would find it? This stupid youth? The audacity of the inexperienced young man seemed ridiculous when great warriors had been thrown to the sidelines in the battle ground! Courage was good indeed! But this was inspired idiocy! He wanted to take advantage of Kunti thinking that she was a simple woman. May be he had been encouraged in this endeavour by some other rascal. The insect had to be ready to die if it wanted to touch the burning flame. Otherwise, it should come to its senses before it got burnt and turned to ashes. No one could save him if he was a victim of his curiosity and the impetuousness of youth.

Seeing Kunti lost in thought, the youth persisted, "Perhaps you find it hard to believe me. Proper education and employment for children and women have now become part of the government programme. Mothers and children have been suffering the consequences of the atrocities perpetrated by men over the ages. The country is not able to move in the path of progress only because men have terribly neglected women in this country.

"Please consider this. It is our collective responsibility to build a healthy society. I am convinced that an enlightened person like you who has been a victim of social taboos and superstitions will definitely help me in my research work."

Kunti did not know whether to laugh or cry. She was not very sure that the man understood what he was saying. Young men these days were verbose in speech. She had been hearing such loud-mouthed talk since her childhood. When women's committees were newly formed in the village during her childhood, the women also talked in the same way without comprehending anything. Father had beaten up mother for that very reason. Kunti would not be arguing with the young man here today had her mother understood then what she was talking about. Even Sumitra Devi! Had she understood what she was talking about? Her personal lifestyle was in stark contrast with the lectures that she delivered on stages. Why else would Kunti be at this place? How many leaders have analysed the state of women with love and affection? Did they have any other motive except beating their own drums?

Kunti sat down on the chair. Her head reeled these days when she started thinking about all these things. While she was swirling around like a piece of straw in the womb of time, this youth had come forward to block the speed of that time. Fah!

The young man was standing still looking skywards. How much of life had he lived and what was his experience in life! Even if he had some, what were the circumferences of land and water in that? He looked so delicate that it would hurt Kunti to say anything harsh to him. And yet it would be suicidal to encourage him to progress on this path.

Seizing the opportunity of the silence and indecisiveness of Kunti, the young man said, "Please do not misunderstand me, Madam. Many important people of this city have advised me to meet you. The kind of heavy burden that you have assumed at this young age ... there is no parallel of the kind of social service that you do forgetting your own conveniences. My research would remain incomplete if I don't include the experiences and sacrifices of your enterprising life. You might have read many essays. But there are no suggestions for reforms. Only information ...."

Kunti wanted to ask what he meant by a life full of sacrifices? Did it mean finding a stellar role in society for women and thoughts of the future of children? Not just that. She wanted to harass the young man by asking several other questions. But it all seemed to her these days like the rehashed words of a pet parrot. Even if it struck a few chords within her for a few moments, the feeling passed immediately afterwards. How annoying!

Anyone would be amazed by the infamous history of Kunti and the stupidity of the young man in dreaming of a prosperous life for himself using the helplessness of unwanted boys and girls. And yet the important people of the city had advised him ....

The young man suddenly stood up and said, "You see, if you desire it, I will not publish your name. All information shall remain entirely confidential. I have come here because of the advice of Satyabrata Babu, i.e. Laltu Babu. I will not do anything to compromise you. I will come some other day if you are busy today. Please tell me when it will be convenient for you to talk to me. I will need at least one hour per sitting. We can complete everything in seven to eight sittings ... I think the work can be completed within one month."

Laltu Babu was otherwise known as Satyabrata Babu. Oh yes. She knew that name. Yet she did not know it. He had sent the youth to do research on social work. What a strange personality he had!

She had gone to attend many meetings with Sumitra Devi. She had heard a great deal of lectures on the emancipation of women and developmental programmes for their upliftment. Many learned *pundits* from across the country discussed women and children sitting in air-conditioned rooms and shedding copious tears. Loads of papers were used for preparing bound volumes and other materials containing the research information. Pictures were taken by television channels. The proceedings were published in the newspapers in a sensational manner. That was all. Everything was quiet after that. Time rolled on as before.

Kunti suddenly felt pity for the youth who had made no analysis of profit and loss in coming to her. He had come out of sheer curiosity. By way of explaining, she said, "See here! I am addressing you in a more familiar manner because you are almost my son's age. But, believe me, I do not have a son. I have been running around to make all the people on this earth my own. But no one is my own. Whatever I have been doing till today is for the only reason that I think it is my duty to do so. Every person must do something or other. Otherwise, how would he live? As far as I am concerned, I believe God has perhaps directed me to do what I am doing. What experience have I gained that I will provide you with information for your thesis? But I would like to ask you a question. Didn't you get any other topic or problem on which to undertake research? What is your idea about this world?"

The face of the youth turned crimson. But he did not want to give up. In an angry voice, he said, "Why do you think that the topic that I have selected is irrelevant? Do you think that

I have chosen the topic out of curiosity? Or do you believe that I plan to become famous overnight?"

Kunti looked at her wrist watch as if she was getting delayed for another appointment. She said, "I am not thinking of either. But it is nothing but sheer stupidity for a young man to show interest in these matters."

The young man became angry at this dig. Anyone would have felt insulted. But he knew that he was not going to achieve anything by getting angry. Hence, he said in a controlled voice, "Why do you think that the topic I have chosen is insignificant or irrelevant? The entire world is discussing this topic enthusiastically. The United Nations, the socialist countries and even the capitalist countries are busy finding solution to this problem. You must be aware of the meetings, discussions and plans that are being made on this topic. The country has come to a standstill situation today. Can't you know that it is impossible for this country to develop unless there is a marked improvement in the state of the mothers? I am doing research on this topic because of this reason ... I believe that I can find some new way to solve this problem. Who knows? My research might even open the eyes of a blind society. A new age might dawn."

Wonderful imagination! Momentary excitement of the youth! The march of the insect to put out the fire!

Kunti lost her patience. The youth perhaps thought that she was a terribly helpless person. Hence, he was encouraged to lecture her with his hand raised and face grave. She had grown tired of hearing lectures like this. She did not want to listen to any more. She had heard it from Sumitra Devi. She had heard it from Tapan. Many plans had been started in the country with helpless women and children in mind. Many social workers had been working day and night for this. Many authors had earned accolades in the process of publishing books on the subject. Even films had been made on the subject for the awakening of the common people. Numerous meetings and seminars had been held. Everyone said that not enough research had been made on the subject. The work would be over if it were enough. How could the social workers play politics with it if the work would be over!

Kunti's patience wore thin. There was a limit to tolerate and digest things. She got up from the chair and said in a harsh voice, "That's enough. Never come here again to bother me. I cannot waste my time in providing fodder for your research, the plans of the government or the so-called social workers. Do you think I am not aware why young people like you are taking up assignments of this kind? Remember, I have seen much better social workers than you. I know what their real intentions are. Go ... leave this place ...! Don't you ever dare to come to this place to bother me again!"

Kunti turned towards Sri Bhavan and quickly walked away after saying this. The children were standing on the verandah with curiosity in their eyes. No one ever came to Sri Bhavan to bother Shakuntala Didi like that. Didi always went outside to talk with people. She never discussed those things when she returned to Sri Bhavan. This was a new and fascinating event for the children.

The young man suddenly ran down and blocked the path of Kunti. He said, "Madam! Madam! Please listen to me for a moment. You are like my mother. Please do not get angry with me. Please forgive me if I have offended you in any way. But please do not drive me away like this. I will be finished, Madam! There is no possibility of a future for me without quality research in this competitive age. Have pity on me, Madam! Please have pity on me!"

As the hands of the young man folded together in the manner of making a supplication, Kunti seemed to have lost her senses. As if she had seen a cobra raising its hood to strike her, she shrieked in anger and hatred, "What do you people think of yourselves? Do I have no freedom just because I am living with a few helpless women, children and handicapped people? Am I going to oblige anyone and everyone who walks in with all kinds of weird requests? Why? This society and its Brahmins will take all kinds of advantages trampling on my body and mind. And I will be singing paeans to them being scared all the time? This body of flesh and blood of mine has had to pass the test by fire in the garb of Sita or has taken five baths in fire everyday in the garb of Panchali for ages. It had either been the victim of the impetuosity of Kunti or had spent sleepless nights in the garb of Urmila. And what have I received in lieu of all these? Hatred, insults and contempt! I have crossed all limits of tolerance today. Hence, I am not going to provide any explanation to you. Will you get the hell out of here this moment or shall I make arrangement to throw you out? Go … get lost."

Kunti was startled to hear sounds behind her. She had no idea that Padi Apa, Shukuti, Kamali and the children had gathered hearing her outburst.

The young man looked at everyone. He looked at Kunti again. Without wasting a moment, he turned towards the main road.

But the strange humility that was displayed in every footstep of his as he turned back disturbed Kunti for a moment. Her throat seemed to be choked with grief. She ran inside her room and bolted it from inside. Looking at the photograph of Maa, she wanted to say – Maa, Maa! You have cursed me in this manner just because you provided me with a bit of shelter! How could you not know that a woman's life was nothing in the absence of wealth, security, tradition and lineage?

But she could not say anything. The two eyes of Maa were looking extremely sad inside the framing in the pale evening and the frightened breeze. So … so, had she been able to know that the life of a woman in the absence of any horn or strength or status was always as painful as this? Did she have no other experience besides this? Why did she fall quiet that day even if she wanted to say something to Kunti? What hopes had she cherished within her? She had perhaps developed a soft corner for the helpless after losing her husband and children in the accident. But why didn't she make any arrangement to ensure the continuity of Sri Bhavan after her demise?

Who was going to provide answers to all these questions? Time? No, the stupid Time also did not have the power to judge. Strong personalities had plundered all that. Time had been forced to accept slavery under them.

Were Kunti, Kuntala, Kala or Shakuntala destined to be oppressed throughout their lives and become victims of strong personalities? Why, no one had been able to provide any proof regarding this! So, were these research, discussions and seminars only farces?

Didn't Kunti have enough information with her to dismiss all this nonsense? Hadn't God provided enough strength in her soft body to overcome all the humiliation and sufferings? That meant she had never objectively tried to test her own strength and capabilities! She had always been scared looking at the outside world. She hadn't been able to hold herself in her own grip and test her own capabilities.

She stood up. No, no, Somehow or other, she had to arrange two horns. Couldn't she do it? She had to do it, come what may. She had accepted everything until now like a doll. She had never expressed her own wishes. She had laughed it off saying that nothing was the matter even when she was under tremendous pressure. She had consoled herself and walked yet another mile. But, her limit of endurance had already been breached. It was no longer possible on her part to live a moment longer if she did not produce some vitality from inside her.

But....

Padi Apa came and stood near her. Looking at her, Kunti knew that either someone else had come or Laltu Babu had sent the car for her. She said softly, "Padi Apa, I am not feeling well today. I will not go anywhere. Send them back."

"Who should I send back? A boy has come on a cycle. There is a letter ...!"

"Kick him out, Padi Apa! That fellow is a rascal! He has no other job except running after women! Call Dhania, Gobi and Pitabas. They will throw him out on the road. Hey ...."

Padi Apa looked through the railings of the window and said, "You are unnecessarily getting rattled. It is not that man. This is a new one. He does not even have a moustache. He has come with a letter from someone. He is breathless. I asked him many questions. But he is not telling anything to me. He insists on handing over the letter to you and talking to you. It is extremely important, he says. A life and death situation. Tears are running down his cheeks, Didi!"

Padi Apa was always a gullible creature. She could never speak a harsh word for fear it might hurt someone.

Who else could it be? Another person had arrived casting the net of pretensions with the excuse that it was urgent. Kunti might otherwise refuse to meet him. Besides, whose letter was he carrying? Laltu Babu never sent any letter. He never left any evidence of his involvement anywhere. Everything was by the word of mouth ... a lot of blah, blah. He was also calculating and intelligent.

The sound of the cycle bell was coming. As if the doomsday had arrived! Padi Apa said, "Why don't you go and get the letter? You may go or may not go after that. What sin has the boy committed?"

The pain of the boy in waiting at the gate was perhaps turning into a physical torture for Padi Apa.

Kunti suppressed her irritation and came outside. She had a start on seeing the face of the boy in the hazy light of the evening. Who was it? Who was it? She had seen him somewhere. Had known him for ages. As the boy saw Kunti, he came running to her and handed over the letter. He said, "Do you take as much time as this to come out from your house? So why are you so eager to serve the country? You had seen me on the street crossing in the morning. Do you remember? Or have you forgotten that? You had become angry because I had pulled Tapan Sir away while you were still talking to him. I remember that.... Forget it! Our procession has been severely stoned. Many are in a serious state. Twenty to twenty five persons are very serious."

Kunti was apprehensive.

"Tapan Babu went after everyone else was gone. I hope nothing has happened to him?"

"That is the beauty. They endanger hundreds of people in the process of attacking a few chiefs."

"Who are they?"

"Who else? The opposition. They have plenty of money and weapons with them. Apart from that an indirect concurrence of the establishment is also with them. We do not have anything with us except our supporters. Forget all that! I have given you the address of the hospital. You will go there. I am off!"

"Stop! Stop for a while! What is your name? How is Tapan Babu?"

"The damage is considerable even though it is not very serious. You will know for yourself when you go there."

The bicycle seemed to fly away in the air. Kunti opened the paper with the address of the hospital. Oh yes. She knew the handwriting. She was Tapan's student for some days. It was not difficult to recognise the handwriting. Nothing else was there on the paper except the address of the hospital. The piece of paper flew away in the breeze. Suddenly, Kunti seemed to have lost all her senses and stood up. Things had been moving so fast these past few days that it was not possible to make heads or tails of anything. She had met Tapan on the street only a little while ago. Things had been getting more and more complex since that time. Kunti could not comprehend anything. Even she did not have a moment to herself to think about Tapan. The news of his injury had arrived before that.

As Kamali picked up the piece of paper and handed it back to Kunti, she asked, "Who was that boy, Didi? Why did he run away like that? You know him, don't you?"

Kunti did not answer. There was nothing to say. She had run out of resources to clarify everyone's doubts.

"Who is sick, Didi? The boy was asking you to go to the hospital ...."

Padi Apa stopped midway. The change in expression on Kunti's face had stopped her.

Had Kunti ever thought that the last decision of life would be taken so soon? Where had Tapan remained hidden? He was standing before her raising his head from the dense fog! Everything else was pale and dark there. Tapan stood on one side with father, mother, the memories of the village, Sumitra Devi, Laltu Babu and his friends, the shackles of society, problems and responsibilities of Sri Bhavan and the thoughts of the future on the other.

She changed her saree in an absentminded and worried mood. She put some money in the bag and came out. Everyone had been staring at her. She had started out very early today and had not called Padi Apa to leave some instruction as she did on other days. She had not even reminded the children to concentrate on their studies. She went near the gate very carefully. She knew that everyone was questioning her silently.

After a long time, she had started out on her own personal work of an urgent nature. There was neither any account of profit and loss nor was there any apprehension of getting or losing something. There was only an anxiousness ; the same anxiety with which she had run by the side of the canal to touch the sky, spreading both her wings to draw a line on the still waters, to go from one bank to the other in order to call the earth her own ; the same eagerness that she had to sing along with the cuckoo in the mango grove in lonely afternoons ; the same avid desire to play hide and seek with the wayward clouds in moonlit nights. Kunti could see a born-timid girl who had suddenly arrived on the highway and was looking around her in amazement while walking very carefully on the side of the street. Was it really possible? Yes, this was only read in stories. But, there were times when life was more eventful and stranger than fiction. She had never imagined that she was again going to confront the world that she had left behind after coming out from the dark fortress. Where had the past been sleeping inside her present life? It had started spreading its empire after yawning and getting up from where it had rested. Kunti did not have the power to dethrone it.

She entered the hospital ward crossing the people who had thronged outside. The noise was deafening. People had been standing in groups and were busy in discussing things among themselves. Kunti had the corner of her saree over her head. She had been walking on the verandah very carefully trying to hide herself from prying eyes. That boy was lurking somewhere. He ran towards her like a vulture swooping down on its prey and shouted, "Madam, come this way. You have already left the bed...."

Kunti followed the boy quietly.

Tapan's head been bandaged. It was soaked in blood. There were bandages on his hands and legs too. He had been sleeping. A doctor was standing near him and checking his pulse. Kunti could not see the face of the doctor clearly. The doctor said something in English to two or three young men standing on the other side of the bed. Kunti could not hear anything.

The boy silently indicated at a chair for Kunti to sit. The doctor turned around and said, "There is nothing much to worry about. No one should disturb him tonight. The blood pressure is a bit high. Besides, if he becomes emotional at this stage ... I mean ...."

The doctor's gaze fell on Kunti. Kunti had also been staring at the doctor. Who was he? She had a feeling that she had seen him somewhere. A very familiar face indeed! The memory was knocking a chord somewhere. All Kunti's consciousness seemed to shiver, the dead past and the blossoming future. The doctor recovered after a moment. He wrote something on the chart hanging from the bed and walked away quietly. Kunti wanted to run after him and enquire about his antecedents. She wanted to ask many things. But she could not ... she was overtaken by unnecessary restraint and shyness. What was the point of asking anything? Other people might misinterprete her curiosity. What was the standing of her personality in this society? Besides,

Kunti had gone through a thousand metamorphoses already. Who was going to accept her new incarnation?

Many people had gathered around Tapan. The elections were ahead. A heated discussion was going on about the heinous acts committed just before that. Kunti had sat behind everybody. That boy came back and told her, "Madam, you have to wait for some time. Tapan Sir had himself requested you to come. We did not know whom to inform and what to do when he became unconscious after being hit by stones. He had never told us anything about his family members. Luckily, we had met you .... He wrote down your address on a piece of paper and handed it to me after the stitching on his head was over. I was forced to disturb you because of the trouble he took in writing the number of the bed and the name of the hospital even though his hand was hurting."

Kunti smiled a bit and said, "There is nothing to worry about that. You have done the right thing. May I know your name? There is a great deal of problem if one does not know any names here."

The boy acted coy. He said, "That's right. I had forgotten to tell you, Madam. Sir calls me Shashi. My name is Shashanka ...."

"It's all right. I will call you Shashi too. Okay, do you know the name of the doctor who was examining Tapan Babu?"

"I cannot say. There are so many doctors in this hospital. Who knows about all of them? Many famous doctors had gathered to examine Sir. The press people, politicians and police officers had come here to take his statement. Who remembers everyone's names?"

Kunti said, "You were saying that he had become unconscious. I too find that he is not in sense. When did he do so much work?"

Shashi laughed and said, "Madam! I find that you do not understand politics at all. Leave it .... Sir had regained consciousness for some time. He has been administered sedatives at present. He will explain everything to you when he gets up. Let me make a round of others in the meantime."

"No, Shashi! Wait for a while. I want to know how and why your Sir was stoned like this."

Shashi became grave. He looked strangely at Kunti. He wanted to say something. But he checked himself.

Kunti held his hand emotionally and requested, "You are a wonderful boy! Please tell me the truth. Who could mount an attack on an innocent man like Tapan Babu?"

"You are wrong here, Madam! Tapan Babu might be innocent for us. But the opposition wants to eliminate him out of their way."

"That means, that means ... O God .... Shashi, are you telling me that Tapan Babu is contesting the election? Why did he show this audacity? How many times does he have to be tricked in life to know how dangerous can be the conspiracy of animals?"

Shashi did not answer. He was smiling. He seemed to have a lot of dreams in his eyes, manifestations of many possibilities. Kunti shook him and said, "Why aren't you saying anything? Do you believe that your Sir is going to win this election?"

Shashi burst out laughing. Somehow he controlled himself and said, "I find you totally disinterested in everything. General election is going to be held in the country. But a distinguished lady like you is totally unaware about things. And yet what unshakeable faith Sir has on you!"

Kunti lowered her face. She did not know politics – she was not even interested in reading any news about elections in the newspapers. There were plenty of newspapers available. But she had neither the time nor the inclination to read all that. It did not matter to her whether Laltu Babu won or someone else won the election and came to power. No one was going to save her from the hell and take her to the heaven!

"You are perhaps hurt by my words. I just said that off the cuff! Please do not mind. Sir is not contesting the election. But, his close friend Parsuram Babu is contesting. You must know about that."

Kunti did not answer. She did not wish to tell him that she did not know anything about Parsuram Babu or his plans. She was smiling silently.

Shashi said cheerfully, "It may not be this time. But Sir will surely contest the next election. Sir has got a lot of contribution. Sir will definitely contest from some constituency within six months. And he will definitely win too. He will never allow Satyabrata Babu to win. He is his biggest enemy! Sir has promised to fight till the last with people like him who wear masks of pretensions and suck the blood of the common people in the name of politics. I am sure you must have heard this from him. Not once, but a hundred times."

Kunti looked at Shashi's face in amazement. She knew that he was assuming that Kunti was privy to a lot of information. Tapan had perhaps confided in him about Kunti in some weak moment. Tapan must have turned emotional too. How else would an eighteen year old boy be so effusive? But he was helping Parsuram Sabat and opposing Laltu Babu. And he will fight the election directly if the opportunity presented itself. O God! What kind of intoxication was this! Was there no end to the desire for power, fame and money? Why did Tapan wish to play this game endangering his own life? Sumitra Devi had driven him out of her house after humiliating him. She had driven out the helpless orphan who had grown on her leftovers without bothering to find the truth and out of her own arrogance. Events took a different turn after that. How could Kunti know that the fire under the ash did not get extinguished, that it again started burning in the waves of time. And it destroyed everything in sight once it started burning. She was not aware what changes had taken place in Tapan with the passage of time. She had not bothered about anything else except keeping Sri Bhavan afloat. She had even not bothered about herself. To switch on to another topic, Kunti asked, "He is not seriously injured, is he?" Shashanka did not answer. His gaze was fixed on the screen hanging on the door. Kunti turned around. Who was it? It was that doctor.

As her gaze fell on the doctor, he turned around and went away. Shashanka suddenly followed the doctor.

Kunti moved from the chair and came to stand near Tapan. He was sleeping in a deep sleep. He seemed to be very exhausted. Why had he sent for Kunti? Kunti had kept no news of him even though five years had passed in the meantime. She had never thought that she was going to meet him again. But this was what life was. This was the work of that invisible hand!

Suddenly, Shashanka entered the room along with the doctor. The doctor asked directly, "Please do not misunderstand me. How are you related to Tapan Babu?"

Avoiding the entire question and the harshness of his glare, Kunti asked angrily, "Why do you think that I am related to him? I just know him."

As the doctor checked his pulse, he said, "No hard feelings. Tapan Babu will recover his sense in a short while. Please do not have an extended conversation with him."

Kunti answered in a deep-throated voice, "I have that much of common sense. Besides ...."

"What? Why don't you speak?"

The doctor was looking at her face anxiously.

"No, nothing. I know that he is sick. I won't talk to him."

"Good, you can talk tomorrow morning. I am in the duty room. Send for me if you need me."

Kunti did not look at him. She did not reply either. She had no doubt that the doctor had been staring at her face. Was the question that was bothering her also bothering the doctor?

Shashi and the doctor left the place. Kunti wiped the face of Tapan with the corner of her saree. She kept waiting for him to regain consciousness. Only Tapan had taught her a new *mantra* of living when she had been exhausted after crossing many hurdles in life. And he had sown dreams in her mind. He had held out many possibilities for the future both directly and indirectly. But all flowers did not blossom. All dreams did not come true. Tapan had gone out of her life in a sudden storm. He had again arrived at the wrong time when she had crossed her youth and got exhausted carrying the weight of her body. She recalled that terrible scene of pretension in the morning. Laltu Babu was so concerned on seeing her. And yet he had promised that he would do anything for the happiness of Kunti in order to do penance for his sin. But he could not provide shelter to a helpless girl for one day in his house. How could he be a leader of men in that case? Could he win the battle simply by maiming his adversaries?

Shashi came inside with a tiffin box in hand. He smiled at her and said, "I have already eaten. There are bread and sweets in this. You can eat that."

"Oh, no! Why did you bother? I am not hungry."

"I will sleep now. You wake me up when you feel sleepy."

Kunti smiled at Shashanka. The boy was really innocent.

"Why did you take all that trouble? Where did you find this tiffin box?"

"It is not a problem to find a tiffin box. The doctor provided this."

"The doctor gave it? Why? Is he known to you?"

"No! We got acquainted here. He asked me to get some food for you. He was really concerned about you. I thought …."

"What did you think? Why don't you come clean? I do not even know the name of that doctor."

Shashanka laughed and said, "You are getting me all wrong! That doctor is also the same. He is asking me many things about you. Tell me, Madam! Did I know you earlier? We have met this afternoon only. But the doctor is not willing to believe it."

Kunti seemed to be worried. She asked, "But this is strange. Why does the doctor want information about me? Is it because I am a woman?"

Kunti's feet were trembling a bit.

"No, no. Why do you think like that? This doctor is not like that. You won't get a god-like man like him elsewhere."

"What does he want to know about me? Is it my relationship with Tapan Babu or something else?"

Spreading a bedsheet on the floor, Shashanka said, "Wake me up if there is any problem. I am sleeping. The doctor is also available in the duty room ...."

Shashanka lay down on the bedsheet and closed his eyes. He seemed to be positive that Kunti could take the entire responsibility of Tapan. A silent wave of confidence was playing on his childish face. Kunti looked at Tapan once and then at Shashanka. She fell quiet. The tiffin box and a glass of water had been placed on the small table. Kunti leaned back against the chair and closed her eyes.

Laltu Babu might have sent word for her in the evening. The driver might have returned with the car. Some great festivity might have been arranged not because the opposition had been defeated but because it had been made moribund. He had arranged a feast for the poor and the handicapped. Scores of photographs had been taken. Won't the gods punish him for the terrible situation he had created half an hour after that for his own selfish ends? Using goondas to bash up the opposition! Won't the ordinary public know the man behind all this mayhem? Shall this country be held to ransom for all time to come? A few people would be achieving their own selfish ends in the name of democracy and social service! Was no one going to oppose this?

Without being aware of it, tears rolled down from her eyes in a stream. She had forgotten the surroundings having been immersed in her own thoughts. Shashanka was snoring softly. The boy seemed to be terribly tired. Tapan was also in a deep sleep. Who knew when he was going to recover his sense?

Kunti was lost in thought. The tiffin box had remained closed on the table.

It was irritating and tiring at times to search oneself within herself. Sometimes, one felt pity too. Some other time, she got lost. One's own existence seemed to be less than dust contrasted with the extensiveness of any experience. The exhaustion of the last four or five days took Kunti to its lap in no time.

Someone placed his palm on hers and called her softly. Startled, she woke up from sleep. The sky beyond the window was getting lighter. Had the night passed so quickly? Her eyes fell on Tapan. He had been staring at her. His left palm was on Kunti's right palm. Kunti looked around to make sure that no one was there. Shashi was still sleeping soundly. The hospital was quiet. Very few people were outside. The mornings of the summer arrived even when the night was still there.

"You haven't eaten anything in the night? Kuntala, have you ben sitting throughout the night on this chair? Your body must be aching!"

"It's nothing. I am used to it. How do you feel now?"

"I am okay now. Initially, I felt the pain. Then an apprehension rose in the mind. After a long time, I experienced fear ...."

"Why?" Kunti withdrew her palm from inside the palm of Tapan quiely.

"The fear of death. And apprehension for others – those people for whom I had seen some dreams."

Kunti feigned as if she had not heard anything. There were many things which could not be told explicitly.

"You may not know it, Kuntala. I came to know about your misfortune for the first time the day Sumitra Devi humiliated and drove me out. You could have told it to me before that ... perhaps you were too shy to discuss that with me. I still clearly remember the tantrums thrown by Sumitra Devi even before I knew what had happened. I had told you about her social service before that. Sheer selfishness ...."

Suddenly, Kunti placed her palm on Tapan's mouth and said, "No, don't talk that. She had helped us at one time when we were in trouble. You know her condition now."

Pressing the palm of Kunti in her own palm, Tapan said, "I know. She did not tell me where she had dropped you. She forced me to go to Nagpur on an urgent work. I returned after fifteen days. You had already left her place by that time. Where could I have looked for you in such a huge world? Laltu Babu came back after a month. There were two English women with him. Mother and son had a fight that continued throughout that night. I had been sitting in the ground floor.

"The doctor was called early in the morning. He went to the first floor. I too went upstairs. Sumitra Devi was bleeding from the ear and she was hallucinating. Laltu Babu talked at length with the two English women. They went away towards noontime.

"Two or three days passed. Laltu Babu had stayed confined to his room. I could not take it any more. I went upstairs on tiptoes. Laltu Babu saw me and came out on the verandah. He told me, 'Maa has gathered enough reputation by providing shelter to rascals like you. There is no further need for you at this place.'

"I said supplicatingly, 'I am not responsible for anything. I will meet Maa for a moment and then go away.'

"'You are not responsible? That's wonderful! Who is responsible for Maa's condition? Who has maligned her?' Laltu Babu's eyes were deep red. He had advanced towards me with his hand raised.

"I was mad. He had ruined the lives of so many girls. There was no count of the number of helpless people he had looted. No one else might have known. But I knew everything. He had an unspoken fear towards me. Hatred too. Hence, I had always maintained a distance from him."

Tapan was breathless. Kunti caressed his forehead and said, "Let it be. You can tell me some other day. The doctor has forbidden you to talk."

"Don't make that mistake, Kuntala. If something has to be done immediately, never defer it until later. I have repented throughout my life because of that."

"Okay, talk slowly. There is no reason why you should get excited."

"It's not morning yet. In a little while, doctors, nurses, press reporters, party members, etc. would arrive. I cannot get you near me any more."

Kunti was silent with her head bowed. The soft touch of love was creating a never-felt-before emotion for the first time in her body and mind. She was not able to gauze its definite shape and features.

"After that I insisted that I must go. I requested him. Sumitra Devi had been staring at me sleeping on the bed. Tears were rolling down from her eyes. I was concerned. Laltu Babu suddenly caught me by my neck and said, 'I am not running a charity here to take care of beggars like you. All the properties including the balance in the bank have already been transferred in my name. If you desire, you can come back to claim her dead body.'"

Tapan again became breathless as he said this and asked for some water. There were tears in his eyes. His face had turned crimson in anger and hatred. When he saw that Kunti was concerned, he said, "It's nothing. A little bit of weakness persists. Hence ... oh, forget it! I could have picked up Laltu Babu in one hand at that time and thrown him down. But I could not do it. He pushed me out of the house taking advantage of my weakness. I have kept a tab on his movements since that time. But, Sumitra Devi could not bear the atrocities perpetrated on her by her son and became stark, raving mad. It is painful when you think about it. I have been running all the time to unmask this farce of service to the nation. The election will be held the day after. All our workers are in the hospital. Selfishness and money are finally going to triumph. Can you tell me, Kuntala? How long man is going to continue persecuting man like this?"

"Please calm down. This is not the time to lose patience. Laltu Babu's weapons might backfire on him," Kunti replied.

"I want to laugh. In which book have you read all these?"

"No, no. I strongly believe that truth will prevail ultimately. I have read the story of the last truth of battle in books like *Ramayana* and *Mahabharata*. God will never be so cruel."

Tapan burst out into a guffaw.

"What did you say? God? Do you still believe the invisible hand?"

Kunti did not give up. She answered, "Yes, I do! God is not there in the temples. God comes in the shape of human beings. Who knows ...!"

Kunti stopped short as she had started out to say something very emotionally. Two drops of tear dropped on the open palm of Tapan.

"Please continue, Kuntala. Why did you stop? I do not want to lose the opportunity to hear something from you after a long time. Please speak, Kuntala."

The dam had burst. Kunti pressed her face on Tapan's palm forgetting her surroundings. Her thin frame seemed to be trembling in some terrible typhoon. Tapan became still for a moment. He thought that the spine of the earth will get crushed if he moved by as much as a millimetre. He said softly, "Kuntala! It is dawn already. Open your eyes and look at me."

Kunti played Holi with her tears likewise and said, "You took your time about it! What am I left with today? The dreams have run their course. The hunger for living is also over. I am bereft of everything today...."

Smiling slightly, Tapan said, "Is there a proper time to come, Kuntala? Nothing gets finished on this earth. The important thing is to search for it and find it. You are too much worried about the body. Have you ever thought of the mind?"

Kunti answered as if she had been mesmeried, "I am extremely helpless. I have suffered enough harassment just to breathe a bit more peacefully and to be not able to take it any more. I do not have the patience. I do not have the courage. I am disintegrating ...."

"Why Kuntala? Have you learnt only this much from the battle of life?"

"The society calls me a fallen woman. The established persons of the society do not have any respect for me. And the people for whom I have fought all my life doubt my credentials. Of course, I have not been doing this job in the hope of getting anything in return. Still, if I make a review of my earnings, I am without a dime in this society."

"Enough! Enough! That is enough, Kuntala! I had waited for the moment when you would turn pauper after giving away everything you have. I had waited for you to be totally liberated afer abandoning your own control over yourself. Assume that that time has arrived now ...!"

"Kunti raised her head and looked. There were all kinds of questions in her body and mind. She was amazed! Was she listening correctly? Was Tapan in his senses? Or was he still under the influence of sedatives?"

Tapan had been staring at her leaning against the pillow. There was a light of joy and ecstasy on his face and eyes. It was not possible for Kunti to look at him straight in the eyes. Bright light had entered inside the room. The rays of the sun had entered through the window in the east and spread throughout the room.

The doctor came inside the room. The nurse tagged along behind him.

"So you have woken up? When did you get up?"

The question was directed at Tapan. But the doctor's gaze was fixed on Kunti. Kunti got up from the chair and called Shashi. Kunti knew .... She knew that all impossibilities of the world were going to be possible in one day. Who was this doctor? The face that was raising its head from the ashes of the past – was that this doctor? How could it be so? The doctor was busy examining Tapan in the meanwhile. The wound mark on the right hand cheek on the doctor's face was suddenly visible to Kunti as he had bent down to examine Tapan. Oh yes. It was the same wound mark. Mother had thrown a piece of burning wood from the hearth at Nima Bhai in anger. The burn mark remained on his face. Neither age nor his medical education had been able to wipe it out. Oh! Kunti's head started reeling. She held the door for support as she started to move outside. Shashi held on to her out of concern.

Tapan asked, "What happened? Doctor, please see what has happened to her."

The doctor came near her and checked her pulse. He examined her eyes. Kunti had been drenched in sweat and was sitting on the chair. Her eyes were closing of their own accord. O God! Please save me if you are at all there!

The doctor said, "She is extremely acnimic. She must be feeling weak. Take this tablet and tonic. Okay, what's your name? And age?"

Shashi said, "Sir, I do not know her name. Madam ... please tell your name."

Tapan replied before Kunti could say anything, "Her name is Shakuntala Das. She is thirty five."

The doctor wrote out the prescription. He said, "I will come later. Take a bit of rest now. Everyone cannot take the strain of being awake throughout the night."

Kunti opened her eyes after the doctor left. Shashi was busy in wiping off the sweat from her face.

Tapan said, "Shashi! Go and drop Madam at her place. It is time for Parsuram Babu and other party members to come. Oh yes. Buy the medicines on the way. Kuntala, do not come here any more. I would be leaving this place soon. There is nothing the matter with me. I will come to you after two days. That is, once the elections are over."

Kunti's displeasure was obvious when she said, "I will take care of myself. But you cannot leave this place so soon. Is there no one else to serve the people?"

"I have come to you even if there is a delay. And is there any specific time to come?"

Luckily, Shashi had wandered into the bath room. Kunti could not give any answer to a simple question.

"Why are you quiet? Can't you answer a simple question? There does not seem to be anything inside that head of yours!"

Kunti laughed. Tapan had taken such digs at her when he used to teach her in the house of Sumitra Devi.

Shashi emerged from the bathroom and said, "Sir, I am making a move. Keshab will come now. You get ready. Madam, let us go."

Kunti looked at Tapan silently and then moved out to the verandah. As she got down the staircase, she came face to face with the doctor. He asked in amazement, "Where are you going? I told you to take an hour's rest!"

Kunti stepped aside and moved on with the corner of her saree above her head. The doctor shouted from behind, "What's this? Why don't you say anything? And how can you leave in this state? The newspapers will hold me responsible if anything happens on the way. The reward of treating politicians. Hey ... stop!"

Shashi laughed aloud. He said, "Doctor saab, can't you understand? I mean ...."

The doctor had crossed the staircase and was almost near her. Shashi said, "Can't you understand ... she is mute .... Mute!"

The doctor was staring amazedly. He seemed to be unwilling to believe it. Kunti went hurriedly and sat on a rickshaw along with Shashi. Oh!

Resting for a while and wiping the sweat off her brow, Kunti asked, "Shashi! The doctor seems to be a nice man. He is taking a lot of care of Tapan Babu. He could not be so well in a day otherwise."

"Oh yes. He is good. But he is an obstinate person. He had asked me about your antecedents twice last night."

Kunti's chest heaved. So her conclusion was correct. Nima Bhai had made no mistake in recognising her. He had been busy in his own efforts since yesterday.

"What did you say?"

"Nothing. I said I did not know. Sir had forbidden me to talk about you."

"Shashi! What is the full name of that doctor?"

"Everyone calls him Dr. Nirmal. I do not know his surname. Everyone will know if you say that much."

"Oh!"

"What happened? Is your head reeling?" Shashi seemed to be worried.

"No, something fell in the eye. You get the medicines from that shop. I am sitting here."

As Shashi got down, Kunti realised that her body was actually trembling. God! What impossible things were taking place! She thought that one of her feet was in the heaven and the other was in hell. Why did Nima Bhai arrive at the wrong time? He must have done hard labour to bcome a doctor after leaving home at that tender age. But he had not been able to change his appearance or the burn mark on his cheek. Had he been able to recognise her? Kunti was not going to introduce herself ever in this life. She was not going to look for fire under the ash and burn herself in the process. Enough was enough! Let the past remain buried.

"Madam! Hold the medicines. I will go elsewhere after I drop you off. There is a lot of work to do today. Tomorrow is the election day. You are going to vote for our party, won't you? Do you remember our symbol?"

Kunti laughed looking at the innocent face of Shashi.

As she had placed her foot inside her bedroom, Padi Apa came and said, "Didi, the man who was talking to you yesterday near the jackfruit tree has come again. What shall I tell him? He had come at the dawn before your arrival. I had forbidden him to come again to this place. He must have waited for you somewhere nearby. He has come running immediately after you."

Kunti was angry beyond words. These people were not going to allow her to rest in peace for a moment. There were people all the time. Everyone had been running to satiate his curiosity or for some selfish end. It was unbearable! There seemed to be a dense illusion all round and Kunti seemed to be getting lost inside that. Her head seemed to be in a continuous swirl. She had no joy in living any more. She did not even want to put up a fight for others in order to wave her own flag of victory. Why should she not live the rest of her life the way she herself wished in that case?

Who was that stupid researcher? The young man had entered inside the circus-like life of Kunti as a joker! Kunti felt like laughing. The imbecile had thought that he was going to find solutions by collecting information about neglected lives. The entire world would be lighted by his new invention!

What audacity the young man had! It was even greater than a dwarf raising his hand to touch the moon. The poor fellow did not know that the signs of his soft feet would be obliterated in a moment in the limitless sand of the sea and under the footsteps of numerous men and women. There were so many unsolvable problems, intriguing stories and weird experiences in this life that they could not be arranged in a straight line over the ages. Those who have done something have done so in order to beat their own drums. And this fellow was a mere student ... without any resources or lineage. He wanted to build his own future by collecting spices from the experiences of other people.

"Why don't you say something? I will tell that to him."

"Tell him to come later. I am busy."

As Padi Apa retraced her steps slowly, she said, "Didi, I would like to say something. Don't get angry with me. How many times would the kid go back from this place? You tell me when you can find an hour for him. I will ask him to come that day. He would curse all of us ...."

Kunti burst into a laughter. There was such intensity in that laughter that Padi Apa looked amazed. She asked, "What makes you laugh like that? Did I say anything bad? The curse of a man is worse that the bite of a cobra. It burns a man alive ...."

Still laughing, Kunti said, "Padi Apa! What a simpleton you are! You are sleeping peacefully because you are so simple. But you have no idea how many such curses of men have I digested already. Tell me, Padi Apa! Aren't we human beings too? Can't we curse? And is there no poison in that?"

Kunti shook Padi Apa emotionally. Padi Apa was confused. She wanted to say something. But she only kept looking at Kunti's face. She had never heard so many things from the person who was ordinarily silent.

"So, you are not able to answer me!"

Padi Apa wanted to leave. She pulled Kunti's hand and said, "Is that so difficult? Don't you know this much? The Kali Yuga is coming to an end. Some day, we will get justice. The Lord is staring blankly sitting mute in His temple now. But I know that he would come out with his twelve feet sword in the end and kill the wicked. And then everyone would be equal. Let me go. That boy must be waiting."

Kunti said, "Tell him, Padi Apa. He should come after the election. Let him come any time after that. I do not have any time right now."

"What is that? He should come after what?"

"After the voting is over."

"Yes. See here. People have left so many papers here for voting. What decision can we take? In which symbol should we vote? You wait. I will get the papers."

"You first go and pack off that boy. He must be standing since a long time. You are hurt more than him, no?"

Kunti smiled. Padi Apa went away. Really, how simple and innocent these people were! Padi Apa was thinking that Kali

Yuga was coming to an end and the Lord was going to kill the wicked with the twelve feet sword in hand. The fallen and helpless people would get justice ...! Dreams! Only dreams! She herself had had also seen dreams like that. But not a single dream ever had come true.

Sumitra Devi had explained that a new age was going to dawn. No one was going to make any distinction between rich and poor, and men and women in that age. But what happened to that dream? She had floated away in that dream and had been in the wilderness. Laltu Babu had also raised hopes of some possibilities in the game of light and shade. After being lost for a long time, Tapan had come floating in the waves. Sitting on the shore, Kunti had suddenly caught hold of him. That was not all. The tide had also brought Nima Bhai in its wake. Someone, who had melted in the darkness after assuring that he would be back in a short while, was also extending his hand and asking to be lifted to the shore. But Kunti could not continue doing it. She did not have the strength to pull out two persons at the same time. Even if she had the strength, she could not go on dreaming any more. She did not have any further desire to run on the bank of the river or catch butterflies by their wings.

Tapan was standing before her holding on to sheer truth. He too had once spread the net of dreams. She had no idea what might have happened to her if she would have been caught in that net. But she had been the victim of another hunter before she got caught in Tapan's net.

What irony of fate! Her still, mute body and mind had been standing between two diametrically opposite persons. There were illusions and grey sand on one side. The game between the clouds and the sun on the green earth was on the other. Nothing was visible clearly ... and the earth on which she was standing was shaking all the time. There were earthquakes and storms every moment. Who had her ever-careful, fear-struck womanhood waited for? Who? Freedom? She had been praying in some enclosed cave of a mountain from the ancient times only to taste the untasted juice of freedom! She had lost her freedom at every footstep! Only she knew how harshly she had kept the handcuffs pressed on her wrists. All her friends and well-wishers had added one more handcuff to her wrists. Kunti was getting breathless under the weight of all those handcuffs. Still ... still someone seemed to be riding fast towards her sitting on the Pakhiraj horse. The dawn seemed to be breaking. Hundreds of demons and poisonous animals had surrounded the Pakhiraj. And yet, he was coming quite fast without bothering about anything. Its footsteps were creating a hundred thousand sensations in her blood. She could not ignore that! So had she waited for this even while suffering in hell? Who was it? Whose advent was causing so much sensation, shiver and eagerness in her untainted mind?

And still ....

"The poor man was disappointed. I have explained things to him. To come at a more suitable time. Auspicious work is not started on any day or at any time."

"Auspicious work? What auspicious work? What did he tell you?" Kunti was taken aback.

"Why? Is it not an auspicious work? He is going to write a book about us. Other people will come to know about us. Even the government will come to know. Isn't he doing a fantastic job, Didi? Who wants to know about us in this country?"

"Padi Apa!" It was not clear whether or not she understood the irritation in Kunti's voice.

"Don't be so obstinate, Didi. Our time is over. But think about these children whose future is dark. Let them be someone in society! Everyone should know about our travails ... we should not shy away from that!"

Kunti was in no condition to explain things to Padi Apa. How could she make her understand that everyone knew of them. The past and the future of the children were known. But there was no limit to the game in which they were nothing better than pawns. A thousand Kunti, Kuntala and Shakuntala might be sacrificed in that *yajna*. But there was not the least hope of creating a Bharata. But she did not want to kill the dream in Padi Apa's eyes. Her entire life had been spent under the hot sun. She was like a daily labourer. Even now she was going round and round like a wheel. Kunti envied her because Padi Apa slept peacefully in the night while she herself spent sleepless nights. Let her dream. Let her be elated by dreams. There was no problem in being awake throughout the night. She had been lying in an inanimate sleep for a long time in a house full of cobwebs. The shadows of dreams even could not disturb that deep sleep. Okay, a streak of light was now entering through an opening in the window. Let it .... Kunti was not going to close that window. To switch to a different subject, Kunti asked, "Have you kept the name and address of that man? How do we get a copy from him when he writes a book?"

"Why, won't he give us a copy? I have told him to give a copy to us first. Then he might give others. But I have forgotten to take his name and address. Won't he come again? This time I will jot them down."

Padi Apa put a knot in the corner of her saree. Someone from within Kunti was reassuring her that he would definitely come again. It was his work. But if he did not come? If he stopped doing his research because of the humiliation? No one was going to be any worse off. Nothing would come to a grinding halt on this earth because of that.

But ....

In that case? What would happen? Padi Apa would not be able to listen to the story of her struggles in her life!

There was restlessness which had spread itself inside and outside the house like a dense fog. The sky was overcast.

She developed an affection within her for that unknown young man. Her heart missed a few beats. He must be really disappointed to return like this again and again. Who knew whether he had any money with him or not? Where did he live? Kunti had never asked him any such question. It was wrong on her part. She had never done any such thing in her life before. A deep breath escaped her.

Kamali came and stood near her. Perhaps Timi had become even more sick. Why else would her face look so sad?

As Kamali started sweeping the room with a broom, Kunti took it away from her hand and said, "Let it be. You don't look very well. How is Timi now? Is she taking her medicines in time?"

"She has become well only because of you. But her head is reeling. She does not have a drop of blood in her body." Kunti looked at her handbag. Shashi had bought two large tonics for her on the way. She did not need them. She will get well in due course. How could she take any medicines when there was an ailing girl in the house? She opened the bag hurriedly and extended the bottles towards Kamali. She said, "I had forgotten. The medicines were in the bag. Give her two spoonfuls after food everyday. You will see. Timi will start running in two days."

Kamali wiped her tears and said, "May you live for a hundred years. But don't talk about running. She has earned this because of running. Puni showed the way to everyone .... Didi, you are doing so much work. You know so many people. Couldn't you do something for me?"

"What?" Kunti's chest again hit against the unknown question.

"Only this. The children do not care for anything these days. Couldn't you get these girls married off? After that, it is their own fate."

Kunti suddenly blurted out, "Kamali! You had got married and set up home, no? You had your husband, father-in-law, mother-in-law, etc."

"Everyone does not have the same fate. The five fingers on a hand are not equal."

Life came to an end and turned to ashes. But dreams did not die.

"You go now, Kamali. Wait for a while. I will definitely make some arrangement. Let the election be over."

With a great deal of reassurance, Kamali folded her hands and made obeisance to the gods. Then she left.

Kunti was startled by her own words. Was she going to fulfil everyone's hopes after the elections? All fantasies would come true? Who put this language in her mouth? What relation had she with the election? She knew that there was going to be an election. She knew Laltu Babu and Tapan were fighting against each other. But what relation had she with all that? She hadn't even gone once to a voting booth to cast her vote. She had never personally experienced the excitement of an election.

Padi Apa called her for lunch. She was going to sit with everyone for lunch today. She did not enjoy eating by herself. Today was a holiday for her. She did not have to go anywhere. There were no meetings in the evenings. There was no need to visit Tapan in the hospital. There was no apprehension of that nagging researcher turning up either. Today she was going to spend time with herself and the inmates of Sri Bhavan.

She would take rest after lunch. She would water the plants in the evenings. She would join the children in prayer. Then she would discuss the studies of the children. She would tell them stories. What story? Stories of kings and queens? No, she was going to tell them true stories. She would sow dreams in their minds while telling stories. As they would be overtaken by dreams ... her chest pounded. The dawn would be breaking ... the sky would be getting lit with the rays of the sun. He would be riding the Pakhiraj horse and coming from some distant land! He will come definitely! It might be delayed a bit. But he will surely come. There was neither age not time limit for him to come. Hence, he will come. He will come, he will come, he will come!

Kunti went to have lunch. There was an unspoken joy among the inmates of Sri Bhavan today. That Mahani, who cried at the drop of a feather, was such a small and thin kid when he had arrived at Sri Bhavan. Now he looked quite good wearing clean clothes. He was studying at the school. When he saw Kunti, he said happily, "Didi, you will give us chocolates today. You will give us sweets. We will vote for you."

Kunti picked her up. There were many questions in his innocent eyes. But he did not know that he could not vote.

"Who would vote for me? I am not contesting the election. Who told you about all this?"

"A gentleman had come. He has given leaflets to everyone. He gave us chocolates and sweets. See the leaflets."

Laltu Babu's election symbol had been printed on the paper which the child took out from his pocket and showed. Parsuram Babu ... that is Tapan's leaflets. Had they not reached this place?

Suddenly, Banu extended the leaflets of Parsuram Babu to Kunti. She said laughingly, "I bet that my symbol will win, Didi. You will give me chocolates and sweets, won't you?"

Kunti was holding the two leaflets in both her hands and weighing them. Who was going to win and who was going to lose? Who should she ask them to vote for?

Mahani had held one of her hands. Banu had held the other. They were simple, obstinate children. What could make them happy except chocolates and sweets?

She had no further interest in having her lunch. Somehow, she gulped something and got up. Padi Apa said, "We have to take a decision, Didi. Stay back a moment. Tell us who we should vote for. We have never gone to vote. This time people will come with vehicles. We will go by cars and come back. Whatever we do, we will do the same thing. We will vote for the person you vote for."

Kunti stared once at everyone present. So these people were asking her to undergo a fire ordeal finally! Why else should they ask her such an unanswerable question? So these people have understood the meaning of winning and losing in an election? Who knew what else they were aware of?

"Didi! Why don't you say anything? Whom should we vote?"

"You cannot vote for anyone. Young children do not vote. And, Padi Apa. You vote for anyone you wish. Why do you ask me? For that, the government ...."

Padi Apa said, "Who is voting secretly? They are all talking among themselves. We will also take a decision. You know what is what. You rub shoulders with many people outside. Shall we not honour it if you tell us something?"

Kunti looked at both the leaflets. She knew why these people were asking her question after question. They had seen Laltu Babu. He came with his car at any time of the day or night. Of course, he rarely came inside the premises. Yet everyone knew that she returned alone with him at the weary hours of silent nights. Hence, they were perhaps eager to know whether or not Kunti was interested in voting for him.

Shukuti came near her and said, "The boy who called you to the hospital yesterday evening had given this bundle of leaflets. He made such entreaties. You too followed him to the hospital. When could we have told you ...?"

So Shashi had finished his election campaigning at this place! She had not been able to say anything or see anything because of her absentmindedness.

Kunti tore the two leaflets into small pieces. She said sadly, "You vote for anyone you want. I am not going to vote at all."

Kunti walked fast towards her room. Noise could be heard behind her. They had expected that she would advise them to vote for Laltu Babu. But Shashi had turned the apple cart. She could not recall that the inmates of Sri Bhavan were so interested in voting anytime before. Everything had turned topsy turvy this time. Disasters were coming into her life from all sides. Laltu Babu and his rich friends were on one side. Tapan and Nima Bhai had surrounded her on the other. She was only playing merry-go-round in between the two. If she stopped for a while, someone from either side was going to grab her. Hence, she had to go round and round as long as there was a bit of strength left in her body.

And, finally, there was that young researcher. He wanted to pick up the story of her playing merry-go-round.

Kunti went and lay down quietly. She had remained awake throughout the night even though she had closed her eyes and pretended that she was asleep. She had only passed into a light sleep towards the early morning. But the touch of Tapan's palm had carried her away to some unknown country.

The hurt, tired face of Tapan again came alive in her mind. She had spent a few moments of her life with him without any fear. Tapan had always been able to restrain himself. Kunti had developed a lot of affection for him. She had even come to depend on him a little bit . But hot breeze started blowing all on a sudden. It was not possible on the part of Kunti to know at that time where Tapan had been blown away in that breeze. Still.... That breeze had again blown the yellow leaf and thrown it in front of her. It had shaken her and then again quietened her. It had sown dreams in her body and mind. A couple of days back she had thought that she could not proceed any further with her withered body. There was a deep depression in her mind. But it had again come alive after being touched by the hand by someone. He had even wanted to create a strong impression in her mind that there was no date and time for either going or coming. But how could she look at the future omitting the past altogether. The earthen house that she had built had disintegrated a number of times. How could she dream of building a palace? Still .... The closed eyelids of Kunti were opening and closing alternately. Things were going on their course somehow . Why did Tapan arrive again to block her path? How long was she going to live after all that she would hold out hopes for other people!

Tapan's words hit her ears the moment she closed her eyes. His eyes and face came alive before her. She looked at the photograph of Maa. She prayed to her silently. But she could not discard Tapan from her thought process. The afternoon passed in terrible agony.

The afternoon's sun was getting milder. It would set after a little while. Then the night would come. The voting would start once the night was over - the game of victory and defeat.

"Didi, the sun is about to set. Why are you sleeping?" Padi Apa was calling. Kunti yawned and closed her eyes again pretending that she was getting up from a deep slumber.

"Didi! Get up. That man has again come since a long time." Kunti's body started burning as if someone had stuck a stick of fire to her. She roared, "Kick him out of this place. I find that no one will allow me to die in peace here."

"I forbade him. But does he listen to me? He is going away. And again he is coming back. He said that he would force his way in to meet you when I restrained him. He has some urgent work. He was handing over a letter... but again took it back... the boy is busy in voting work, you know!"

"Voting work? What voting work does he do?"

"Why? His master is contesting!"

Kunti stopped in her tracks like water thrown on burning fire. What had gone wrong with her? Shashi had perhaps come with some urgent message.

Kunti went outside without letting anyone know about the urgency. She had been so immersed in her own affairs that she had even lost her ability to judge a situation. She could not open her mouth to say anything even if she was worried about her own impetuosity. What would Padi Apa think?

Shashi was standing outside the gate. He ran towards her and said, "Madam! Had you been sleeping so long? It is almost night. I have already come here four times." Kunti only smiled at him.

"Are you all right now? Did you take the medicines? Sir is extremely worried about you."

"How is he now? I hope he does not have a fever...?"

"No, no. It's nothing. He has survived greater attacks on him. He has already been discharged from the hospital. Tonight is the most important night for us. All calculations go wrong on this night."

"Why did you leave Sir and come here wasting your time?"

Shashi laughed and said, "Now see, Madam! Sir has asked me to get news about you whatever be the time of the night. He has even asked me to wait all night. And you are asking me why I came here. I do not know what I should do. I am going to sit on the street crossing."

Kunti felt like laughing. But she said gravely, "I am all right. Ask Sir to take rest. Let the election result take its own course. When can I meet him?"

As if he had not heard anything, Shashi said, "I am leaving in that case. I will come after a couple of days. Madam! I have a request. Please keep these leaflets. Make sure that all your people vote for our party. But don't tell Sir anything about this."

"Why?"

"Sir had forbidden me. He has strict instruction not to talk anything about election at this place. But I cannot keep quiet. Even one vote can make a difference. The opposition will distribute bags of money tonight. Where is that kind of money with us? You know the kind of man Sir is. I am on my way. Please do not tell anything to Sir."

Shashi flew away on the bicycle without waiting for an answer from Kunti. Only his white shirt was visible till the street crossing through the darkness of the night.

The children had started singing the prayer song. Kunti went there slowly and sat down. O God! Let this terrible night pass without incident!

Sri Bhavan had a routine life. Everyone abided by that. In the evening, children concentrated on their studies after prayer. The elderly people stitched or did some other useful work. Sometime, they sat down together and gossiped. Then they had their dinner and slept. Someone remained awake sometime as an exception to the rule. If someone was sick, the whole of Sri Bhavan remained awake. Kunti sometime made sure that it was quiet all around. Only Padi Apa kept staring. She locked the gate and then she too fell into a deep sleep. But she stopped snoring at the slightest of the sound. The entire Sri Bhavan slept peacefully depending on her. No one bothered too much if Kunti stayed out even till midnight.

There was no change in the routine today from the evening till late in the night. The only deviation was the presence of Kunti throughout the day and the night. The deviation was Kunti talking happily with everyone, inquiring about their welfare, consoling Kamali, and explaining Padi Apa and the children about the process of voting. Even she had played hide and seek with the small children. She had joined them in playing merry-go-round. She had felt lighter after sweating a great deal in the process. She just wished to get rid of the pains and sufferings which had formed layers on her chest since ages. Somehow she wanted to spend her days in pursuit of lighter pleasures and then fly away to some fairyland with an unburdened mind. Wouldn't someone fix the wings of a butterfly on her shoulders? She had read so many stories. She had heard the fairy stories of the grandmother and the stories about the prince and his sidekick. She had heard impossible stories of strange lands from her friend Jharana. Why didn't something like that happen in her own life? Everyone would come to know of it in the morning ... what?

She could not think of anything. She was tired of searching for that 'what'. Death was knocking on the door. But she had not been able to understand that 'what'. She had been searching for that thing and had been trying to give it a shape since a long, long time. That was why that researcher was returning from her doorsteps everyday. Kunti had silently read the question on his face and eyes. Hence, she was asking him to go back every time. He was also in search of that precious 'what'. But that young man was not going to spare her. He would definitely get enough time some day to confront her. Then ....

Half of the bed was already wet with her sweat. The breeze had stopped from all sides. The waves of the moving clouds in the sky were stationary. Not a leaf shook on the trees.

Carefully, Kunti opened the door and came outside. Strange! Everyone was sleeping on the verandah in one line. There was total silence on all sides. As if the earth had been sleeping since some primal time ....

The gate had not been locked today. Why was it so clearly visible today? The lock was hanging from the chain. Padi Apa had perhaps thought that Kunti might go out in the dead of the night. Or perhaps someone might come in the night ... why should she bother about these routine matters? Padi Apa did not lock the gates when she did not feel well.

She came to the last step. A cemented pandal had been constructed by Maa in front of the gate. A mango tree had grown from inside that pandal. Neither the sun nor the moon could touch that pandal through the dense leaves and branches. There were flower plants, casurina trees around the pandal. Mango, jackfruit and coconut trees were there behind the pandal. Sometime, Maa sat there in the nights. Some other time, she slept there too on a makeshift bed. Some other time, she even slept on the cement pandal itself. The night passed. She kept looking at the sky. Some time she snored in deep sleep. Kunti used to think of a lot of things in the beginning. About whom did Maa think sleeping there? Gradually, it did not matter any more. When curiosity arose in her mind, she suppressed them. Yet, Maa used to say that she had a great many things to tell Kunti. The cruel time did not permit that. Even what she tried to tell at the last moment was not at all intelligible. That is why, she had not been able to draw the shape of 'what' in her mind. Anytime she had tried to fix two wings to her two arms, the wings had always fallen off. She could imagine the next phase of the unseen shape only if she could fix those wings. She might have been able to count the number of stars in the sky, the greenery on the wet chest of the earth, the depth of the waves on high seas or the quantity of lonliness present in the outer space. She would tell the world the stories of her victories. But .... She would perhaps live with these 'buts' till the end of her life. She could not explicitly say what she had desired, what she had looked for, what she had dreamt and ... and .... Aw! There was no end to it once you got thinking about something. Only the head reeled.

She went walking near the gate and removed the chain and the lock from the gate. Then she walked back. The first room of Sri Bhavan was hers. There was a large verandah to the right. Then there was a hall where everyone kept their clothes and provisions. She again restlessly walked back near the cement pandal. The pandal seemed to be beckoning her again and again. There was a large stone lying near the pandal. A heap of small stones had been lying to the left of that since a long time. Maa had a great desire to extend the pandal a bit more. But she could not succeed in doing that. Padi Apa had asked the children to collect stones from the road. They had been put in a heap. She had been asking Kunti to build a narrow road from the pandal till the gate. The road became muddy in the rains. Padi Apa got rashes on her feet walking on that muddy road. No one had ever tried to move the large stone from that place. Who had the strength here to move that stone? Children climbed up on the stone and jumped down. They wrote their names and drew pictures with chalks. Sometime they stumbled against it and bled. The stone had become a part and parcel of Sri Bhavan.

Kunti slowly walked near the pandal and sat on it. The horns of a few cars could be heard intermittently in the quiet of the night. There was no need for any car to go through this street. Laltu Babu and his friends had been busy with the elections for the past three nights. The intoxication of the elections was perhaps the biggest intoxication of all. It was not a big thing who was going to win and who was going to lose in this game which had started everywhere and where lives and money were at stake. But when would this farce started for the benefit of the common man come to an end? The game would continue to be played as long as man is not free from the demon of hunger.

Thousands of Kuntis would sacrifice themselves in that. Numerous feasts would be organised for feeding the poor. Children like Mahani and Banu would be dreaming of chocolates and sweets everyday. Young men like Shashi would be going around aimlessly even while they would be aware of everything. And lakhs of unemployed young men would be prisoners in research laboratories. A few wealthy persons made use of their knowledge as weapons to satisfy their own selfish ends. They kept quiet even though they knew everything. The reason was they did not have the ability to be free from the demon of hunger. Wherever she had gone from the time of her birth, Kunti had seen different shapes of that demon. That was why, the butterfly had flown away farther and farther; her singing along with the raging wind by the side of the river had stopped ; listening to entangled songs of the open earth had come to an end ; and her lips had been forcibly shut to block the path of truth. In spite of herself, she had died everyday to come alive again. For whom? Who was it? Was this battle for banishing hunger or to get freedom from hunger? She could not understand properly ...! Who was going to provide her that freedom?

Kunti stood up. The night was getting deeper and deeper. The clock on the fire station building struck three.

A car suddenly screeched to a halt near the gate shattering the silence all around Kunti. Who might come at this hour of the night? As the horn of the car blew twice, Kunti ran near the gate. She was worried about someone getting up from sleep in Sri Bhavan in the dead of the night. It did not look like Laltu Babu's car. He could not be easily free from the intoxicating effects of election. Then ... then ...!

Someone opened the door of the car and came out on seeing Kunti. Why, this was Laltu Babu! The colour of the car was deep black. There was a black trouser and a red shirt on his body. There was a strange hat on his head which had kept his eyebrows covered. He had brought it from overseas. He covered his bald head with that when he was in a happy mood or on auspicious occasions.

But ... this was the wrong time ... he should not have come out of his house just before the election. He had been so much concerned about his own reputation when she had gone to meet him the day before. He had sent her away quickly in front of people just to prove that he had no relation with any woman. How come he was here at this hour of the night...!

Laltu Babu was busy in locking the door of the car at that time. He had indicated to Kunti to remain quiet. As if he had come to discuss something extremely confidential. Kunti had been staring at him leaning against the gate.

Swaying from one side to the other, Laltu Babu came near the gate and said, "Kala! Open the gate. It is not safe to remain outside for long."

Kunti opened the gate. What was this? Laltu Babu was so drunk that the place was stinking like a brewery. He could not walk straight. He was swaying like a tree swaying in a strong breeze. What had happened to him? Why had he come to this place where he should never have come? What was his grief? The election would take place in the morning. Hence, he had not been able to recognise Kunti in the afternoon. Why did he suddenly arrive at Sri Bhavan in the middle of the night?

As he moved towards her room, Kunti said, "Wait! Why are you going in that direction?" Laltu Babu turned around. The light from the street was falling on his face. What was this? This was the ghost of Laltu Babu! The ghost that she had met in the prayer room of Sumitra Devi in some distant past. Oh God! What was this!

Leaning against the gate, Kunti gathered courage and said, "Why are you agitated like this? The election is tomorrow. You cannot afford to lose your patience today."

"No, no! I am not worried for the election. I have made all arrangements for that. My victory is certain. I am not at all bothered about that. I am worried only for you. Only for you!"

Kunti was a little scared. But she said in a controlled voice, "Please don't worry about me. I am all right. Sri Bhavan is okay.

All of us will vote for you. You have been providing food to all of us. We cannot pay back the kindness that you have shown during our bad days. Please get back home now and take rest."

Laltu Babu's hand extended towards Kunti. He needed to hold on to something to steady himself.

He did not have enough strength in his feet to carry the weight of his body.

Things happened in a flash. Laltu Babu grabbed her palms. His hand was trembling. He said, "Don't misunderstand me, Kala. I could not help you at that time because of the circumstances. My conscience has been biting me for that reason constantly."

Kunti tried in vain to free herself. She said, "No, no. On the other hand, I put you into trouble. I should not have gone there at that time. You are unnecessarily worried about it."

Laltu Babu's face brightened with happiness. He seemed to have been freed from all his sins because of the benevolence of some goddess. Kunti tried her best to free herself from the grip of Laltu Babu. But she did not succeed. What had got hold of him? Was it excessive drinking or the prospect of definite victory in the election? He was not aware what he was talking about. Kunti too could not make anything of it. Who knew what might happen in a moment?

Kunti held him by the hand and moved towards the cement pandal. He would perhaps become quiet if he sat down for a while. Laltu Babu embraced Kunti tightly only after taking a couple of steps. Was there so much strength in the trembling hands? Kunti became breathless inside his strong chest and said, "Leave me alone! What are you doing? Leave me!"

But Laltu Babu was not listening to anything. His drunken lips had pressed down on the lips and cheeks of Kunti. Kunti was burning with anger. She did not know what to do. No words could get inside piercing the stony chest of Laltu Babu. He could not even hear if anyone called.

Kunti made an all-out effort to free herself and say something. Laltu Babu stopped her by putting his palm on her mouth and said, "I know that you are angry with me. I have not been able to come here as I was busy in the campaigning. I have not been able to help you at the time of the election. I am sorry for that. You punish me with your own hand, Kala!"

He bowed his head dramatically after saying this. He threw his hat on the ground. Kunti understood that he was talking like a mad man because of excessive drinking. She pulled him by his hands and said, "Please sit down on this pandal for a while. It's cold out here. I have not been hurt in any way. You are unnecessarily getting worked up."

As Kunti advanced a couple of steps and reached the large stone, Laltu Babu again embraced her. He took his mouth near her ear and said, "Listen to me, Kala! I am definitely winning this election. And then I will positively become a minister. You won't be staying here at that time. You will stay near me. I have received enough punishment because I had forced myself on you once. But I want that you should surrender yourself before me of your own accord. You cannot send me back today as you have done until now. I have been waiting for you since a long time ...."

Pressed inside the embrace of Laltu Babu, Kunti had been staring at him. She had only seen the mask of Laltu Babu until now. He had kept his real face hidden. It had raised its ugly head from behind the mask when it had found the opportunity. Didn't Kunti know that one had to die some day if she lived with the snake! Didn't she know that the snake did not turn into a pet animal just because it is fed with milk and bananas!

She had suffered in silence throughout her life. She had just about started breathing when grief had again struck at her door. The poison of Laltu Babu had started affecting her entire system. It was not possible to understand what he was saying in the excited, drunken state.

Kunti stared at his face again. That all-destroying hunger was in his eyes. Suddenly, all fear vanished from her mind. In its place, there was an extreme hatred and the desire to battle it out to save herself. She had never got such an opportunity ever before. Her weak frame had been injured time and again against her will. She had no desire today to save her chastity or her dharma. She had no love for her body either. Laltu Babu had been waiting for Kunti to surrender herself of her own accord. How could he know that she had lost all sensations since ages by the curse of some evil spirit?

Again the lips of Laltu Babu pressed down on her forehead and eyes. Her body was bleeding from the wounds made by a hundred spears. The earth beneath her feet was shaking. The sky had created all-destroying clouds in her eyes. The universe was going around and around on all sides of her. No ... no more ... no more ....

Kunti gathered all her strength in one breath and pushed Laltu Babu with both her hands. In a flash, he fell on the ground. His bald head hit the large stone with a sickening thud. He lay prostrate there after emitting a shriek. Kunti had kept herself ready to attack again. What was this? Was Laltu Babu bleeding so profusely from the head or was she imagining things? As Kunti advanced a bit and stared, she found Laltu Babu making an effort to get up. He had extended his hands towards her. No, she was not going to allow him to get up. She was not going to listen to what he was trying to say. Let him get up. Then Kunti would deal with him. She was ready to make the last compromise of her life.

Kunti extended her legs downward sitting on the pandal. Laltu Babu had been sleeping under her feet on that large stone. Blood was flowing down from both the sides. Let it flow. Some time it was going to stop. Then he would be able to understand the meaning of his misdeed. And these people were going to be leader of men!

Suddenly, his legs seemed to tremble. He was perhaps making the pretension in order to get up at the first available opportunity. Then Kunti could not match him any more in strength. Oh yes! His head was shaking. His feet and knees were jerking. Kunti did not know what to do.

She looked around her and her gaze fell on small stones. She picked up two of the larger ones and smashed those on the chest of Laltu Babu. The stones seemed to weigh tons in her hand. But as the stones hit him, his mouth turned into a grimace. As if the two rows of teeth had been mocking at her. They seemed to be making fun of her and telling her that death did not come so easily. No one could kill him. And Kunti was only a weak female.

His hands seemed to be scraping the earth. It seemed that he was going to get up any time and finish off Kunti. He seemed to be groaning....Perhaps he was making an effort to say something. If someone in Sri Bhavan would get up hearing the sound he was making... or if some unknown man going on the street entered.... Everything would come unstuck in that case.

Kunti picked up two more stones and took careful aim at Laltu Babu's head. She dashed two more stones on his chest.... The same chest which had gone berserk clasping her in a tight embrace. Let everything turn to ashes. Laltu Babu's teeth still seemed to mock at her even though there was blood everywhere. It seemed to be telling her – go ahead and hit me. I am not going to die, I am not going to die.

What happened? He won't die! Okay....

Kunti collected all the larger stones and put them on the cement pandal. She looked at Laltu Babu. He was still thrashing around. The head seemed to be bending to a side. His back and neck were still on that stone. From waist downwards, there was a jerking movement. He had a lot of strength indeed! If he got up this time, he was going to devour her alive.

She picked up a very large stone and threw it on his chest. The red shirt was sticking to the half open chest. Blood started coming out from the chest in a spray. Was there a hole in his chest? Like a wild tigress, she caught hold of his shirt and tore it to pieces. Let all his blood flow on to the earth inside Sri Bhavan. Kunti was going to sit around to see the big festival of blood today. She would find out how much blood was there in his bosom...!

She leaned down. The chest was drenched in blood. A gaping hole could be seen on the chest. Laltu Babu had fallen asleep with his eyes open. The two rows of teeth still mocked at her. They were perhaps asking her to look at his chest. Let her see as much blood as she wished to see. But let her surrender herself to that chest. Kunti had still been looking at the chest. The blood was clotting all around. What was there inside those round balls of blood? Whose face was this? This was not Laltu Babu! Then who was this! Hey ... this fellow was Manua. Who else would have such crimson eyes? Laltu Babu never had such huge moustache and uneven teeth. Ha! Look at his cheek! How he was staring at Kunti. What audacity! Just because he had won once, he had thought that he would keep on enjoying her throughout the life!

Kunti stood straight. She picked up another large stone and said, "Rascal! You have come again! Once you had your teeth on my flesh after smoking *ganja!* Was that not good enough! You had decided to whisk me away to Kolkata and suck my blood there every moment of the day! You could not do it then. So you have come again today! Wait, just wait. I will settle all accounts today!"

She hit a heavy stone on that face resembling a blood mask. The face still did not hide itself. She picked up whatever stone she could lay her hand on and started hitting the body on the chest. After there was a heap of stones on the body, she sat down on the pandal breathing peacefully. There were many stones lying nearabouts. Manua could not get up. Even if he tried to get up, Kunti was going to hurl stones at him and make sure that he lay there. There was nothing to be afraid of... nothing at all. Kunti wiped her face with the corner of her saree. She found blood on that. Bloodstains were there all over her saree. Ah! She smelt the blood using her nose. She looked at the heap of stones. She looked at the chest and the shattered face of Manua. The eyes were dilated and looked at her in the same fixed manner. What cheek this Manua had! Kunti had kept staring quietly. The legs seemed to be twitching at times. Hadn't Manua died yet? Was he still bleeding from the chest?

She got up. She removed the stones and looked at the chest. Blood had clotted there. But Manua seemed to be dead already. She removed the rest of the stones and looked again. What was this? Where was Manua? Someone else had been staring from near that chest. His lips were red with chewing *paan*, there was a red towel around his shoulder and a bead necklace around the neck. There was humility in his eyes. As if he would go on rubbing his palms until they fell off from his wrists! Someone seemed to be scratching Kunti playfully under her feet. Who was this fellow really?

He had been staring at her face with a basket of gold ornaments… he wanted to give her a massage on the back…. again he was feeding her a laddu forcefully while fanning her with a hand fan. He was banging his head against the wall if Kunti did not eat. Oh dear! Oh dear! That eunuch Radhu Mahajan was still alive! Didn't he get a bit of poison or the village pond that he had come running to this place in the middle of the night! Look at his confident stance! As if he was a very capable male! Not one – he had sat thrice on the marriage pandal and had married three women. Wasn't he capable indeed!

Kunti was again furious. She was in this state today only because of that scoundrel. He paid money to her father and bought her off. He paid money to Manua and got his wife ravished through him. His only intention was that the son born from the womb of his wife would be known as his heir. And how he succeeded in saving his dynasty! Whatever he did, he did! But what pride he had that he had come running to this place at midnight! Had he come to die here? Very well! If he had so much love for death, no one was going to deprive him from the good fortune of dying in the hands of his wife.

Kunti held two large stones in her hands and looked at the face of Radhu Mahajan. Why was he so scared? Why had he closed his eyes? There seemed to be a sadness in his face. He was a coward till the last. When Manua looked at him in anger, he purred like a cat before him.

She hurled both the stones simultaneously on the chest. She did not look at the body any more. She again put the small stones together in a heap. It was over! Radhu Mahajan had turned into pulp. After all, he was her husband. She was not going to look at her bleeding dead body!

By that time, there was a large heap of stones lying on the body of Laltu Babu. His head, hands, legs, etc. could not be seen. Still there were many stones lying around.

Kunti was getting exhausted. Her body seemed to be getting heavier. She got up on the pandal and sat there leaning against the mango tree. She was not going to sleep however tired she might be. Who knew when Radhu Mahajan would come out of the heap of stones or may be Manua might come out! And Laltu Babu will definitely be on his feet after resting for half an hour. Not only would he get up. He will come running to suck out all her blood. How could she go to sleep at a time like this!

Leaning against the mango tree, she was looking up some time and then looking down. She was getting flown away with the floating clouds of the sky to some distant past by the cool breeze of the dawn. Someone suddenly snapped off the wings of the young girl who was moving in the mango grove and riverbank among the butterflies. She had hid herself in a corner and was crying. Her feet was falling on the velvet back of the deep red *Sadhababohu** as she walked around. She was wailing loudly because the *Sadhababohu* had died. As she started out to the village road with a bag of books and unkempt hair, someone was snatching away the bag of books and throwing it away. She was returning home wiping her tears with her left hand. The floating clouds too moved fast! The girl was thinking of the ways of the world and fainting near the dead body of her friend Jharana. The complexion was creamy. Unkempt hair on the head. Red lips, sharp nose and blue eyes. But why was there so much tear in those eyes? Why? The girl would be so happy if she could only smile a bit....

A few cuckoos started singing in unison.

---

* a red, velvet smooth insect seen in the rains.

Was it already dawn? The black car was still visible near the gate in semi-darkness. It had been waiting for Laltu Babu....

There was not a bit of strength left in Kunti. She could not even walk one step ahead. She had locked Sri Bhavan from outside. How was she going to open that door?

Let it remain locked. Kunti could not get up. Her body had been totally exhausted by carrying three dead bodies at the same time. She could go down from the pandal only if someone would move the dead bodies away. She could walk and talk only after that. Now her eyelids were drooping out of sheer exhaustion. Who knew when she would get over this tiredness and move again? Wouldn't someone come before that?

Wouldn't that researcher come now? He had made such an effort to get an insight into her life's experiences. If the young man would come now, Kunti would explain to him, "My dear fellow, it is sheer stupidity to use a battle axe when you could cut something with a pocket knife."

As her eyes started to close, she thought that someone was calling her. Her eyes opened again.

It seemed that Time had felt suffocated in some deep cave and sat up after many ages. The hot air exhaled had drawn blood from all sides of consciousness.

The sound "Om" was emerging piercing the chest of the earth!

Who? Who was coming? Whose footsteps were they? Who was there?

Kunti went to a deep, peaceful sleep before any further sound could be heard. The eastern sky was gradually turning crimson...!

INDEX

J

K

L

M

N

O

P

R

S